Blake,

Nationalism,

and the

Politics of Alienation

JULIA M. WRIGHT

Blake, Nationalism, and the Politics of Alienation

OHIO UNIVERSITY PRESS ATHENS

Ohio University Press, Athens, Ohio 45701

Ohio University Press books are printed on acid-free paper ⊗ ™

12 11 10 09 08 07 06 05 04 5 4 3 2 1

Cover art credit: William Blake, "The Vision of Christ," *Illustrations of the Book of Job* (1825).

Library of Congress Cataloging-in-Publication Data

Wright, Julia M.
Blake, nationalism, and the politics of alienation / Julia M. Wright.
p. cm.
Includes bibliographical references and index.
ISBN 0-8214-1519-0 (alk. paper)
1. Blake, William, 1757-1827–Political and social views. 2. Nationalism and literature–Great Britain–History–18th century. 3. Nationalism and literature–Great Britain–History–19th century. 4. Political poetry, English–History and criticism. 5. Alienation (Social psychology) in literature. 6. Nationalism in literature. I. Title.

PR4148.P6W75 2003
821'.7–dc21

2003056309

Contents

Illustrations

Acknowledgments

I would like to begin by thanking Tilottama Rajan and Angela Esterhammer for their invaluable support and guidance during the development of this study; their generosity as readers of the manuscript from its earliest stages greatly enriched not only the project itself but also the experience of writing it, and I continue to be grateful for, as well as to draw on, that experience. To Tilottama Rajan I owe a special debt, not only for her advice on this project, but also for her pervasive influence on my research, teaching, and professional life. Much of what I do right I learned from her, and much of what I do wrong I strive to correct with her example in mind. The work of Stephen Behrendt has significantly shaped my approach to Blake, and his cogent comments and encouragement on this study came at a key juncture, helping me through the final revision stages.

Along the way, at conferences, in hallways, and through e-mail, others offered generative insights or, even more heroically, patiently listened while I tried to ramble through a problem out loud. One such person is Joel Faflak. Words are inadequate to express not only the importance of his friendship to me but also the value of his intellectual companionship; thought-provoking conversations over many a cup of coffee have helped to fuel my academic work and my enthusiasm for it. He has also, along with others, sustained my belief in the value of intellectual community within and beyond the university's walls in times when an economics with limited material vision would reduce academic activity to the cold equations of c.v. lines, class sizes, and marketable patents. Special thanks in this regard in general, and for this book project in particular, are also due to Daniel Wilson, Nancy Batty, Jackie Jenkins, Grace Kehler, Ann Mayer, Cameron McFarlane, Christine Thorpe, and Ranita Chatterjee. Thanks, too, to Dennis Denisoff, James Good, Brian Greenspan, Kristen Guest, Elizabeth Harvey, Michael Holmes, Balachandra Rajan, Elizabeth Sauer, and my colleagues at Wilfrid Laurier University, from whom I have learned and continue to learn so much.

The financial support of the Social Sciences and Humanities

Research Council of Canada over the years has been essential to the completion of this study, and the research support that I now so fortunately receive through the Canada Research Chairs Program made it possible for me to prepare the manuscript for the press with the able research assistance of Holly Crumpton and James Allard. I am also deeply grateful to the Northeast MLA's Book Award Committee and Executive for the wonderful honor of the 2002 NEMLA Book Award for this manuscript, and would like to thank those who anonymously read it in the course of that competition and passed on their useful insights. Thanks are due, as well, to David Sanders and others at Ohio University Press for their help with the preparation of this manuscript for the press.

Portions of various chapters have been presented before audiences generous with their comments, at departmental colloquia and conferences such as "Reading Romanticism" (Durham, North Carolina, 10–13 November 1993), "William Blake 1794/1994" (Twickenham, England, 13–15 July 1994), and the annual meetings of the Northeast MLA (Buffalo, New York, 7–9 April 2000) and the North American Society for the Study of Romanticism (Tempe, Arizona, 14–17 September 2000); of particular value were comments by Anthony Campbell, Robert N. Essick, and Martin Kreiswirth. Earlier and shorter versions of two chapters have appeared in print before, and I would like to thank the anonymous readers of those essays for their comments as well as the journals' editors for their kind permission to reproduce that material:

- A version of chapter 1 appeared as "The Medium, the Message, and the Line in Blake's *Laocoon*" in *Mosaic, a Journal for the Interdisciplinary Study of Literature* 33 (2000): 101–24.

- A version of chapter 4 appeared as "'And None Shall Gather the Leaves': Unbinding the Voice in Blake's *America* and *Europe*" in *European Romantic Review* 7 (1996): 61–84.

Thanks, as well, to the Library of Congress, the editors of the William Blake Archive, especially Joseph Viscomi, and Robert N. Essick for generously providing the illustrations included here.

Lastly, and most importantly, I would like to thank Jason Haslam, for making everything seem possible and every moment worthwhile. He and I might not have known each other when this project was begun, but without his encouragement, advice, and laughter, it would never have reached this conclusion.

Abbreviations

References to all of Blake's writings, except *The Laocoön,* will be to the *Complete Poetry and Prose of William Blake,* rev. ed., ed. David V. Erdman (New York: Doubleday, 1988), and all references to the Bible will be to the King James version. Blake's texts will be cited by line, plate, and chapter numbers where applicable, and by Erdman's page number where not. All references to Blake's engravings will be to *The Illuminated Books of William Blake,* 6 vols., gen. ed. David Bindman (Princeton: Princeton University Press, 1998), cited by the plate number in the Erdman edition, unless otherwise specified. Because of editorial issues discussed in chapter 1, all references to the texts of *The Laocoön,* except where editions are specified, are my own transcriptions from reproductions of the design (with reference also to various editions of the texts), with the quadrant in which the quotation is located being indicated by A (upper left-hand), B (upper right-hand), C (lower left-hand), and D (lower right-hand).

The following abbreviations will be used for Blake's works:

Am	*America; a Prophecy*
Anno. Reynolds	Annotations to *The Works of Sir Joshua Reynolds*
Anno. Bacon	Annotations to Bacon's *Essays Moral, Economical, and Political*
Anno. Wordsworth	Annotations to Wordsworth's preface to *The Excursion*
BU	*The [First] Book of Urizen*
Eur	*Europe; a Prophecy*
J	*Jerusalem*
L	*The Laocoön*

M	*Milton*
MHH	*The Marriage of Heaven and Hell*
PA	*Public Address*
SE	*Songs of Experience*
SL	*The Song of Los*
VDA	*Visions of the Daughters of Albion*
VLJ	*A Vision of The Last Judgment*

Introduction Nationality, Individuality, and Defamiliarization

> Every people has . . . its own individual character; and in virtue of that character, is the interest inspired by their fortunes. Even that strong sympathy which waits upon the events of life, is not sufficient in itself entirely to attract us; and our interest in their history is imperfect, except when the distinct individual conception of their character as a people accompanies the relation. . . . Every one who has applied himself with interest to the theory of a nation's literature . . . will most probably remember, that in the works he then read, there seemed opening up to him, not the mind of a new author, but the mind of another nation. . . . He will recollect . . . a new and strange feeling of visiting an unknown land, and of standing for the first time among an unknown people.
>
> *Anonymous,* "OF A NATIONAL CHARACTER IN LITERATURE" (1818)

In *Jerusalem,* Los declares, "I must Create a System, or be enslav'd by another Mans" (*J,* 10.20). Los's assertion is frequently quoted because of its utility as a succinct formulation of William Blake's insistence on the necessity of escaping the constraints of "another Mans" system. But it is an unusually revolutionary formulation of Blake's resistance to externally imposed systems. Los's solution in *Jerusalem* is revolutionary in principle, as well as politics, because it replaces one system with another. Blake, however, indicates no such economy of substitution in earlier texts. In *America,* Orc's position is closer to that of a nihilist than a revolutionary:

> That stony law I stamp to dust: and scatter religion abroad
> To the four winds as a torn book, & none shall gather the leaves;
> But they shall rot on desart sands, & consume in bottomless
> deeps;
> To make the desarts blossom, & the deeps shrink to their fountains,
> And to renew the fiery joy, and burst the stony roof. (*Am,* 8.5–9)

The "fiery joy" is not a means to an end, like Los's created system, but the end itself—the absence of system and so the release from the weighty, constricting caves of plate 23 of *Jerusalem*. It is energy rather than structure, and "Uncurbed" "Passions" rather than "Cool Blooded Design" (*VLJ*, 564). While Los's declaration can justify Blake's creation of a mythology and geography through which to stage his interrogation of systems, Orc's speech makes Blake's later collection of occasional characters into an organized pantheon appear to be a lapse into the very structuring practices that he so vehemently opposed.

With the notable exception of *Jerusalem*, an exception I will address at length in chapter 6, Blake is concerned almost exclusively with attacks on the existing system, bursting the limiting, stony roof of art theory, poetic form, gender coding, neoclassical nationalism, and various other enforced cultural norms, and hence his idolization as a fighter of the good fight for individual liberty. But in Blake's larger corpus, as I shall suggest in the following pages, individual liberty is inseparable from, though often at odds with, the dominant concern of *Jerusalem*: an engagement with community, particularly national community. Whether Blake only jars his readers into recognizing some of the contours of their conformity, or assaults a notion of community with a dramatic axe, the texts that he engraved and printed for circulation insistently engage the difficulty of disengaging the individual from the communal and the ways in which discourse, and particularly its extension into print, serves to mediate between the individual and the communal. An extreme example of the latter is the printed book, which enforces and propagates cultural norms, but it also includes more complex examples, such as Oothoon's pleas to be heard by Theotormon. Blake's characters may rail against the dominant order and constraints on individual freedoms, but free individuals are not hermits: they require audiences, fellow citizens, lovers, and families. Blake thus often represents his most oppressed and oppressive characters as solitary figures in bounded spaces. The ultimate boundary in Blake's corpus, however, is the temporal line. Unidirectional and infinitely narrow, such linearity emerges in Blake's corpus as an enslaving metasystem: it naturalizes national progress, locks individual improvement into an educational and iterative narrative rather than an inspirational model of transformation, and everywhere drags thought through the fixed sequence of words strung out on a page.

Nations, Communities, and Individuals

I am opposing the individual to "community" here, rather than "society" or "Romantic-era England," to stress at the outset the ways in which a community is presumed to cohere through shared values, language, and interests, and on terms that resonate with representations of the family and the nation. Nationalism is, for this study, less an "imagined community" (to use Benedict Anderson's famous phrase) than a means for instituting a coherent community through disciplinary mechanisms.[1] As an ideology—or, rather, a related set of ideologies, given the variety of nationalisms at the moment of the emergence of the post-Enlightenment nation state—nationalism enforces homogeneous community by translating uniqueness from the individual to the nation. Against the divides of rural and urban, male and female, aristocrat and laborer, and even radical and conservative, nationalism emerged to claim that the nation defines all of the individuals who belong to it, and that all of its members have a stake in the continuance of the nation on those terms. The flexibility of nationalism is revealed by the variety of agendas it was used to reinforce in the British Isles: British imperialism, Irish resistance to British colonial control, antiquarian returns to various native pasts (including Welsh, Scottish, Saxon, and Druidic), and technological quests for futurity, to name just a few. But in the Romantic era it consistently elides individuality within the category of "national character"—in Ernest Gellner's phrase, *"nations maketh man"*[2]—and co-opts cultural work to further the national agenda rather than challenge, complicate, or supplement it. And so, as the anonymous author of the epigraph above argues, foreign literature provides access to "not the mind of a new author, but the mind of another nation,"[3] echoing, likely unwittingly, Blake's assertion a quarter of a century earlier that "the sayings used in a nation, mark its character" (*MHH,* 6).[4] In Blake's time, nationalism in its modern form was a new phenomenon. Blake was very much concerned with the ways in which the nationalism promulgated by the state and its institutions was not only repressive for the individual, in the Althusserian sense, but also a disruption of a nativist art and imagination as the uncorrupted expressions of individuality. As Gellner notes, "Far from revelling in the defiant individual will, nationalists delight in feelings of submission or incorporation in a continuous entity greater, more persistent and more legitimate than the isolated self."[5] While non-hegemonic nationalisms could be espoused defiantly, they necessarily take as their basis the notion of a collective will rather than an individual will. There can be no nation of one subject, thinking and acting in isolation.

In *Ideology and Utopia in the Poetry of William Blake,* Nicholas Williams charts the significance of utopianism as "the only concept which simultaneously allows the breadth of a universal concept of ideology and the possibility of ideology-critique."[6] If utopianism requires the idealism of "no place," nationalism is its material correlate. Nationalism idealizes the space of the nation, and offers to transmute fallen and divided existence into harmonious participation in the organic body of the nation; instead of utopianism's promise of ahistorical and ideology-free transcendence, nationalism asks the community to cohere in order to achieve very material and political goals, whether freedom from an oppressor, imperial expansion, economic success, cultural development, or the defense of land and property against an invader. Indeed, it at least tacitly insists that those aspirations will fail if the nation does not cohere: all must act as one, or the all that is greater than the sum of its parts will be shattered.

For the national subject, the "tension between the self as subjective, alienated, even solipsistic, and the self as integrated into a universal Humanity that gives it status and meaning"[7] that Leopold Damrosch describes is an internal tension, like that between body and soul: "Man has no Body distinct from his Soul for that calld Body is a portion of Soul discernd by the five Senses. the chief inlets of Soul in this age" (*MHH,* 4). In other words, the national subject as defined by nationalist ideology is an individual extension of the universalized national character, insofar as each national character is consistent within its respective nation and every nation is presumed to have its own national character.[8] Moreover, the distinction between the individual and the universal that circulates through Blake criticism—and, as Damrosch notes, collapses in the poet's definition of the "individuality of vision" as universal[9]—is reflected on the mundane plane as a tension between the individual and the communal.

As a consequence, the space of struggle between disciplinary pressures and individual desires is frequently a public space in Blake's poetry, making Blake's writings radically different from those which M. H. Abrams describes as addressing "a central Romantic subject: the growth and discipline of the poet's mind, conceived as a theodicy of the individual life . . . which begins and ends in our experience in this world."[10] While the individual life has a comparable centrality for Blake, it does not ground the narrative perspective of his writings, nor is it understood to be a work in progress, as Abrams describes it. The individual life is either constrained by public discourses, or epiphanically frees itself from at least some of those constraints. As a consequence of this focus, the subjective interiority of these figures is rarely represented in Blake's texts: with few exceptions, mostly in the early *Poetical Sketches* and *Songs of Innocence and of Experience,* there are no soliloquies that are not marked as public addresses or addresses about the public, there are no transcriptions or paraphrases of the internal thoughts of his characters, and there are no lyrics in the conventional Romantic sense of private poetic expression. The characters' private thoughts are always represented by publicly perceived actions, such as speeches, laughter, rejoicing, howling, and cursing, telegraphed as they would be on a stage rather than described by an omniscient narrator with full access to their interiority. Blake's works are constituted as public performances and his characters are constituted as public performers, visibly caught in and struggling with a maelstrom of cultural forces and currents while their inner struggles are concealed from view. Thus, instead of a mental theater, like that discussed by Alan Richardson, Blake paints a public theater in which the individual strives to free himself or herself from the extensions of hegemony: Oothoon struggles with patriarchal violence, Orc fights British colonial domination in the United States, Milton arises newborn when he frees himself from the errors of dogma and court politics, and Urizen wrestles with the constraints of time and space.

As I have already noted, the term "communal" suggests individuals who are grouped under shared terms (culture, ideology, region, nation, religion, and so forth), but those competing forces are not readily disentangled. The individual is, in a sense, caught between the utopian unity-as-divine-and-universal and the national unity-as-fallen-and-specific, and remains caught between those two controlling vehicles of individual identity. There is a further complication in considerations of Blake's handling of nationalism that arises from the sometimes interchangeable use of England and Britain (as the island and/or the political union of Scotland, England, and Wales) in Romantic-era discourse, and the complex ways in which "British" national identity was variously traced in this period to English origins through the Magna Carta and to British roots through the Glorious Revolution or, in Blake, through an antique name for the island as a whole, "Albion." As Linda Colley's important study, *Britons: Forging the Nation, 1707–1837,* helps to make clear, the development of a British national identity that would supersede those of England, Scotland, and Wales was neither simple, nor decisive, nor quick, nor, arguably, ever clearly successful and complete.[11] I have tried to be discriminating in my use of the terms "England" and "Britain" (and their cognates), judging shades of appropriateness by the terminology of the text in question and the historical forces being brought to bear on it, but they are blunt instruments at best to deal with this Gordian knot.

A nation space defined through overlapping and often competing categories of "British" and "English" provides a useful synecdoche for the culturally entangled and politically contested exteriority—of Blake, the model subject, and specific characters—that is at issue here. This exteriority is fundamentally hybridized, crossed by all of the discourses to which Blake had direct or indirect access, and all of the models in which those discourses are formulated, just as the public domain is traversed by those discourses and models. But if each individual is unique, as Blake often insists, then any sense of community must require the suppression or elision of some elements of that uniqueness, and therein lies the rub. Nationalism in particular is susceptible to this difficulty, and hence its utility as an avenue through which to address the problem of the socialized individual in Blake's work. While sexism and racism have generally been used against those that they attempt to define most thoroughly, so that sexist and racist thinkers generally do not obviously lose anything by their subscription to such a repressive -ism and are usually expected to gain some form of social power, nationalism is used to unite and flatter those that it describes. This formulation is, of course, greatly oversimplified. Such a construction fails to address, for instance, the constraints that patriarchal pressures place on men or the temptation to accept, at least in part, a disempowering ideology in order to be recognized by those who do hold power. But it does draw out a nationalist quandary: nationalism seeks to establish a communal paradigm as interior and inherent to each subject and, by offering communal power, seeks to set aside any other interiority. Thus, an Englishman is not a Protestant because of personal faith, or even acculturation and legislative pressure, but because England is a Protestant nation. As Blake writes in his Annotations to Bacon, "The Hirelings of Kings & Courts . . . make themselves Every Body & Knowingly propagate Falshood" (620). To offer another sense of national identity, or to claim individual identity against the collective, is to show the falseness of this communal interior as well as to challenge an exclusionary paradigm from within. Thus, as "enemies" of nationalism, in Gellner's colorful term, writers such as Blake "teach us not to take nationalism at its own valuation, on its own terms, and as something self-evident."[12]

Defamiliarizing the Self-Evident

The question of the "familiar" emerges significantly in Blake's verse and criticism of it as a way of grasping the "self-evident." The term "familiar" is derived from a word for genealogical connections, "family," yet implies an experiential rather than a genetic acquaintance. "Familiar," with various prefixes and suffixes, is an oddly common term in Blake criticism. David V. Erdman writes that he can decode Blake, and so demonstrate that his work is allusive rather than absurdly idiosyncratic, because he has "learned to read the idiom of current allusion with sufficient familiarity" and has "become familiar, too, with Blake's use of sources in the ironic manner which historians of painting call witty quotation," while W. J. T. Mitchell argues, "We have to make Blake strange again. . . . We have appropriated him and familiarized him, made him safe for modern consumption."[13] Conversely, Susan Fox writes that Blake "makes even the most familiar places and things ominously unfamiliar," and Damrosch asserts, "After several generations of Blakeans have banged their heads against the brick wall of artistic form, we can safely conclude that Blake's poems do not possess form in any familiar sense."[14] One particular derivative of the term "familiar," "defamiliarization," is a useful tool in attempts to consider some of the implications of this strangeness. The word often appears in literary criticism in general, and Blake criticism in particular, but is generally divorced from its origin as the English translation of a term coined by the Russian formalist Viktor Shklovsky in his essay "Art as Technique."[15] I mark that source here not to privilege origins, however Romantic that might be, but because Shklovsky's term is more complicated, and for my purposes more useful, than its usual English translation suggests. The original term is *priem ostranenija,* often abbreviated to *ostraneniye.* The full phrase is usually translated as "the device of making strange," while its shorter version is variously translated as "estrangement," "making strange," "alienation," and, most commonly, as "defamiliarization."[16]

There is an odd chiasmus in these translations, between terms that refer to the perceiving subject's sense of the artifact's belonging and those that refer to that subject's own sense of belonging, between "making strange" and "estrangement." It is in this chiasmus that the formalist term, I would argue, becomes useful in cultural studies, particularly in attempts to analyze the formation of cultural codes that establish the slippery domain of the familiar. While apparently innocuous, the category of the "familiar" often slides into constructions of what is "natural," "civilized," "right," or "proper," codes that, in Althusserian terms, interpellate the subject into the ideologies in which they are invested, and it is this interpellative dimension that is exposed in the doubleness of strange and estranging. In *Melmoth the Wanderer* (1820), Blake's contemporary Charles Robert Maturin makes a pertinent observation on the power of codes that are formally invested with familiarity: "However extraordinary these injunctions appeared, the manner in which they were issued was so imposing, peremptory, and *habitual,*—it seemed so little a thing of local contrivance and temporary display,—so much like the established language of an absolute and long-fixed system, that *obedience to it seemed inevitable.*"[17] Blake makes a similar point, but more obliquely: "well wrought blandishments, / And well contrived words, firm fixing, never forgotten, / Always comforting the remembrance" (*J,* 12.34–36). In this context, *priem ostranenija,* or "the estranging device of making strange," disrupts the interpellative effect, separating the subject from the comfortable familiarity of cultural codes and so making obedience to their injunctions seem less inevitable. In this moment of alienation, then, the tension described by Damrosch is produced and the struggle begins. It is in this sense that Blake's texts "make strange."

Making strange is not only potentially liberating, but it also permits innovation, admitting strangeness itself into the lexicon of normality. In *The Marriage of Heaven and Hell,* Blake writes, "If the doors of perception were cleansed every thing would appear to man as it is: infinite. / For man has closed himself up, till he sees all things thro' narrow chinks of his cavern" (14). The chinks of Blake's cavern are similar in function to the censorship that Pierre Bourdieu discusses in his essay, "Censorship and the Imposition of Form":

> The metaphor of censorship should not mislead: it is the structure of the field itself which governs expression by governing both access to expression and the form of expression, and not some legal proceeding. . . . By imposing form, the censorship exercised by the structure of the field determines the form—which all formalist analyses attempt to detach from social determinisms—and, necessarily, the content, which is inseparable from its appropriate expression and therefore literally unthinkable outside of the known forms and recognized norms.[18]

Bourdieu limits such structures to academic disciplines, but this statement could be extended to other governing codes, from genres to ideologies to scientific theories and aesthetic norms. All such structures select what is visible, and what is thinkable: they are the cracks in the stony walls, and the stony roofs. They offer valuable glimpses not of open vision, but of structured vision, a vision that is mediated by codes that determine what is visible and how. As Shklovsky's analysis in "Art as Technique" implies, however, the code and its selection of visible signs are codependent: not only does the code determine the selection, but the selection also reinforces the code.[19] Shklovsky suggests that the introduction of an element that does not fit into a text unsettles the reader's decoding of it, arresting the process of comprehension so ably described by Bourdieu: "To understand also means to understand without having to be told, to read between the lines, by re-enacting in the mode of practice (in most cases unconsciously) the linguistic associations and substitutions initially set up by the producer."[20] The unfamiliar, the irreconcilable, halts the chain of substitutions mapped by the code, making possible the production of other codes and metacodes, including the recognition of the codedness of the reading process.

History against Ideology: The State of Defamiliarization

During Blake's lifetime, defamiliarization and its simplification, reversal, were common strategies in the political sphere. Ideological cacophony and political chaos, as well as international and domestic crises, led to an unusual level of conflict and uncertainty about English (or British) identity and the place of the individual within it. England's status as an imperial and quintessentially "civilized" nation was challenged from all quarters: from the colonies, from imperial competitors, and from within English society. Major uprisings in nations under its imperial control had taken place throughout the eighteenth century, from the Scottish rebellion in the 1740s, to the American Revolution in the 1770s, the conflict with Tipu in India during the 1780s, and the Irish uprising of 1798. England successfully suppressed all except the American rebels, but military failures and debilitating costs mitigated any sense of imperial security and further aroused domestic dissent among a population that was paying high taxes and losing sons to the military efforts. These military efforts extended beyond the boundaries of the British Empire to include an unsuccessful attempt to "liberate" San Domingo, then a French colony, from a slave revolution and, of course, the trials of the wars with the United States and then with France.

From 1788 to 1795, to add fuel to the fire, the impeachment of Warren Hastings, governor-general of India, exposed British colonial rule as corrupt, exploitative, and greedy. In a speech on the occasion of the trial's opening, Edmund Burke makes the impeachment a test of national legitimacy and Hastings's actions a blot on the national record:

> my Lords, the credit and honour of the British nation will itself be decided by this decision. My Lords, they will stand or fall thereby. We are to decide by the case of this gentleman whether the crimes of individuals are to be turned into public guilt and national ignominy, or whether this nation will convert these offences, which have thrown a transient shade on its glory, into a judgment that will reflect a permanent lustre on the honour, justice and humanity of this Kingdom.[21]

Hastings was acquitted. He was acquitted even though Burke, the defender of rank and the author of *Reflections on the Revolution in France* (1790), was willing to vilify Hastings, "the first man in rank, authority and station,"[22] the governor-general of India, and suggest that members of Parliament might, against the interests of national integrity, overlook the executive's crimes because of national bias:

> God forbid that, when you try the Cause of Asia in the presence of Europe, there should be the least suspicion that the Cause of Asia is not as good with you, because the abuse is committed by a British subject. . . . God forbid it should be said that we in this kingdom know how to confer the most extravagant and inordinate power upon public ministers; and that we are poor, helpless, deficient and impotent in the means of calling them to account for it. God forbid it should be said that no nation under heaven equals the British in substantial violence and informal justice.[23]

These words would soon ring prophetic. In the following decade, mutinies exposed a comparably ugly side of that cornerstone of British imperial power, the navy, especially abuses of power by officers, while political agitation kept the question of civilian rights in the public eye. The flurry of trials that followed the mutinies, the protests, the radical publications, and the formation of political societies played out, over and over again, the struggle between invested power and its adversaries for the claim to the moral high ground, a struggle the former usually won, often by pitting legislators, judges, and paid, less-than-reliable informants against defendants charged with subversive activity. While the civil façade of British culture was being stripped away throughout the empire, the French Revolution offered another challenge to its aristocratic hegemony, and then, out of the ashes of the Terror, came a military threat to Britain's imperial rule and power position in Europe—Napoleon.

Against this tumultuous backdrop, in which elements of the established order were examined, exposed as abusive, defied, overthrown, and reinstated, radical writings proliferated and conservative reaction was consolidated. In pamphlets, periodicals, books, caricatures, and speeches, radicals challenged the sociopolitical order—which had been previously justified as natural, divinely sanctioned, and rational—by establishing alternative value systems, particularly that system derived from Thomas Paine in which rights were equal and inherent and social hierarchies were supposed to be culturally rather than naturally produced. Through legislation, the establishment of a considerable network of informants, and prosecutions, as well as propaganda that competed with radicals for the hearts and minds of the general populace, those who wished to retain the current system tried to stamp out revolution as if it were a series of small fires in a parched forest. But radical writers continued into the breach, so to speak, storming the halls of political power through the failures of established systems (despite their escalating efforts) to successfully invoke social closure, further destabilizing the systems to which they objected as well as generating new sites of stability. Of these writers, Blake is perhaps now the best known.

But these writers were, in significant regards, not so different from those that they opposed. While I completely agree with Steven Goldsmith's observation that Blake has a "stubborn commitment to making representational acts visible" as a means of "revealing the play of power within language," and that this "insistence on a wary vigilance, and the role that representation plays in that vigilance, characterizes both Blake's texts and the democratic discourse that appeared simultaneously,"[24] the same sense of vigilance and the power of representation appeared in hegemonic discourse. At issue here is not the "liberating potential of discursive practices,"[25] but the pan-ideological competition to control the representation of the individual and, more crucially, the community through which the individual is defined. The era saw innumerable skirmishes between different political groups—from religious sectarians to nonsectarian democrats, from Paine-inspired radicals to Burke-emboldened conservatives, and from feminists to proponents of feminine propriety—and those skirmishes were fought in the streets, the media, and the courts. But, because they were fighting against each other, these groups often used the same weapons. Paine offered one political vision, Burke offered another, and Blake offered a third, and the same culturally constituted, rather than politically specific, polemic strategies circulate throughout their representations of social errors and utopian ideals. All three, for instance, use the family as the basis of their societies and implicitly share certain assumptions about what "family" means ontologically as well as ideologically. They disagree only when it comes to extending the familial model to the national community. In other words, despite some key political differences, the mode and terms of their discourse exhibit a number of family resemblances—once again calling to mind Blake's interest in the tension between communal similitude and individual difference. These family resemblances are not all-pervasive, of course, and Blake's handling of genre and media, I would suggest, is one of the sites of resistance to the established terms of political debate.

Blake, Nationalism, and the Defamiliarization of Form

As the preceding pages imply, I am greatly indebted to Erdman's comprehensive study, *Blake: Prophet against Empire,* and the stream of Blake criticism that it inaugurated. But I also agree with Jon Mee's point, in the introduction to his important study of Blake, that Erdman's "tendency to identify the political dimension of [Blake's] poetry and designs with the representation of historical events . . . means that, at its very outset, historicist Blake criticism underestimated the radical significance of the formal dimension of his work."[26] This "tendency" recalls Northrop Frye's defense of Blake in *Fearful Symmetry,* a defense that, to a large extent, depends on Frye's claim that Blake is an allegorical poet. Both Frye and Erdman base their arguments on the assumption of a referential system in Blake's work, a system in which Rintrah must represent something coherent and distinct from "Rintrah," whether "wrath," as Frye argues, or William Pitt, as Erdman suggests.[27] A third great voice of early Blake criticism, S. Foster Damon, however, draws attention to a point often only implicit in Erdman's work or used to establish value in Frye's: "Blake was content not only to record: he wanted to force his reader to think along with him."[28] It is the means by which this performative force is exerted that concerns me here, and it is, I would argue, largely exercised through the "formal dimension of his work," to use Mee's phrase.

By challenging forms that support genealogical justifications for the present, by subverting homogenizing discourses, and by representing certain constructions of the political body as diseased or uninspired, Blake critiques the tools as well as the agenda and ideology of the prevailing nationalist discourse. Nationalism, because it generates a national character, a national history, and a national ideology, is the ultimate familiarizing vehicle, and the vehicle used to reinscribe familiarity over the sociopolitical uncertainty of the Romantic period. Whether we follow Benedict Anderson, Anthony Smith, and others in locating the origin of modern nationalism in the late eighteenth century, or Gellner in tracing it back to the effects of the Industrial Revolution,[29] its growing power to unite the British public and direct that public's energies toward specific commercial and military enterprises is beyond question. Nationalism is efficacious in part because it produces a large community along familial lines, enforcing genetic, genealogical, and cultural ties, as well as requiring the loyalty associated with familial relationships. It also establishes a national identity with which all who belong to that nation will be comfortably familiar. To defamiliarize its constituent constructs is to pry open its totalizing impetus, complicate its familial genealogy, and, finally, to create at least the possibility for an alternative community that establishes different terms of familiarity through what one revolutionary tract termed "the witchcraft of a proclamation."[30]

Insofar as he had an ideology that he wished to have dominate the national scene, held dogmatically to certain beliefs as right and good, used public forms of discourse to argue for that agenda, and verbally abused opponents of that political vision, Blake was not very different from those he opposed. As John Barrell notes, Blake's theory of the social effects of art is much the same as that of Reynolds in its operation, if not in its content: "For Blake, as for Reynolds, the point seems to be that by the exhibition of ideal forms, we will learn the grounds of social affiliation; . . . because the ideal forms are fitted, are designed for action, Blake believes that they will teach us (as the central forms of Reynolds do not) that the sense of community among the varieties of character is to be achieved by deeds which are of service to a Christian community."[31] Similarly, to return to another Blakean nemesis, Burke, William Richey argues that Blake used the same paradigms as Burke but inverted their associations. Thus, for example, "Since Burke has consistently presented the revolutionaries in the worst possible light—comparing them to madmen, savages, and, at times, even devils—Blake simply treats the *ancien regime* in a similarly derogatory manner."[32] At issue here is not Blake's ideology, but the formal and rhetorical strategies with which he sought to propagate that ideology—hence my decision to limit this discussion, almost exclusively, to Blake's printed works. By defamiliarizing the dominant cultural codes in the public domain, on however limited a scale, Blake disturbs the existing "grounds of social affiliation" (in Barrell's phrase) to inaugurate his own. Blake disrupts the linearity that informed the hegemonic totalizing myths of progress, represents characters casting off the shackles of gender and other social codes, and turns the tables, so to speak, on nationalist discourse by identifying such nationalism with the very figures that it used to mark the alien that it wished to exclude. Each of these approaches requires the representation of the existing structure as an alien constraint, and therefore posits a proper national collectivity beneath that structure that can be released. As Barrell notes, for example, "for Blake the English audience is only a public when it exhibits (as it rarely does) the qualities necessary to appreciate his work, or Barry's, or Fuseli's, or the works of the Roman and Florentine schools."[33] It is this conflict between definitions of the proper and the alien within the identity of Blake's British public that is traced in the following pages.

Vital to this conflict is Blake's repudiation of linearity in favor of instantaneous transformations and his replacement of communal ideologies with personal vision—or, in other words, his substitution of epiphany for personal growth and revolution for progress. The key volume of essays, *Nation and Narration,* demonstrates the ways in which nations are constituted in and rely on narrative. As the editor, Homi K. Bhabha, suggests in his introduction, recent studies of nationalism "contest[] the traditional authority of those national objects of knowledge—Tradition, People, the Reason of State, High Culture, for instance—whose pedagogical value often relies on their representation as holistic concepts located within an evolutionary narrative of historical continuity."[34] From validating genealogies to the march of history and the myth of progress, English (and British) nationalisms were predicated on the authority not of the "bounding line" but of the directed line, with its beginning, middle, and end. I thus begin, in chapter 1, with Blake's contestation of formal linearity in *The Laocoön*.

The directed line is, however, also an infinitesimally thin bounding line, marking the inside of "Englishness" or "Britishness," "art," and "civilization." Breaking up the directed line disrupts the limiting line that it implicitly validates: a discontinuous national history threatens to produce a hybrid national identity, just as a continuous history supports a safely homogeneous definition. While Charles Bernstein's volume, *The Politics of Poetic Form,* is concerned with "how radically innovative poetic styles can have political meanings," my argument here is that discursive styles had political significance during the "crisis of literature" in which Blake wrote.[35] Blake thus argues that literary form itself participates in political oppression:

> When this Verse was first dictated to me I consider'd a Monotonous Cadence like that used by Milton & Shakspeare & all writers of *English* Blank Verse, derived from the modern bondage of Rhyming; to be a necessary and indispensible part of Verse. But I soon found that in the mouth of a true Orator such monotony was not only awkward, but as much a bondage as rhyme itself. . . . Poetry Fetter'd, Fetters the Human Race! Nations are Destroy'd, or Flourish, in proportion as Their Poetry Painting and Music, are Destroy'd or Flourish! (*J,* 3; my emphasis)

From the ballad, appropriated by those of Blake's contemporaries who wished to promote nativism or speak to the lower classes, to the epics, selected to promote particular views of the nations they depicted, and the epistolary satires that Thomas Moore used to critique the private face of the aristocracy, the formal components of political discourses insert their contents into the domain of assumptions and conventions with which those forms are associated.

This study falls into two parts, and three, a double segmentation that reflects the interpenetration of the discussions of content and form. The first three chapters address Blake's disruption of linearity and closure as a defamiliarizing strategy, while the latter three discuss his representations of the alienating effects of such strategies. The first third of the study examines Blake's contravention of the artistic conventions (particularly those related to linearity) of media and genre, especially as they support nationalist narratives (with special attention to Blake's *Laocoön, Poetical Sketches,* and the Lambeth Books); the second third focuses on his representations of alienation and heterogeneity in *Europe* and *America,* representations deployed to disrupt the idea of a coherent collectivity that underwrites prevailing ideologies; and the final third narrows that focus to the (re)construction of the infected national body, primarily in *Milton* and *Jerusalem,* as it returns to the concern of the first two chapters with nationalism.

In chapter 1, I examine the form of Blake's idiosyncratic engraving, *The Laocoön,* in terms of the debate among contemporary art theorists about *ut pictura poesis* and the privileging of linearity, particularly as chronology. Linearity lies not only behind form, but also behind the formation of genealogies that Blake identifies with the progressive, often nationalist, Romantic theory of the development of art that he repeatedly contests: "If Art was Progressive We should have had Mich Angelo's & Rafaels to Succeed & to Improve upon each other But it is not so. Genius dies with its Possessor & comes not again till Another is Born with It" (Anno. Reynolds, 656). The engraving, a single plate, consists of a drawing of the classical statue of Laocoön and his sons battling the snakes; around the drawing are pieced, like a textual mosaic or jigsaw puzzle, a considerable number of short texts in English, Greek, and Hebrew. While these texts are often cited individually in support of various assertions about Blake's thought, I am concerned with the implications of their unusual arrangement in terms of the Laocoön debate in late-eighteenth-century art theory. The verbal content of the texts in Blake's *Laocoön* challenges existing histories of art by claiming, for instance, that classical art is derived from Hebraic art, while Blake's arrangement of the texts challenges G. E. Lessing's oft-cited theory that writing is linear and visual art is spatial. Blake thus offers a two-pronged attack on the priority of linearity in theories of art in the period, particularly theories of art implicated in nationalist genealogies of cultural progress. This attack is consistent with his verbal assaults on the state of British art and the art establishment's conviction that artistic value is transmitted from generation to generation.

In the next chapter, I continue to discuss the mutual determination of form and nationalist genealogies in relation to Blake's repudiation of conventional histories. While Mee has ably addressed "republican antiquarianism" in the 1790s, my concern is with the formal framing of the antiquarian and the nationalist (rather than the radical) investments in it. In the *Poetical Sketches* and the Lambeth Prophecies, Blake, I argue, appropriates antiquarian discourse in order to subvert historical linearity and thus the nationalist narratives that antiquarian scholarship helped to construct. Blake establishes a nonlinear model for national renovation, rather than the evolutionary, linear, often genealogical, models favored by antiquarian nationalists such as Warton, Percy, and others. Blake's model is most vividly expressed in *Milton,* a text of notorious fragmentation and repetition that, I would suggest, appears so fragmented and repetitive because it reflects Blake's interest in nonlinear, even nontemporal, change:

> Every Time less than a pulsation of the artery
> Is equal in its period & value to Six Thousand Years.
> For in this Period the Poets Work is Done: and all the Great
> Events of Time start forth & are concievd in such a Period
> Within a Moment: a Pulsation of the Artery. (*M,* 28.62–29.3)

The nonlinear reading invited by *Laocoön* helps to clarify Blake's handling of the past in his pseudoantiquarian works; in such works, Blake offers nonlinear national histories, undermining the prevailing model of a Whig history that is linear, progressive, and dogmatically nationalistic. Blake's nationalized resistance to the "classicizing tendency," to use Stuart Peterfreund's phrase,[36] is part of a larger, contemporary movement to cast off the totalizing, universalizing impetus of the imperial march toward civilization by turning toward localized, disjunctive models of communal identity.

In chapter 3, I turn to these disjunctive models as they appear in *Visions of the Daughters of Albion, Europe,* and *America,* arguing that Blake uses narrative devices to emphasize the destabilization of the ideological closure of the communal space. Blake defamiliarizes conventional social codes to subvert the ease with which they are accepted and demonstrate their failure to totalize a social space that is finally more heterogeneous than such codes can allow. He achieves this defamiliarization, in part, by disrupting the reader's identification of a character with whom to affiliate his or her point of view or a narrative voice in which to trust. Drawing attention to the separation of Oothoon from Bromion, Enitharmon from history, and the mythic world of *America* from the historical, by, for instance, fracturing dialogues into a series of monologues unheard by other characters, Blake not only represents the mutual alienation of characters within his texts, but also alienates his reader. The reader necessarily occupies the intersection of the different, isolated and isolating, systems represented in Blake's poems, at the margins of all and included in none. Alienated by a world that not only is constituted through words on a page and an unconventional book, but that also uses unusual names, stages generally recognizable events in unfamiliar ways, and denies the reader a surrogate through whom to be introduced to this new world, the reader is held back from the text. It retains its unfamiliarity, its strangeness, and its estranging effect. The reader is consequently placed in the space in which revolutionary transgressions of the homogeneous societies are possible. This is finally what we can take from Blake's description of *A Vision of The Last Judgment* (1810): "I have represented it as I saw it[.] to different People it appears differently as . . . every thing else does" (*VLJ,* 555). While Paul Youngquist suggests that *Jerusalem* "resists easy assimilation to prevailing norms of reading, replacing the pleasures of understanding with an anxiety about its possibility,"[37] I would argue that such resistance disabuses, rather than abuses, the reader, by refusing to assimilate the reader into norms to which Blake objected in theory and practice.

In chapter 4, I focus on *America* and *Europe* to examine Blake's use of heterogeneity—particularly in the sense defined by Molly Anne Rothenberg—to subvert this kind of enforced uniformity.[38] In the preludiums to *America* and *Europe,* Blake ties his critique of gender paradigms to his subversion of bibliographical practices through the childbirth metaphor, a trope in which art meets the politics of gender and the body meets the book. The production of texts that totalize the field of social relations and the convention of linearity that totalizes the narrative are thus mapped onto the females' assimilation into the dominant gender codes and the unified identity that those codes presume. On the verge of being incorporated into a system that views them only as fecund wombs, the females of the preludiums resist that assimilation by complicating their identities through the addition of a voice that is productive in ways that exceed, and are alien to, gender codes, generating the same kind of destabilizing hybridity as that discussed in the previous chapter. The voice not only articulates their alienation from gender codes, but marks that alienation by its very existence. As in *Visions of the Daughters of Albion,* Blake produces a female character who defamiliarizes prevailing assumptions about gender from a position on the margins of that totalizing system. Through the childbirth metaphor, moreover, the implications of such resistance are extended to the reader's assimilation into the totalizing paradigms that govern the hegemonic text. Blake aligns mass-produced texts with the alienated uterus through which the women are reduced to silent fecundity. Just as the women resist their reduction to reproductive receptacles by rendering their identity self-alienated—representing themselves as an assemblage of parts with varying interests—Blake resists his works' implication in the production of readers as reproductive receptacles, passively repeating what they are told, by splitting his texts into an assemblage of textual and visual parts with varying significatory interests. The preludiums to

America and *Europe,* through the childbirth metaphor, establish a crucial link between the discursive incorporation of individuals into an ideologically invested norm and the normalizing effects of ideologically invested discourses on individuals. Through their resistance to the interpellative effects associated with the book, the shadowy females offer strategies for the struggle against social homogeneity and enforced uniformity that have not been recognized by previous feminist readings of these prophecies.

In the final chapters, I return to the problem of a specifically national community in which individuality is subordinated to the production of nationalist norms and essential characteristics. Cultural studies did not have to draw attention to Blake's nationalism; drawn with greater force, in many ways, than that of his better-known contemporaries, Blake's nationalism has long been acknowledged. But it has not been much studied in Blake criticism, and its complexities—and alterations during the course of Blake's life—have yet to be explored in depth. The subject has received some attention in recent books, such as those by Stephen Behrendt and John Lucas, as well as the occasional article, such as those by Seymour Howard and Susan Matthews, but an ideology key to most of the major and minor works of a canonical Romantic poet deserves far more discussion and debate. Blake's nationalism is, moreover, a kind of nationalism that has not yet been given much attention by cultural critics: the nationalism of an English Nonconformist radical, it expresses neither the resistance of the colonized nor the self-justification of the colonizer. Nationalism is not a coherent, stable ideology, particularly in the early years of its development. As Lucas suggests in *England and Englishness,* Blake's is only one of the cacophony of voices competing to establish "*their* vision of England" in the late eighteenth century.[39] Blake's shifting nationalist vision thus not only offers insight into the complexities of his politics and antinarrative strategies, but casts light on the nationalist debate of his day.

In *Milton,* as I demonstrate in chapter 5, Blake attacks the prevailing, neoclassical brand of British nationalism and begins to define his own national utopia. Blake decries the hegemony's exploitation of the neoclassical valorization of duty and self-sacrifice to further its militarist and imperial agenda, condemning the classics as artificial agents that corrupt native English culture and consequently personal imaginative vision; he establishes this unusual causality by using the national bard, Milton, as the personification of national culture. Restriction is revealed not only as a damning constraint, but also as a cultural structure that is incompatible with Blake's cultural ideal for a renovated England, an incompatibility that

Blake represents as an alienated body: "This is a false Body: an Incrustation over my Immortal / Spirit; a Selfhood, which must be put off & annihilated alway" (*M,* 40.35–36).

In *Jerusalem,* this notion of cultural infection making the political body strange to itself reaches its most elaborate expression, and that is the subject of chapter 6. The epic employs extensively a figure that I term the "vital/viral paradigm," a model of textual propagation in which ideologically acceptable works revitalize society as they circulate, directing the nation to its ideal state, while more controversial works spread like disease, invading the nation with alien interests and imperatives. I briefly trace this trope from Plato to William Cowper; but it became, I argue, particularly important as a means of decisively marking what is strange and dangerous, and what is good and beneficial, during the explosion of radical discourse at the turn of Blake's century and the ideological uncertainties that attended that explosion. It appears in writings by authors across the political spectrum, from radicals such as Mary Wollstonecraft and William Godwin to conservatives such as Francis Jeffrey and Burke, as Blake's contemporaries used the visceral impact of the medical trope to impose moral clarity. After reviewing a few of the figure's Romantic avatars, I examine its deployment in Blake's poems, particularly in Blake's more nationalist works, *Milton* and *Jerusalem.* In *Milton* and *Jerusalem,* Blake extends the implications of *America* and *Europe* to hybridize the body politic, fragmenting the national population according to its inspiration or infection by textually embodied ideology. Disease and cancerous growths, in this context, figure the transformation of individual identity in ways that can be limiting or liberating, depending on the transformative textual agent and the ideological perspective of the pseudomedical authority that claims the power to classify texts as viral or vital. With *Jerusalem,* Blake attempts to vaccinate the body politic against the diseases of "error." But, through the formulation of this vaccine, his own discourse, by the very logic of vaccination, is brought uncomfortably close to that which it is supposed to eradicate. This is the danger. In his early works, Blake limits himself to the nihilistic subversion of prevailing paradigms or, in other words, to bursting the stony roof. In *Milton,* however, Blake begins to cobble together his critical stances to form his own vision of the renovated nation, a vision that is completed in *Jerusalem.* Although he retains subversive strategies, such as multiperspectivism and defamiliarizing settings, Blake can use only hegemonic strategies to put his own system into place. Submerging difference in a totalizable system and imagining a countercolonization that sweeps the globe, Blake's discourse itself becomes hybrid, infected by the very paradigms that he had so long contested. I thus depart from traditional recuperations of *Jerusalem* as a profoundly religious or imaginative work to explore its darker side, particularly Blake's erasure of religious and national differences to expand his own homogeneous, colonizing nation.

The progression from chapter 1 to chapter 6 thus follows Blake from his subversion of the linearity that enables neoclassical nationalist narratives, to his critique of the replicated text, to his own replicating imperialist vision: "Therefore I print; nor vain my types shall be: / Heaven, Earth & Hell, henceforth shall live in harmony" (*J*, 3.9–10). While *Jerusalem* has, until recently, been read as a religious utopia, its assimilatory strategies and rhetoric connect it to contemporary imperialist practice and discourse. Not uncoincidentally, *Jerusalem* and *Laocoön* are roughly contemporary: together, they mark the unresolvable tension between nonconformity and comprehensibility that saturates Blake's work, and has troubled so many of Blake's readers. Blake resisted conventional standards and paradigms but could not, ultimately, defeat them because of his engagement with the structures that he wished to overturn—and the power that they offered.

THE LINE OF PROGRESS

Blake's *Laocoön* and Classicist Theories of Art

> So you see how I have run away from Wordsworth, and Milton; and shall still run away from what was in my head, to observe, that some kind of letters are good squares others handsome ovals, and others some orbicular, others spheroid. . . . If I scribble long letters, I must play my vagaries. I must be too heavy, or too light, for whole pages—I must be quaint and free of Tropes and figures—I must play my draughts as I please, and for my advantage and your erudition, crown a white with a black, or a black with a white, and move into black or white, far and near as I please—I must go from Hazlitt to Patmore, and make Wordsworth and Coleman play at leap-frog . . .
>
> Have you not seen a Gull, an orc, a sea Mew, or any thing to bring this Line to a proper length, and also fill up this clear part; that like the Gull I may *dip*—I hope, not out of sight—and also, like a Gull, I hope to be lucky in a good sized fish—This crossing a letter is not without its association—for chequer work leads naturally to a Milkmaid . . .
>
> *John Keats,* LETTER TO JOHN HAMILTON REYNOLDS (3 MAY 1818)

John Keats's whimsical corporealization of writing divorces the inky shapes on the paper from their verbal denotation and literary reference points.[1] "Free of Tropes and figures,"[2] his letters dance on the page as shapes rather than signifiers. Writing in Keats's letter becomes not only a verbal act of representation, but also an act to be represented, a multimedia performance that includes the painting on the page that must fill the surface of the canvas, the black-on-white plane of motion that mirrors the leaping of checkers across a game board, and the ballet of the hand's flying motion across the page and over to the inkwell. By celebrating the physical act of writing, Keats reminds us of its materiality, of the need to grasp the pen and shape the letters, of making choices and submitting to conventions regarding how they are shaped, of the gritty feel of a fountain pen scratching across a thick sheet of 100 percent cotton bond or the roll of a ballpoint across the grainless expanse of recycled paper—or, in our own day, percussive strikes on mildly resisting squares of plastic.

In *Writing Matter: From the Hands of the English Renaissance,* Jonathan Goldberg notes the intellectualization of the act at the expense of its physicality in Renaissance writing manuals; but writing was further decorporealized in the eighteenth century through the decisive separation of the arts (visual, verbal, aural) under the rigid codifications of neoclassicism.[3] However, Blake's own expositions of the visual, checkerboard effects of writing, most notably in *The Laocoön,* both resist and refute such abstracting pressures with effects that are less playful, and more urgently directed, than those of Keats's letter. In *The Laocoön,* emphasizing the spatiality of writing is part of an attack not only on classicism and its separation of the arts, but also on causality and linearity; by challenging conventional constructions of the properties and proprieties of the arts, Blake also removes the reader from the tyrannies of causality and sequence by producing a version of what Roland Barthes termed a "writerly" text, a text that approaches hypertext in its malleability for the reader and subverts, on the level of form, the dogmatic and rigidly linear narratives from Whig history to national narrations to scientific causality.[4]

Blake's resistance to classicism is a well-established tenet of his aesthetics but, as David Punter notes, it is also implicated in Blake's politics: the "classical regulation of form is seen as one among many manifestations of that fear-induced alienation by which humanity constrains and binds itself."[5] Classicism imposes formal standards that, in effect, standardize the artistic structures through which human experience is represented. In such works as *Understanding Media,* Marshall McLuhan has provoked an interest in precisely this problem, namely the ways in which form, or medium, silently configure the mass reception of cultural artifacts. One concern of McLuhan's, and of Blake's, is the impact of the mass-produced book: "Printing changed learning and marketing process alike. The book was the first teaching machine and also the first mass-produced commodity. . . . The psychic and social consequences of print included an extension of its fissile and uniform character to the gradual homogenization of diverse regions."[6] I shall discuss Blake's critique of the homogenizing power of the mass-produced book in chapter 4, which deals with the circulation of identical dictates throughout the social domain, but I want to emphasize here the standardization of form implicit in such productions.

In the Western tradition, books have a well-established conventional form: regular type, lines that read from left to right and from the top of the page to the bottom, pages that are read from the front of the book to the back, partitioned illustrations (if any), page numbers along an upper or lower edge, and often, in Blake's time, catchwords in the lower right-hand corner. This format produces page after page that is formally identical to every other page in the book, and formally iterative of every other page in every other book, completing the "perfection" sought by the writing handbooks examined by Goldberg in the handless and perfectly regular lettering of the printing press. While the mass production of texts homogenizes society by widely distributing identical messages, the standardization of bibliographical format homogenizes it by enforcing identical reading patterns and strategies. Every feature of the standard book format is, in one way or another, designed to support linearity: the arrangement of words and pages, as well as catchwords and pagination, provide clear and unimpeachable emplotments of the line of the text, while the separation of word and illustration, and the effacement of typographical difference through normalized typeface, enforce the perception of writing as a transcription of speech rather than as a graphological signifier that operates independently of its transcription.

Jacques Derrida has drawn attention to the latter in *Of Grammatology,* that is "the literary element," or "what in literature passes through an irreducibly graphic text, tying the *play of form* to a determined substance of expression."[7] While McLuhan quips, "The medium is the message," Derrida posits a dynamic interplay between form and content of a kind that has often engaged Blake scholars in readings that go beyond the text to the illustrations, erasures, and pagination of Blake's work. At issue, however, is not just the expanded framework in which we read Blake's works, but the contravention of norms that they present and the implications of such contraventions for reading as a verb rather than a noun. It is the standardization of form that submerges the "play of form," as the corollary to Shklovsky's observation that the unfamiliar holds our attention is that the familiar does not. By contesting the familiar, formal imperatives of mass-produced texts, Blake defamiliarizes both bibliographical conventions and the strategies by which theories of media and genre shape our perception of, and engagement with, words and pictures. He thereby generates a space for reading in which alternative strategies can be produced, rendering the modes of reading heterogeneous rather than uniform.

Some of Blake's more extreme contraventions of traditional bibliographical form can be found in the untitled design known as *The Laocoön* (see fig. 1).[8] While the texts pieced around the statue are often cited in support of various assertions about Blake's thought, they are generally removed from this multimedia context. The work is of uncertain date but has usually

Fig. 1 *The Laocoön* (copy B), Collection of Robert N. Essick.

been placed in the 1820s and is believed to be roughly contemporaneous with the design "On Homers Poetry"/ "On Virgil"; Robert N. Essick and Joseph Viscomi have recently produced compelling evidence that places the print's production circa 1826.[9] The design is certainly derived from the drawing Blake produced for Abraham Rees's *Cyclopaedia* (1819), in which a variety of subjects are surveyed pictorially through technical drawings and, in the case of sculpture, with sketches of famous works.

The engraving defies generic classification and is unique even in Blake's corpus.[10] It apparently denies the usual benefits of engraving through its single-plate and single-state production, as well as its limited print run. Generically, it at once suggests an illustrated essay, by surrounding the drawing of the sculpture with various assertions about art, and recalls a Renaissance emblem book, by placing the pictorial component in the foreground and piecing the verbal portion around it as an implicit gloss on the illustration.[11] Blake also follows this format in his *Illustrations of The Book of Job* (1825), commissioned in 1823,[12] but while he limits the amount of text on each design in *Job* and usually organizes the lines of text along architectural frames or within drawings of scrolls and books, the sheer textual plenitude of *Laocoön* forbids even such limited gestures toward generic recognizability.

The design recalls a jigsaw puzzle more than a page from an emblem book, graffiti more than an engraving, and marginal annotations more than aphorisms on art. *Laocoön*'s unrecognizability reflects its resistance to the conventions of the book and therefore to the models of reading that they presuppose. The multimedia performance of *The Laocoön,* combining sculpture, engraving, writing, and drawing, reminds us that the signifying process, for Blake, was technological and visual as well as textual. At issue here is not Blake's message but Blake's media. Mark Poster has recently argued, "Changes in the configuration or wrapping of language alters [*sic*] the way the subject processes signs into meanings, that sensitive point of cultural production,"[13] extending McLuhan's point about media to include variations on a formal level in ways that are useful for examinations of Blake's multimedia works. Transcriptions of the design included in editions of Blake's writings elide the work's "configuration" by erasing its contestation of "bibliographical codes" and so submerging the ways in which Blake inserts the work into a debate about the nature of art and, to bring us back to Punter's useful remarks, about the classicist valorization of linearity and causality in particular.

Lessing, Fuseli, and Blake: Laocoön *and Late-Eighteenth-Century Art Theory*

In *William Blake's Theory of Art* and, more recently, in *The Counter-Arts Conspiracy,* Morris Eaves has shown that Blake was deeply involved in the controversies and the concerns of the visual arts community in his day.[14] One controversy that has not yet garnered any attention from Blake critics, however, is Gotthold Ephraim Lessing's critique of the doctrine *ut pictura poesis.* In *Laocoön: An Essay on the Limits of Painting and Poetry* (1766), Lessing argues that the content of a work is determined by its medium: painting can deal with only a single moment, but can present various objects simultaneously; poetry can narrate a sequence of events, but cannot escape its linearity to present two objects at once.[15] Lessing did not choose his central example at random. During the eighteenth century, especially among German critics, the Laocoön was a recurring example in discussions about classicism, art theory, the relationship between the arts, and art history. Lessing's nemesis, Johann Joachim Winckelmann, used it extensively in *Reflections on the Imitations of Greek Works in Painting and Sculpture* (1755) as well as in the copious *History of Ancient Art* (1764). While it is generally accepted that "Winckelmann and Lessing rather decisively set the German debate about the Laocoon in terms of both the *querelle des anciens et des modernes* and *ut pictura poesis,*"[16] a host of other critics contributed to the debate, including Johann Wolfgang von Goethe, Johann Gottfried Herder, and Friedrich Schiller, as well as Johann Heinrich Füssli, or Henry Fuseli, as he became known after moving to England.[17]

In Blake criticism, Lessing is cited rarely and in passing, and usually not with reference to Blake's *Laocoön.*[18] In "Space and Time in *Milton:* The 'Bard's Song,'" Yvonne M. Carothers offers a rare exception, but she still compares Lessing's *Laocoön* to Blake's in nongenetic terms. She identifies Lessing's essay as "exemplary of the aesthetic principles operative in the arts of the latter eighteenth and early nineteenth centuries" and moves from a summary of Lessing's thesis to the assertion, "Of course, Blake would object to Lessing's theory of the imagination," but she does not address how closely the two *Laocoöns* are linked.[19] While Morton D. Paley maintains that "Lessing's *Laocoön* . . . does not seem to have been known by Blake at all, though it could have been through reports and fragmentary translations,"[20] there is significant evidence that suggests that Blake did know of Lessing's *Laocoön,* as well as textual evidence in Blake's *Laocoön* that strongly suggests that Blake actively engages the Lessing-Winckelmann debate in that engraving.

Although it is generally assumed that Blake knew virtually nothing of his German contemporaries, Blake's friend Fuseli was clearly familiar with Winckelmann's and Lessing's writings.[21] Fuseli, to whom Blake was particularly close during the 1790s, often figures prominently when the Laocoön debate surfaces in English: in 1765, he translated Winckelmann's *Reflections* into English;[22] in 1766, Johann Caspar Lavater asked Fuseli to review Lessing's *Laocoön;* in 1789, Fuseli ranked the Laocoön among the best three classical statues as he discussed his own aesthetic theory with a correspondent of Fanny Burney's;[23] in 1801, he cited Lessing's *Laocoön* and repeated its central thesis on the relationship between verbal and visual media, following Lessing's wording closely.[24] Furthermore, Lessing's text is mentioned in the *Analytical Review,* an interdisciplinary periodical published by Joseph Johnson and Thomas Christie that frequently printed contributions from the Johnson circle—including from Mary Hays, Mary Wollstonecraft, and Fuseli—as well as reviewed some of Blake's work.[25] In November 1794, the journal published a review of a book on the sublime; the review, by "R. R.," a regular contributor who has been identified as Fuseli by Eudo C. Mason, cites and names Lessing's text.[26] In the *Review,* R. R. accepts the basic premise of Lessing's argument, as Fuseli does in his *Lectures,* but also suggests that Lessing did not go far enough: "The futility of such mutual inroads of poetry and painting on each other has been shown by a late German writer of great acuteness and some taste, though on a tame principle, and without drawing the inferences that obviously derive from his rules."[27] He footnotes his reference to a "writer of great acuteness" with the remark, "G. E. Lessing, in a treatise entitled Laocoon; or on the limits of poetry and painting."[28] Moreover, Fuseli's third lecture, which summarizes, if not plagiarizes, Lessing's text, was written during the 1790s, at the height of Fuseli's and Blake's friendship. It was published in 1801, and was reprinted in 1820, the year after the publication of Blake's sketch of the statue in Rees's *Cyclopaedia.* Lessing's text would also have been of particular interest to the two colleagues because it deals at length with an issue important to both Fuseli and Blake, that is, the transformation of verbal material into a visual medium: Fuseli often based his paintings on passages from texts, illustrating the works of Aeschylus, Plutarch, Dante, Edmund Spenser, William Shakespeare, John Milton, and Thomas Gray, to name a few, while much of Blake's visual art, of course, consists of illustrations to his texts and others' writings.

There are also a number of correlations between Blake's work and the Laocoön controversy that suggest that Blake was aware of the debate and its key issues. Blake, for instance, identifies the sculptors of the Laocoön as "three Rhodians" (*L,* C), a claim made in Pliny and discussed at length by both Lessing and Winckelmann (the attribution is important to Lessing's interest in the textual source for the sculpture, should one exist). In his *History of Ancient Art,* Winckelmann discusses antique gems immediately after his analysis of the Laocoön,[29] while Blake ascribes the Laocoön and "Antique Gems" (*L,* C–D, D), both classical artifacts, to Hebraic sources. Lessing is concerned throughout his work with the question of unity, particularly in Homer, and Blake addresses the same issue briefly in *Laocoön* and more extensively in "On Homers Poetry," a text that also mentions the sculpture; "On Homers Poetry," moreover, is part of an engraving generally taken to be contemporary with Blake's *Laocoön.* There are also a number of correspondences that are too common in aesthetic theory to clearly indicate a connection, but are nevertheless suggestively similar. For instance, Lessing writes, "I grant that there is also such a thing as beauty in clothing, but what is that when compared to the beauty of the human form? And will he who can attain the greater be content with the lesser?" (39), while Blake asserts, "Art can never exist without Naked Beauty displayed" (*L,* B).

There is, however, more compelling evidence. Contesting some of Winckelmann's conclusions about the identity of the Laocoön's sculptors, Lessing begins with a piece of information that, he acknowledges, Winckelmann was "the first to publish" (146): the signature of the sculptors was inscribed on the recently discovered base of the Laocoön statue.[30] Blake usually signed his works along the bottom edge of either the plate or, in the case of some of the work that he did professionally, along the outer circumference of a design. But he signed the *Laocoön* engraving across the top of the statue's base (*L,* C–D), in a clear reference to Winckelmann's discovery, if not Lessing's challenge to Winckelmann's identification of the sculptors. Thus, Blake not only had every opportunity, by the 1820s, to learn of the Laocoön debate—whether from conversations with his friend Fuseli or from Fuseli's English writings and translations—but refers to information prominent in that debate in designs that refer to the statue.

Evading Genealogy and Chronology: Constructing a Nonlinear History

Given this context, it is important to examine Mason's suggestion that

"Blake's own *Laocoon* sheet of aphorisms on art [is] a body of art doctrine utterly opposed to everything Fuseli stood for."[31] The case is overstated, not least because many of the so-called aphorisms are not directly relevant to art, but it is nevertheless a useful observation, particularly in light of Essick and Viscomi's point that "the engraving reinterprets [the statue] textually"[32]: Blake, to some extent, uses the Laocoön to contest Fuseli's theories, especially those he took from Lessing, just as Lessing used the statue to contest Winckelmann's theories. Not only do many of the aphorisms contradict the classicist position that Fuseli advocated, but the form of the work itself, by emphasizing the spatial component of writing and using a nonlinear arrangement, refutes the thesis of Lessing's that Fuseli took to heart.

Lessing's premises are founded on the priority of chronology: the chronology of the various artistic representations of Laocoön's death is the object of much of his research, as he seeks to address the question of whether the statue is derived from a literary version or the converse, while chronology, he maintains, determines the order of his argument and, indeed, all writing. In his third lecture, Fuseli takes up this priority in his own way. After praising the visual arts on the grounds that "[i]n forms alone the idea of existence can be rendered permanent," he argues that, "as bodies exist in time as well as in space," it is necessary to put forms into motion and that "this is the *moral* element of the art."[33] "Invention," given as the title of the third lecture, is itself fundamentally chronological: "to invent is to find: to find something, presupposes its existence somewhere." And, through invention, form "discovers, selects, combines the *possible,*" where "[p]ossible . . . means the representation of effects derived from causes, or forms compounded from materials, heterogeneous and incompatible among themselves, but rendered so plausible to our senses, that the transition of one part to another seems to be accounted for by an air of organization."[34] Chronology thus not only is necessary to artistic ethics, but determines each step in artistic production: invention is a derivative of the possible, and the possible is defined as fundamentally derivative as well as perceived as linear (that is, transitions appear organized), as a derivative of other derivatives through the representation of causal relationships or static forms derived from prior materials. In this complex genealogy, the only nonderivative product is God's creation—hence Fuseli's devout insistence on using the term "invention" rather than "creation" when referring to human productions.[35] Chronology is not just a founding concept in Lessing's and Fuseli's theory of art, but a privileged one that generates value.

Genealogy is an important type of sequence in the context of these artistic debates because it carries with it the promise of transferable value. Classicists posited a history of art that was much like Hegel's history of empires: individual nations rise and fall, and then pass the baton of supremacy to the next imperial nation to rise. First Greece, then Rome, and then Renaissance Italy rose to artistic perfection; and, it was contended, Britain would be next. As Eaves puts it, "As X, so England, with X usually being ancient Greece, whose grace often extended sequentially to ancient Rome and Renaissance Italy. That historical sequence is the product rather than the origin of a more profound idea, that all past artistic success manifested a fundamental evolutionary pattern. The pattern, a gradual development based on the cumulative acquisition of concepts and skills, arrives in many alternative and overlapping forms."[36] This view of the history of art is, as Eaves's description of it suggests, heavily implicated in the motif of progress, in the assumption that success is constituted within a history of positive evolution. This is the assumption that governed pedagogical practice at the Royal Academy, where students were first fully trained in classical art before being allowed to work within more contemporary idioms, enacting on an individual level the historical progression that would authorize British art as descended from and superior to that of the classics.

In his *Public Address,* however, Blake denies that a nation's artistic power derives from such genealogies: "Englishmen rouze yourselves from the fatal Slumber into which Booksellers & Trading Dealers have thrown you Under the artfully propagated pretence that a Translation or a Copy of any kind can be as honourable to a Nation as An Original [*Belying*] Belying the English Character in that well known Saying Englishmen Improve what others Invent" (*PA,* 576). Blake also explicitly refuted, on the level of the artist rather than the nation, the position that success depends on building on the past successes of others: "If Art was Progressive We should have had Mich Angelo's & Rafaels to Succeed & to Improve upon each other But it is not so. Genius dies with its Possessor & comes not again till Another is Born with It" (Anno. Reynolds, 656).[37] Blake's resistance to linearity thus extends to the history of art and the pedagogical practice—learning the classics and the Masters before developing one's own art—that it informed.

Lessing's main concern regarding the statue of Laocoön, however, is its status as copy or original. Lessing begins his essay by seeking to establish that Virgil's *Aeneid* could not be based on the sculpture and closes by contradicting Winckelmann's dating of the work to lend historical support to his earlier argument:

> I must confess that the idea of Virgil's having imitated the artists is, to me, far more incomprehensible than the contrary assumption. If the artists followed the poet, I can account for all their deviations. They had to deviate because those very features found in harmonious relationship in the poet's work would have revealed some infelicities in their own. But why did the poet have to deviate? If he had faithfully followed the group in each and every detail, would he not still have given us an excellent picture? (41)

Lessing's exposition of the reasons in favor of the text being the "original" or a "copy" (45) is somewhat spurious because of the history of the statue, which Lessing elides. The Laocoön statue was found in a damaged state during the Renaissance and restored in a way that modified it: the original statue had Laocoön's arm bent behind his head but the statue's restorers and copiers rendered it outstretched.[38] Blake continues the tradition of revising the statue by altering the version of the sculpture that he would have seen in a number of details, complicating Lessing's easy polarization of "original" and "copy." Essick and Viscomi suggest that "Blake's artistic license is reflected most clearly in Laocoön's face and gown, his sons' positions, and the right son's . . . appearance."[39] In the restored sculpture, for instance, the child on the left extends his arm straight up, but Blake bends it at a right angle, reversing the modification of Laocoön's arm and oddly recalling the posture that Janet A. Warner has argued "connotes sleep or . . . an abandonment to sexual pleasure," but that Winckelmann identifies with suffering in his discussion of Laocoön's attitude in the original sculpture.[40] Further, in the sculpture, the child on the right places the two smaller fingers of his raised hand at right angles to his palm and other fingers, but Blake draws all four fingers parallel to each other and to the palm, almost exactly duplicating the gesture of "suffrager" in Bulwer's *Chirologia*. Also, the snake's head on the right in the sculpture is in profile, so that the viewer can see the jaws extended, but Blake turns the head almost ninety degrees, so that the viewer sees the more innocuous top of the head and not the devouring jaw. Blake's substitution of his own signature, "Drawn & Engraved by William Blake," for the sculptor's, "Athanodorus, son of Agesander, of Rhodes, made it," is another revision as well as one that calls attention to the others. Blake, in short, did not copy but created his own *Laocoön*.

Blake also characterizes his reinterpretation as another restoration that resurrects the original. While Lessing and those whom he cites quarreled about whether the statue was the inspiration for or a copy of the pertinent passage in Virgil's *Aeneid*, Blake, citing the usual passage from Pliny, writes, "יה & his two Sons Satan & Adam as they were copied from the Cherubim / of Solomons Temple by three Rhodians & applied to Natural Fact. or. History of Ilium," beneath the podium (*L*, C–D). Blake enters the debate summarized by Lessing in the early chapters of *Laocoön* by arguing that the statue is not based on Virgil's *Aeneid* or a common prior text, as Lessing suggests (34), but was copied from a Hebraic visual artifact and was appropriated by classicists. Moreover, since one biblical account of Solomon's Temple refers to "graved cherubims on the walls" (2 Chronicles 3.7), Blake is arguably suggesting that he has returned the statue to its original medium, engraving.[41] Blake makes a similar argument on the right edge of the design, asserting that "What we call Antique Gems / are the Gems of Aarons Breast Plate" (*L*, D), once again locating a Hebraic origin for works praised as classical by neoclassicists. Similar references to Hebrew culture appear in the texts that surround the statue: "Hebrew Art is / called Sin by the Deist Science" (*L*, B); "The Gods of Priam are the Cherubim of Moses & Solomon" (*L*, A); "Israel deliverd from Egypt / is Art deliverd from / Nature & Imitation" (*L*, C). Blake thus engages the eighteenth-century debate between the classical and the modern, in which Winckelmann and Lessing were central, by ascribing important classical artifacts to Hebrew art, as he wraps the statue in Hebrew script and references to the Old Testament and Hebrew Apocrypha and presents his own version of the statue as the lost original.[42]

There is more at stake here, however, than the "History of Ancient Art." Recently, Victor Anthony Rudowski and Carol Jacobs have argued separately that Lessing distorts the chronology of his reading of Winckelmann, suppressing his knowledge of Winckelmann's later work in order to sustain his absolute contradiction of the critic for polemical purposes.[43] Lessing's *Laocoön* thus "tells us that *actual* historical priorities are not at stake but rather the very concept of historical priority so thoroughly ironized throughout the text."[44] Jacobs argues that Lessing's concern with imitation—emphasized by his choice of an epigraph from Plutarch, "They distinguish themselves from one another in their objects and mode of imitation"[45]—is implicated in his own anxiety about appearing to be imitating

Winckelmann, so that locating Virgil before the Laocoön becomes tropologically linked with locating Lessing's *Laocoön* before Winckelmann's *History of Ancient Art.* Blake's argument about priority and imitation is itself polemical. It is concerned not with historical validity but with asserting the precedence of Hebrew art to construct classical art as a fall from its precursor, in direct contradiction of the neoclassicists' claim that contemporary art has fallen from the ideals of classical artifacts. In a work contemporary with *The Laocoön,* "On Homers Poetry"/ "On Virgil," Blake makes a more explicit assertion on this point: "Sacred Truth has pronounced that Greece & Rome as Babylon & Egypt: so far from being parents of Arts & Sciences as they pretend: were destroyers of all Art. Homer Virgil & Ovid confirm this opinion & make us reverence The Word of God, the only light of antiquity that remains unperverted by War. Virgil in the Eneid Book VI. line 848 says Let others study Art: Rome has somewhat better to do, namely War & Dominion" ("On Virgil"). Blake cites the same passage from Virgil in *The Laocoön* (*L,* B) and uses the same identification of classical cultures with imperialism and the corruption of art, a charge that is made with even greater force in *Milton,* as I will discuss in chapter 5. In "On Homers Poetry" and "On Virgil," however, Blake opposes to the classics not just the Bible but also the Gothic: "The Classics, it is the Classics! & not Goths nor Monks, that Desolate Europe with Wars" ("On Homers Poetry"); "Grecian is Mathematic Form / Gothic is Living Form" ("On Virgil"). Since, historically, the classical period falls between biblical Israel and the Gothic period in Europe, Blake's chronology is not founded on the sequence of events but on a scale of aesthetic values: "Mathematic Form is Eternal in the Reasoning Memory. Living Form is Eternal Existence" ("On Virgil"). Blake argues that Gothic and Hebrew art are part of "Eternal Existence," transhistorical artifacts that embody artistic values and precede the corruption of those values by militaristic cultures. The paradigm that informs Blake's identification of the Laocoön as a copy of the cherubim in Solomon's Temple is thus not chronological but hierarchical, as it is plotted relative to a range of aesthetic values rather than temporality.

The poet's challenge to the predominant assumption of sequential progression from success to success supports both his rejection of the classics and his insistence that geniuses are born rather than taught. The Laocoön is, in many ways, an eminently suitable emblem of the proclassical tradition that Fuseli and Lessing accepted without question: sculpted by Greeks and then revised during the Renaissance by its restorers, the Laocoön is a bridge between the two traditions as well as proof that the

Renaissance could improve on the Greeks by outstretching Laocoön's arm and so, as Winckelmann put it, preventing it from "divid[ing] the principal attention."[46] Blake, by modifying it himself and claiming that it was a derivative of a Hebraic engraving, inserts the work into his own Gothic-Hebraic coordinates, challenging linearity as a rubric that governs the narrativization of art history in favor of a nonchronological value system.

Transgressing the Line of Writing

Lessing, however, goes beyond this model of artistic progress to apply its linearity to writing itself. Poetry, Lessing argues, is sequential and temporal, while the visual arts are instantaneous and spatial. Consequently, the visual artist must choose a pivotal moment, while the verbal artist must address the whole narrative. Lessing draws attention to the chronology of his writing and reading, asserting in his preface, "the following chapters . . . were written as chance dictated and more in keeping with my reading than through any systematic development of general principles. Hence they are to be regarded more as unordered notes for a book than as a book itself"; then, after expanding on his Blakean opposition to the book as the medium of systems, Lessing adds that he "start[s], as it were, with the Laocoön and return[s] to it a number of times" (5).[47] The critic thus ties the sequence of his work to the chronology of his experiences of other works in a way that recalls his paradigm on the properties of artistic media: he identifies the Laocoön with a point of departure or arrival that can, as on a surface, be approached from many different points, while associating his writing with temporal sequence only. More to the point, Lessing's *Laocoön* is not only about the limitations of verbal and visual media, but also about the transformation caused by those limitations when a particular content is translated from one medium into the other. Lessing's concern with the statue's origin is not a simple question of art history, because it operates as an excuse for moving from the differences of fact between the various artistic representations of the event to the ways in which the media's different limitations enforce variations in representation. The former set of disparities establishes genetic relationships, but the latter establishes generic relationships.[48] It is this question of media that Fuseli singles out in his own "copy" of Lessing: "poetry and painting resemble each other in their uniform address to the senses . . . [and] differ as essentially in their *materials* and their *modes* of application, which are regulated by the diversity of the organs they address, ear and eye. *Successive action* communicated by sounds, and *time,* are the medium of poetry; *form* displayed in *space,* and momentaneous energy, are the element of painting."[49] Blake's engraving challenges this paradigm. While works such as *Milton* also challenge narrative linearity, dealing at verbal length with a single moment from a variety of perspectives as well as combining visual and verbal media,[50] *The Laocoön* is almost a work of daredevilry: it is Blake's cocky demonstration that he can exceed the limitations of painting and poetry delineated by Lessing. The mystic was not immune to the temptation of the occasional swagger, as poems such as "When Klopstock England Defied" attest; his *Laocoön* is a refutation of Lessing's thesis, and Fuseli's dictum, delivered with a flourish.

The linear, orderly structure of verbal media—whether writing, printing, or typography—is undone in the engraving, as Blake instead gives shape to his pieces of text, by bending them in arcs, horseshoes, trapeziums, and even a question mark, as well as more conventional rectangles with indentations on alternate lines, and by fitting them into the interstices left between his drawing of the statue and the borders of the plate. Lawrence Lipking's important observation that Blake defaces Reynolds's *Discourses* by scribbling in the volume's margins to challenge its authoritarian stance is pertinent here.[51] Blake not only revises the great statue in his own way but also scribbles in the margins of the Laocoön and refuses to write a book on art, instead annotating an absent debate. Through the *Laocoön,* Blake iconographically inserts his annotations into the discourse to which they refer while producing a clash of media and texts that not only avoids the pitfalls that he saw in the bookish medium of that discourse but engages, by its very form, some of the questions that concerned his colleagues. The Laocoön was the touchstone of a series of debates that dealt not just with classicism or the unity of the arts, but with the properties of different artistic media. By combining as many as four different media in *Laocoön*—drawing, writing, engraving, and sculpture—Blake puts into play these different properties, engaging the debate in theory as well as practice.

The work offers no beginning and no ending, no top and no bottom, and no grammatical units to follow for more than a brief span. As an entity to be read, the engraving shatters sequence as well as completion: it defies the reader to read all of the words and be sure that all are read, to read all of the words and be sure that the grammatical units are all discerned. Blake refuses to produce a text like that which his twentieth-century editors sought—a linear text that has a beginning and an ending. Unlike in Blake's other illuminated works, the verbal component of the engraving is not presented in the conventional series of horizontal lines. The lines are written in all directions—horizontally, vertically from top to bottom, vertically from bottom to top, and in curves that correspond to the lines of the statue. Only the left and bottom edges are consistent in the directions of their texts, and only the latter edge does not have divisions that are perpendicular to the line of writing, thus making it alone readable in the conventional manner. To read the left edge, the page must be turned sideways and the reader must decide whether to read column by column, or straight across, and accept that neither alternative is facilitated by the arrangement of the grammatical units of words. The remaining space of the engraving conjoins texts that are written in curves, horizontally, and vertically. Where does one begin? It is not possible to read from left to right, from top to bottom, from page 1 to page 2, and each reorientation of the work makes a different group of texts readable. The necessity of repeatedly reorienting the design to make it legible forces an engagement with the physicality of the printed page,[52] recalling the letter that Keats wrote a few years before. The usual organization of a book's textual components effaces its corporeality through an arrangement of words that renders the problems of reading invisible by organizing words into a clear sequence that does not ask the reader to stop, to find a new place to start, to try to keep track of what has been read and what has not, and by following conventions that are so familiar that they are no longer noticeable. But Blake's textual pieces mirror the broken bodies of the snakes: flattened from three dimensions into two, it is impossible to trace their serpentine lines for more than a short space.

The nonlinearity of Blake's *Laocoön* has traditionally been recuperated by the characterization of the work as a collection of aphorisms, exploding the nonlinear work into a nonlinear assemblage of perfect lines—an anthology of serpentine fragments or, as Essick and Viscomi put it, "[A]n onslaught of inscribed axioms."[53] While the textual elements of the design contain assertions that can certainly be classified as aphorisms, there are other texts that clearly are not aphoristic. Before Essick and Viscomi's edition of the design, one that limits editorial intervention to indications of the passages' spatial placement, passages from *The Laocoön* that could not be recuperated as aphorisms were segregated, or even eliminated, in editions of Blake's work, marginalized as graphic supplements to a series of aphoristic doctrinal assertions. Hazard Adams omits the nonaphoristic texts in his selection from *Laocoön;* Geoffrey Keynes places the four texts that are most resistant to aphoristic classification at the four corners of a parallelogram at the top of a list of texts less resistant to that designation; while Max Plowman and Erdman divide the texts into unclassified preludia and writings that are explicitly designated as "aphorisms." The tendency to read the pieces of texts as aphorisms has even guided the organization of the material. Erdman, whose edition is known and lauded for its preservation of Blake's punctuation, ignores many of the line breaks in this particular text or represents them as a series of horizontal spaces, normalizing the spatial arrangement of the texts to conform to standards established for prose fragments. Blake's departure from prosaic form is most marked in a passage in the upper-right-hand corner of the design that is "written out in fair straight lines, with a capital at the beginning of each":[54]

> Divine Union
> Deriding
> And Denying Immediate
> Communion with God
> The Spoilers say
> Where are his Works
> That he did in the Wilderness
>   Lo what are these
> Whence came they
> These are not the Works
> Of Egypt nor Babylon
> Whose Gods are the Powers
> Of this World. Goddess, Nature.
> Who first spoil & then destroy
> Imaginative Art
> For their Glory is
> War and Dominion. (*L*, B)

There are only two other texts in the design that capitalize the first word of a line that is syntactically dependent on the preceding line; the vast majority of texts in which a line is clearly linked to its predecessor do not capitalize the first word of the subsequent line.[55] Yet this passage is almost always transcribed as prose. Such deformation elides line breaks, alters capitalization, and makes the texts look aphoristic. Essick and Viscomi's representation of the design looks very different from the others', with unusual indentations and typographical arrangements that support their characterization of the verbal content of the design as "a dense *web* of axioms and epigrams."[56]

This "onslaught," however, is particularly complicated because it exceeds the generic categories of aphorism, axiom, or epigram. The engraving includes single words ("Good" [*L,* B], "Evil" [*L,* A]), scholarly imperatives,[57] descriptions of the design that cite the original of the drawing and the artists involved, proper names in Hebrew and Greek that are set apart from other words,[58] and biblical-style fragments such as "He repented that he had made Adam / (of the female, the Adamah) / & it grieved him at his heart" (*L,* A–B). The texts of Blake's *Laocoön* thus often depart radically from the genre, particularly as seen in Lavater's *Aphorisms on Man* (a work translated by Fuseli and heavily annotated by Blake)—but not always. The collection of texts that surround the engraving of the statue are generically heterogeneous, calling into question the generic status of assertions that, isolated from this complex context, might appear aphoristic.

In his essay on Blake's mock proverbs, Gavin Edwards notes that proverbs are aphorisms with a history, sayings that have become recognizable by and significant through their common, familiar usage. Writing about the proverbs in *The Marriage of Heaven and Hell,* Edwards suggests that

> Blake knew very well that he was producing aphorisms and not proverbs. He ironically emphasizes the gap between the two by inventing a society in which his aphorisms become proverbs by utopian fiat. . . . In working with proverbs and answering them Blake is not simply proposing alternative proverbs—proverbs of hell against proverbs of the church; he is questioning the finality of proverbs as such, refusing their authority, insisting on replying to these replies, on revealing what proverbs try to conceal, that they are acts of speech among others.[59]

The ease with which Blake's aphorisms in *Laocoön* are taken as authoritative—indeed, the ease with which the design is reduced to an amalgam of aphorisms with its other components elided—therefore needs to be called into question.[60] If Blake's Proverbs of Hell "question[] the finality of proverbs," then a nonlinear arrangement of aphoristic and nonaphoristic texts, an arrangement that offers neither formal nor theoretical closure while mimicking the strangulating movement of the snakes, questions that finality on even more levels. While Lessing's polemic depended, formally and conceptually, on the linearity of writing to insert each point into a validating causality, Blake's nonlinear assemblage offers a collection of loci that can be "hooked up" to other texts in ways that are not predetermined and so do not lock it into a causal frame that contains its signification.

Editing as Transformation: Reading the Nonlinear Text

So, Blake's *Laocoön* disrupts the chronology of art history, the assumptions of causality, the linearity of writing, and the finality of doctrinal statements. But what, exactly, does it offer instead? While the editorial liberties that have been taken with the design suggest that it has no authorial order, I would argue that it does have such an order and that this order is related to strategies for organizing the elements of visual works of art and Blake's suspicion of set linear readings. Blake's organization can be recuperated, in part, with attention to the ways in which editors transform *The Laocoön* into a linear text. Blake's editors almost invariably include *The Laocoön* in selections from his works, but in transcribing its verbal component they inevitably elide the medium of the design in favor of the messages of which the work is supposed to consist. Jerome McGann, discussing Blake's *Jerusalem,* praises Erdman's edition of the work for "translat[ing] Blake's illuminated work into a reasonable set of typographical equivalences," but notes that different "bibliographical codes" are at work in Blake's illuminated work and Erdman's transcription of it.[61] Even facsimile editions cannot duplicate such qualities as the texture of the paper, the layering of colour over the indentations caused by the printing process, and the collection of the pages (leaving aside the perennial question in Blake studies of the variations between copies of many of his works). To one degree or another, Blake's *Jerusalem* is normalized as it is reproduced in new editions: at the very least, such editions generate the bound and duplicated book, which was anathema to Blake, rather than a unique, handcrafted copy; more usually, the lettering is standardized, the designs and coloring disappear, capitalization and punctuation are normalized, and Blake's illuminated works are transformed into a form that is visually indistinguishable from that of the standard book.

Nowhere is this transformation more marked than in transcriptions of Blake's *Laocoön.* "Typographical translations" of the design, to use McGann's terminology,[62] not only eliminate the drawing that dominates the piece and rearrange the lines of text, but also normalize the typography; Erdman, for instance, renders words in Gothic script through block capitals. The commonalities between these different editions indicate an editorial imperative to render Blake's engraving consistent with existing models. It is conventional to place the title of a picture in large type along the bottom edge of the design; therefore the lines "יה & his two Sons Satan & Adam as they were copied from the Cherubim / of Solomons Temple by three Rhodians & applied to Natural Fact. or. History of Ilium" must be the title. It is conventional to read from top to bottom, and therefore the words, after being grouped by grammatical rules, must be published in such an order, although some exception may be made for certain departures from this order. Apart from their treatment of these two features, Blake's editors differ radically from each other. Among the many editions of Blake's works, *Laocoön* is never transcribed in the same sequence twice. Despite the application of similar editorial paradigms, each transformation of the work to conform to bibliographical codes produces a different linear text.

Each edition of the work is finally only one reading of the work, one possible sequence of the lines—and often one that it is difficult to arrive at by reading the engraving rather than taking the "aphorisms" out of that context and rearranging them on another page. For instance, under the statue, Blake writes four lines that Essick and Viscomi, in their edition of the text, designate as the first four lines of the design:

> If Morality was Christianity Socrates was the Saviour
> יה & his two Sons Satan & Adam as they were copied from the Cherubim
> of Solomons Temple by three Rhodians & applied to Natural Fact, or History of Ilium
> Art Degraded Imagination Denied War Governed the Nations.[63]

(This numbering of the lines is, of course, contingent on the convention that one reads horizontally toward the right and then moves downward to the next horizontal line.) In Plowman's edition, the second and third lines are given as the title, and the first and fourth lines are seventh and eighth in a general list of aphorisms. Keynes begins his transcription of the design with a stylized representation of the arrangement of certain words and phrases, then lists the second and third lines under the statue, then the first, and then the fourth. In Adams's edition, the second and third lines are given first, the fourth line is listed nineteenth, and the first line is given third last. Mary Lynn Johnson and John E. Grant print the second and third lines first, in larger type, typographically implying titular status, then the fourth and finally the first; the classification of the middle lines as a title is reinforced by their parenthetical, and newly capitalized, addition to the design's usual appellation, "The Laocoön (Yah and His Two Sons)." In Erdman's edition, the second and third lines are given first, the fourth line appears in the middle of a general list of statements, and the first line is given, as in Adams's edition, third last.[64] Essick and Viscomi are refreshingly sensitive to the placement of the passages in Blake's design, indicating that placement in their bracketed directions and in their retention of some of Blake's groupings of the lines.[65] But still their ordering of the passages skips from segment to segment of Blake's design, from "below the plinth" to "above the serpent's head on the left" and from "vertically in the right margin" to "on the plinth" as they spiral outward along an uninscribed web, circling clockwise around the statue and then the surrounding areas of the plate.[66] There is little consensus among these editions: one of the better-known, if often misquoted, statements from the engraving, "The Old & New Testaments are / the Great Code of Art" (*L,* B), is listed eleventh in Erdman's general list, twelfth in Adams's list, fourteenth in Plowman's general list, ninth last by Keynes, seventh last by Johnson and Grant, and appears as lines 99–100 in Essick and Viscomi's edition. The groupings of the lines also differ radically from edition to edition.

Erdman does not classify the texts by theme until after he has listed two other categories of texts: first, the material normally proper to the title page, namely Blake's signature, "Drawn & Engraved by William Blake" (*L,* C–D), and the two lines that Plowman calls the title; second, a selection of texts that are classified by their proximity to sections of the figures. Then, the rest of the texts are grouped under the heading "Remaining aphorisms, reading outward in thematic order."[67] How, though, does one define "outward"? Erdman gives the horizontally placed statement "Art can never exist without / Naked Beauty displayed" (*L,* B), which begins one line below the upper edge, before the vertical lines "No Secre / sy in Art" (*L,* B), which begin five lines to the left of the right edge. How, especially, does one define "thematic order"? Such an order requires that the words be grouped in particular ways and that each group have a governing theme. But is the group "Where any view of Money exists Art cannot be carried on. but War only / by pretences to the Two Impossibilities Chastity & Abstinence Gods of the Heathen" (*L,* A–B) about war, art, commerce, mythology, or virtue? And what unarticulated notions of "order" govern the other editions? The wide range of editorial solutions to Blake's textual puzzle, within the editorial unanimity about the importance of the two lines under the statue and the necessity of publishing the lines horizontally in a vertical order, demonstrates both an impetus toward a recognizable order and the limitations of recognizable orders when confronted with that which refuses to be recognizable. The editors agree that the words engraved on the design must be given a linear order—a sequence through which the engraving could be read from beginning to end without a word being missed—and share a recognition of the titlelike qualities, typographic and referential, of the description of the statue, while also attempting to address the difficulty of converting to that conventional form a work that does not conform to such conventions.

Erdman, usually scrupulous about editorial interventions in Blake's illuminated works, handles the *Laocoön* in a particularly telling way. By normalizing the typography, even modernizing one of the Hebrew letters,[68] eliding line breaks or representing them as spaces, and organizing the texts into "roughly thematic sequence," he normalizes the texts according to literary conventions; but he also includes a reproduction of the *Laocoön* design in his edition and remarks in his notes, "There is no right way to read [the inscriptions]—except all at once and as the frame of the picture."[69] This is an important departure from the presentation of transcriptions of the design as unproblematic editions, and it brings us right back to Lessing and Fuseli. Given the art theorists' insistence that painting is "momentaneous," Erdman's remark that the texts, as they appear in Blake's design, should be "read . . . all at once" and as "the frame of the picture" seems to offer not a resolution to the transgressive spatial component of the writing but its recuperative translation from a verbal medium to a visual one, in which its nonlinear organization is appropriate. In short, if it is not linear, it must be a picture—a ready corollary to Lessing's paradigm—and experienced in the terms prescribed for that medium. By reproducing the engraving, one of just four illustrations in his edition of Blake, and setting it beside his linear transformation of the plate's texts, along with his editorial note on how to read the former, Erdman splits the work along media lines: first, Blake's engraving as a visual work, to be viewed "at once," in the moment, and then its translation into readable format, a verbal work to be read in the traditional, linear manner. This splitting is reinforced by a printing accident in Erdman's latest edition, namely the inclusion of the reverse image of the design.[70] Instead of the typographically familiar black lettering on a white ground, the reader is presented with the more alien white lettering on a black ground. But this corruption of the textual recognizability of the design restores the whiteness, and so the recognizability, of the statue, reinforcing the illustration's visually defined function in the edition. Erdman's editorial treatment of the work elides the contradiction of the rules of media implicit in the design by producing two versions of the plate, each under the rubric of a different medium, splitting apart its formal hybridity to produce two generically pure works—a "momentaneous" picture of a statue in a frame and a series of verbal aphorisms arranged by theme.

Erdman's measures, extraordinary in editorial terms but conventional in their segregation of visual and verbal forms, thus raise an important question: How does one read a work without a clear sequence? Blake's statements repudiate genealogy and historical timelines, while their very form subverts Lessing's claim that writing is founded on simple sequence. These questions about how we publish verbal material and what that indicates about how we read and what we expect are not simply editorial. Such constructions impinge on the content of the material. Blake's disruption of the conventions of arrangement, from foreground and background to the horizontal orientation of lines and the vertical sequence of those lines, subverts those constructions and the ideologies that produced them. Linearity and definitive order are repressed and so process as an ongoing investigation of alternative orders—none of which is sanctioned by the text or the author—is made possible. The various editorial constructions of *Laocoön* as a linear text, as a text with divisions by genre, subject, or spatial orientation, as a text that conforms to bibliographical conventions, not only foreground the kind of editorial "intervention" that McGann discusses in the second chapter of *The Textual Condition,* but also deflect the possibilities of the text. Each of these interventions is a reading, and the plurality of the editorial interventions indicates the degree to which Blake has challenged the most basic rules of book making. By combining media in a way that contravenes conventional practice and prevailing theory, Blake, in effect, does what Nicole Brossard calls "breaking the habits of reading." She writes, "I believe that a text gives subliminal information on how it wants to be read. Its structure is itself a statement, no matter what the text says. . . . So by changing the perspective, the themes, or the style, somehow you deceive the conformist reader in her or his moral or aesthetic expectations and you annoy her or him by breaking the habits of reading . . . [and] you also offer the non-conformist reader a space for a new experience."[71] *The Laocoön* forces the recognition that we do not read the same way twice and that our access to the text is not transparent, but depends on certain rules: linearity and order (whether thematic, generic, spatial, or formal) conventionally govern our contact with the text but do not totalize it.

In its atelic nonlinearity, *Laocoön* anticipates the modern hypertext. Michael Joyce defines the hypertext not as a stable artifact but as an activity, as "reading and writing electronically in an order you choose; whether among choices represented for you by the writer, or by your discovery of the topographic (sensual) organization of the text. Your choices, not the author's representations or the initial topography, constitute the current state of the text."[72] Like the hypertext, *Laocoön* has no single beginning, no single ending, but innumerable places to begin and end. It is, in V. A. De Luca's phrase, a "wall of words" that calls up both visual and verbal modes of meaning and aesthetic pleasure.[73] The beginning is not defined by the number of the page and its position on that page, but by where the reader chooses to begin, and, as Brossard and Mary Ann Caws point out, linearity is fundamental to conventionality.[74] As with a hypertext, the reader can skip, reread, end, and begin again, without being bound by linearity. In *The Laocoön,* Blake writes, "Without Unceasing Practise nothing can be done Practise is Art / If you leave off you are Lost" (*L,* A): a text without a beginning or an end offers no place at which to "leave off" and be "Lost." Blake mixes scripts, genres, media, languages, and even planes, disrupting the smooth reading that texts such as Lavater's permit, by proliferating "modes of information," to use Poster's revision of McLuhan's central dictum:

> McLuhan's axiom that "the medium is the message" points in the direction of the mode of information but does not go far enough. . . . In the mode of information the subject is no longer located in a point in absolute time/space, enjoying a physical, fixed vantage point from which rationally to calculate its options. . . . In the perspective of Deleuze and Guattari, we are being changed from "arborial" beings, rooted in time and space, to "rhizomic" nomads who daily wander at will . . . across the globe . . . without necessarily moving our bodies at all.[75]

While Poster is concerned with the effects of electronic media—television, the Internet, fax machines, cell phones—his attention to the ways in which constructions of media reinforce particular forms of subjectivity is useful for grasping the radicality of Blake's engraving. Without the fixed points of reference that a stable chronological organization of the text constructs, Blake's readers become "nomads who . . . wander at will" through the work—like Keats's "vagaries." Without the "fixed vantage point" of the upper left-hand corner (so tacitly marked "begin here" that we no longer even notice the instruction), the margins, the lower right-hand corner ("move to the next page, now"), readers are loosed from the "absolute time/space" of the printed page, in which the space of letters strung in a row must be rigidly followed through time.

This is not to suggest that Blake's work is completely chaotic, but to suggest that it requires its readers to open up new routes, and new ways of imagining routes, as Keats does, through a recognition that the words on a page also function visually. The design is traversed by nonlinear orders. "Science" is printed, twice, in Gothic Germanic script, and so are "Death" and "Sin"—but so are "Jesus" and "Life."[76] All examples of that script, moreover, are confined to the lower half of the upper-right-hand quadrant of the design, suggesting an echoing among the terms of these binaries (death/life and Jesus/sin) as well as the taxonomical force, science, that turns the positive terms into their negative avatars. At the same time, two of those texts allude to Genesis: "Art is the / Tree / of Life / GOD / is Jesus" (*L*, B); "Science is the / Tree of Death" (*L*, B). The third passage inserts those two references to the Edenic trees into Blake's argument about Hebrew art, asserting that "Hebrew Art is / called Sin by the Deist Science" (*L*, B). Separating the allusions to Genesis from the condemnation of aspersions on Hebrew art are seventeen lines that associate empire with the destruction of art, an imperial agenda that Blake identifies with Greece and Rome but opposes to the Gothic in "On Homers Poetry" for reasons that could extend to the Hebraic. Thus the Gothic lettering of Hebraic references echoes the two cultures' shared position in Blake's anti-imperial topography, further affirming their cultural redemption from the taint of militarism through art. Similarly, single words echo across the design in geometrical patterns. References to the Antichrist appear at diagonally opposed corners, for instance, while the words "Good & Evil" are engraved over the smaller son's right arm at the top of a triangular formation, with "Good" over a snake's head at the lower right-hand corner and "Evil" over the second snake's head at the lower left-hand corner: "Good" appears to be biting Laocoön's hip and "Evil" is clearly biting the younger son's hip. Numerous other connections are invited by Blake's combination of genres, media, and forms, from the placement of "The Angel of the Divine Presence" over the line "Angel Jehovah" in Hebrew,[77] as a kind of translation, to the suggestive wrapping of "If you leave off you are Lost" (*L,* A) around the priest's outstretched fist, which struggles to hold the snake and impede its dangerous coiling.

These different mediating contexts—genre, script, placement, illustrative relationships, translation, and so forth—suggest that the work goes beyond being nonlinear to being multidimensional, as intersecting planes of signification cross through every element of the work. "Science" is crossed by all of the other occurrences of the word on the design, by its opposition to art, by its different placement on the right half of the design, by its different scripts, by its relationship to knowledge through Genesis, and through that relationship to Blake's condemnation of Reynolds's view of the artist as a student rather than a genius, and so on and so on. Being nonlinear, in other words, does not make the textual fragments disorganized, as the editorial license with which the work has been treated suggests.[78] Linearity is a familiar road—and Blake's *Laocoön* offers a kaleidoscope that needs only a shake to create a new pattern.[79] While Lessing, and Fuseli, separated the arts and delineated their limits, Blake combines the arts and transgresses their limits.

Throughout these controversies about the limits of media, modes of reading, art history, and linearity, Laocoön and his sons struggle with the snakes. Laocoön's outstretched arm, holding a coil of the snake in his tightly clamped fist, figures this struggle with the line while, in the plane of the two-dimensional engraving, his fist succeeds in breaking the serpentine line. A priest who stood at a series of boundaries—between the gods and the people, between the Trojans and the Greeks, between victory and defeat, and at the moment between life and death—and was later located, through eighteenth-century debates about the statue, in a tangle of chronological lines, is a useful figure for Blake's political and formal contestation of the line.

"WHENCE CAME THEY"

Contesting National Narrative

OISIN. O Patrick!—to the Finian race
A falsehood was unknown
No lie, not imputation base
On our clear fame was thrown. . . .
Not thy own clerks in truth excell'd
The heroes of our line.

Anonymous, THE CHASE

In *The Laocoön,* Blake contests the use of linearity as the organizing structure of writing and as the formal means of directing the reader's experience of the text. But this question of linearity and the control of reading is not limited to debates about art theory and art history. The history of art outlined by Eaves is entangled in contemporary nationalist notions of cultural progress. Consequently, in his *Public Address,* Blake not only condemns the progressive model of art history and the copying that it sanctions, but slips periodically into condemnations of a more general, nationalist scope:

> Commerce is so far from being beneficial to Arts or to Empire that it is destructive of both. (*PA,* 574)
> Englishmen rouze yourselves from the fatal Slumber into which Booksellers & Trading Dealers have thrown you Under the artfully propagated pretence that a Translation or a Copy of any kind can be as honourable to a Nation as An Original [*Belying*] Be-lying the English Character in that well known Saying Englishmen Improve what others Invent. (*PA,* 576)
> The English Artist may be assured that he is doing an injury & injustice to his Country while he studies & imitates the Effects of Nature. (*PA,* 578)
> The wretched state of the Arts in this Country & in Europe originating in the Wretched State of Political Science . . . (*PA,* 580)

While, as Eaves suggests, Blake's dominant concern in his *Address* is "a national art vying with the art of other nations," these references to "English Character," "Country," and an "Empire" that is distinct from the "Arts," suggest that Blake is also engaging a broader national agenda.[1]

Traditionalists who believed that progress must be made by building on past successes were not confined to the art world. Political conservatives emphasized tradition as the foundation of ongoing national progress, justifying the status quo through reference to its long life and plotting a slow evolution of society that remained consistent in revealing certain valued features, such as a monarchy or the domestic containment of women. Such a model permeates Burke's notorious tract *Reflections on the Revolution in France* (1790):

> By a constitutional policy, working after the pattern of nature, we receive, we hold, we transmit our government and our privileges, in the same manner in which we enjoy and transmit our property and our lives. The institutions of policy, the goods of fortune, the gifts of Providence, are handed down, to us and from us, in the same course and order. Our political system is placed in a just correspondence and symmetry with the order of the world, and with the mode of existence decreed to a permanent body composed of transitory parts; wherein . . . the whole, at one time, is never old, or middle-aged, or young, but in a condition of unchangeable constancy, moves on through the varied tenour of perpetual decay, fall, renovation, and progression. Thus, by preserving the method of nature in the conduct of the state, in what we improve we are never wholly new; in what we retain we are never wholly obsolete.[2]

Burke's claim that Britain follows "the pattern of nature" not only adds a special charge to Blake's remark "The English Artist may be assured that he is doing an injury & injustice to his Country while he studies & imitates the Effects of Nature" (*PA*, 578), but places the existing state of British society in an uninterrupted quasi-genealogical transmission that begins with nature, and so implicitly, given contemporary British views, with God. This construction of British history faced challenges from radicals who appropriated the discourse of the recent antiquarian revival to validate a national tradition that supported their counterhegemonic position, turning the conservatives' paradigm against them. In his early work,

Blake engages this revival while also contesting, as in the later *Laocoön,* the linear imperative.

In the poems of the 1780s and 1790s, Blake experiments with various genres: *Poetical Sketches* (1783) includes prose pieces, songs, ballads, prologues, more conventional verse forms, and a play; *An Island in the Moon* (1784) is a satire in prose and verse;[3] *Songs of Innocence and of Experience* (1793) recall the children's poetry books that had begun to appear in the previous century; *The Marriage of Heaven and Hell* (1790–1793) ranges from aphorisms to allegory and from poetry to prose; and the so-called Lambeth Prophecies include preludiums, prophecies, books, visions, and songs. But these different negotiations with the rigid parameters of genre reveal an ongoing resistance to linearity, both as a governing structure for national history and, as its corollary, a necessary narrative structure. In the *Poetical Sketches,* self-consciously established as the poet's first work, the more politically radical texts betray a concern with the origin and sequence of events, while the overall arrangement of the poems destabilizes order and chronology. Through *The Song of Los,* Blake inserts two previous works, *Europe* and *America,* into a linear narrative, punctuates that linearity with iterations and pointers that map disparate events of that narrative onto each other, and so produces eddies of circularity and loci of intersecting events. *The [First] Book of Urizen* radically challenges linearity by transposing the ages of history onto the body and identifying them as decisive changes rather than evolutionary stages, so that an organic whole replaces a chronological sequence and the linear narrative form of history writing is disrupted. *Milton* and *Jerusalem* repeat that organic and spatial organization of history, locating historical change not in the linear progress toward "civilization" but in the apocalyptic and epiphanic transcendence of such a construction through the instantaneous casting off of error—change arises from revolutionary prophecy rather than evolutionary epic.

The Iterability of the Bard and the Writing of the Nation

In *Fearful Symmetry,* Frye suggests, "Blake belongs neither to the Augustans nor to the Romantics, either as a representative or a rebel. He belongs to another age altogether; the age, in poetry, of Collins, Percy, Gray, Cowper, Smart, Chatterton, Burns, Ossian and the Wartons."[4] But these poets were not simply non-Augustan and pre-Romantic. Most of them were also actively antiquarian and nationalist: Thomas Percy produced the *Reliques of Ancient English Poetry* and translated some of Paul Henri Mallet's antiquarian research; Thomas Gray translated Norse and other antique material; Thomas Chatterton forged medieval texts that Marilyn Butler has associated with a Bristol-centered nationalism;[5] Robert Burns recovered oral Scottish matter; Thomas Warton made an early attempt to define a millennium-old national literary tradition in his anthology, *History of English Poetry;* and James "Ossian" Macpherson revised traditional Gaelic material. As has been well established, Blake was profoundly interested in and influenced by the antiquarian researches of his contemporaries, as well as the antiquarian focus of his immediate precursors, especially Gray.[6] Stuart Peterfreund has identified the *Poetical Sketches* in particular with an attempt to recoup a national identity, the "northern, nativist alternative" that evades "the classicizing tendency" reviled by Blake.[7] Rather than with Romanticism or the Augustan age, we might align Blake's immediate precursors and early contemporaries with an Enlightenment counterculture. Turning away from the rationalist, neoclassicist progress that posited cultural origins that were often implicated in the hegemony's procommercial, imperial, and generally conservative nationalism, they offered an ideological alternative to which Blake was sympathetic.

In the antiquarian controversies of Blake's day, cultures of the distant past were represented in ways that validated particular views of the nationalist culture of the hoped-for future. Liberty became a critical concept. While Burke argued for a more modern origin for English liberties, antiquarians traced the roots of libertarian values into the premedieval period. Percy, for instance, argues in the well-known preface to his translation of Mallet's *Northern Antiquities* that the "Celtic nations do not appear to have had that equal plan of liberty, which was the peculiar honour of all the Gothic tribes, and which they carried with them, and planted wherever they formed settlements."[8] This odd recuperation of expansionism and colonization as the propagation of an "equal plan of liberty" was not unusual. Lucas argues that the massacre at Culloden in 1746 drew attention to such submerged contradictions in ways particularly discomfiting to libertarian nationalists who traced the British government to "'Gothic' origins": "At about this time [i.e., of Culloden], and for reasons that will often be independent of immediate politics, the Gothic becomes associated with those parts of Britain that are not England. But if the constitution is 'Gothic' then England may not assert its liberty against those other parts without ceasing to be true to the source from which such liberty is derived. England is the aggressor against the very liberty it claims to be upholding."[9] As a consequence of this schizophrenic moment in the development of English national identity, the rising antiquarianism of the colonized nations of the British Isles during the period was echoed within England itself. While antiquarians from Ireland, Scotland, and Wales sought to construct a national identity independent of and superior to the English "civilized" identity that was being imposed on them, antiquarians within England sought to evade their alignment with a colonizing, repressive hegemony, often appropriating the discourse of their Celtic neighbors, including such elements as the power of the poetic voice and oral traditions. Many of these writers looked to the past for the legitimization of the "liberty" that was central to their political agenda, whether they sought the removal of English power from the colonized nations or of tyranny from England itself. As Lucas notes, this antiquarian work "provided the more evident materials out of which it was possible to begin constructing a new image of Britain, one with cultural, historical, and, by implication, social and even political consequences. This new image has at its centre the affirmation of northernness. It opposes and is meant to replace the 'classical' spirit of the Augustan cultural configurations."[10]

Blake operates within this context, valorizing the Gothic culture indigenous to northern Europe, as well as the Hebraic tradition, while deprecating the rationalist and classical culture as one of laws, constraints, and militarist imperialism foreign to the "true" British identity it corrupts. This was not an unusual stance. In *National Identity,* Anthony Smith argues that an ethnic nationalism that looked to the past arose during the late eighteenth century to displace a pan-European nationalism that took classical antiquity as its model.[11] Instead of "a universal history" in which Europe continues the civilizing narrative begun by the Greeks, ethnic nationalism offered a return to a regional sense of a distinct identity; this was more commensurable with the Romantic desire for a return to an idyllic origin and proximity to nature, as well as with the increasing valuation of the individual that was expressed politically in the agitation for "the rights of man." Blake's nationalist resistance to the "classicizing tendency," in Peterfreund's words, is thus part of a larger, contemporary movement to cast off the universalizing impetus of the imperial march toward civilization through the classical world, and instead turn toward localized, disjunctive models of communal identity. Classicism, imperialism, tyranny, and the priority of linearity, which validates their transmission through the centuries, are all represented as corruptions of the indigenous, authentic national culture.

Agreeing on the value of nationalism and historical origins, critics of the status quo maintained that society had lost touch with these traditions because of artificial social structures that had been overlaid onto a racialized character, a character that is, for counterhegemonic nationalists as for many of their opponents, specific to nation and place.[12] The rubric by which these two nationalisms are distinguished is generic as well as political. In one view, the national narrative is continuous and plots the evolution of the nation from its inception onward to its imperial development; the construction of that origin often located England as a branch of the imperial tree that has its roots in Greece, Troy, and Rome. But, from another political perspective, the national narrative has the features of an antiquarian document: lost and existing only in a few tattered fragments, corrupted and destroyed by an intervening history, it survives only as a trace through which the recovery of the original may be possible, but not readily so. Both are antiquarian in emphasis, but the first can be termed "traditional" for its emphasis on the continuation of the present trajectory and the second "revolutionary" because it is founded on a radical return to the distant past. Like the art historians to whom Blake objects in his treatises on art, traditionalists organize validating events in a neatly linear narrative; Burke, for instance, claims, "from Magna Charta to the Declaration of Right, it has been the *uniform* policy of our constitution to claim and assert our liberties," drawing a straight line between two historical points nearly five hundred years apart.[13] Revolutionary antiquarian nationalists, however, sought to break free of that historical model to reestablish an origin that would be compatible with a supposedly essential core of national identity—and so restore and resume the writing of the proper national narrative. Such political agendas arguably promoted the productions of forgeries, of pseudoantiquarian texts that could be used to authenticate a particular political position in the present, as well as of legitimate antiquarian scholarship.[14] Antiquarian and historical endeavors, in this context, were less defined by their authenticity with respect to facts than their authenticity with respect to imputed national truths.[15] It is perhaps in that context that Blake wrote, long after the forgeries of Macpherson and Chatterton had been exposed, "I Believe both Macpherson & Chatterton, that what they say is Ancient, Is so" (Anno. Wordsworth, 665).

In his earlier works, Blake engages both the content of antiquarianism and the political projects that it supported and opposed. But while his emphasis on the "Original" and disruptions of linear progression leads to some agreements with the revolutionary antiquarian nationalists, Blake distinguishes his national concerns from both forms of historically validated nationalism. Blake's rejection of linearity has formal implications for the ideological investments of these competing nationalisms because of linearity's support of closure and totalization: the traditional model views the shared culture as an expression of values and characteristics that enable and constitute the march toward progress, but the revolutionary antiquarian model contends that the shared culture is divorced from a national identity that remains latent in each national subject but only occasionally surfaces in social relations. In Blake's works, resistance to the former and alliance with the latter lies at the heart of the poet's valorization of bards, prophets, and artists as the voices of that submerged identity. But, if this can be narrativized, such a political-generic alignment ultimately leads to increasingly vexed identities in Blake's works, as the national subject and the nation continue to be mutually alienated, creating fissures that prohibit the mapping of the interdependence that defines them. From emplotments of social deterioration in *Poetical Sketches* to prophetic books that are identified with characters rather than nations or continents, to the pseudobiography of Milton and the erasure of nation in personification (see chapter 5), and then to apocalypse in *Jerusalem,* Blake challenges traditional nationalism without ever fully endorsing the revolutionary antiquarian variety. But by subverting the linear and ideological closure of narratives that govern the definition of the national community and replacing them with iterative, nonlinear, and antigeneric works that instead define the national subject as alienated from the putatively national culture and its narrative, Blake consistently seeks to tear away the constructs that inhibit the resurrection of the legitimate political subject from its suppressed traces. My concern here thus involves Blake's early challenges to tradition and the narrative linearity that informs it, primarily in *Poetical Sketches, The Song of Los,* and *The [First] Book of Urizen.* In those works, history disjunctively plots the fall of society, not its gradual progress.

Two figures are crucial to the revolutionary resurrection of an essential national identity—the prophet and the bard.[16] The transformation of the bard from antiquarian object to a figure for the voice of political protest created a prophet-bard hybrid that bears, like a recovered antiquity, the marks of atemporality and discontinuity, as well as some irony. The pre-Norman bard was no champion of subversion or political change during the period of his social prominence, but a privileged appendage of the elite. The transposition of the bard from a culture in which he was close to the establishment to a culture in which he is the voice of the opposition that would like to constitute the establishment is simultaneous with the transmutation of epic into prophecy. Behrendt's analysis of prophecy and epic provides some useful points of reference. Behrendt notes that prophecy had a political status in English representations of Hebraic culture, but as a means of voicing opposition to the ruling order rather than praising it.[17] Epic, however, like Virgil's propagandist work, *Aeneid*, enshrines the established order by glorifying its history and legitimating it through prophecies that are written post hoc, valorizing the origin of the hegemony under which it is written so that the "epic poet's private experience both precipitates and parallels a similarly intense collective public experience."[18] The epic poet is the traditionalist, believing that the values of the origin have been transmitted uncorrupted to the present society, which fully embodies them, while the prophet argues that the genealogy has been compromised, so that society is divorced from its cultural essence and is moving away from, rather than approaching, its fulfillment. Such attempts to return the culture to its proper path posited a national identity that had been lost to foreign or unnatural artifice, except in rural areas untouched by modern innovation—these attempts include Wordsworth's "Preface to the *Lyrical Ballads*." The ancient bard functioned, in many ways, like the writers of classical epic, as a national archive that helped to reinforce the status quo. But the eighteenth-century figure of the bard was not just a remnant of the lost culture but also a prophetlike figure who would, in the present, direct the nation back to the culture in which it was so strongly invested.

Temporality is convoluted here—the bard is resuscitated in the present to lead the way back to the past—through the grafting of the bardic and the prophetic. Prophecy is paradoxical in precisely these terms, as someone in the present has a vision of the future that is often designed to return society to its past. In Blake, bardic declarations take on the atemporality of prophecy: it is "the Bard," not the prophet, "Who Present, Past, & Future sees" ("Introduction," *SE*, 2–3). The prophetic transformation posits a constant cultural truth; the national truth may have been compromised over time but it still continues in its essential validity, and the bard reflects this temporal duplicity. The temporally displaced bard, removed from his native culture to that of the eighteenth century, retains his epic authority while speaking in the present as a prophet in the Hebraic tradition.

In their discussions of the relationship between Blake's juvenilia and a recovered northern culture, Lucas and Peterfreund emphasize the genealogical linking of poets and the valorization of the bardic figure through the insertion of the poet into a tradition of prophetic, authentic voices, which had Milton, despite political reservations, as its exemplar. Moreover, in the case of James Thomson, Gray, and William Collins, this appropriation of antiquity to forge a renovated national identity was implicated in the bardic construction of the poet as one whose "ultimate responsibility . . . was, if not to radicalism, then to dissent."[19] In brief, the bardic figure does not simply have an authentic poetic voice but operates at the crux of three discourses: a nationalist, often anti-imperialist, recuperation of northern European antiquity; the dissenting posture of the prophet in the Hebraic tradition; and the populism that sought to shift the base of political as well as cultural power from the elite to the general public. The bard, like the prophet, lies outside of the contemporary communal culture and outside of temporality, and his task is to forge a connection between a latent national character and the lost culture in which that character enjoyed its full expression. He is not implicated in social evolution, but in cultural restoration.

The atemporal and iterative framework in which the bard's role is defined resonates with a pattern that is repeated throughout Blake's writings: an instant that operates outside of chronological time (and sometimes inside spatiality instead) erupts to disrupt linearity, while iteration destabilizes sequence by establishing achronic connections.[20] These alternatives to narrative not only recall the resistance to linearity and chronological histories in *Laocoön,* as well as Blake's general resistance to causality—"The Word Cause is a foolish Word" (Anno. Bacon, 626)—but also resonate with many of Blake's writings on art. In his Annotations to Reynolds's *Discourses,* for example, Blake contends that genius does not arise out of progressive improvement but is transhistorical and produced outside of such causation: "[Reynolds's Discourse III] Endeavours to prove That there is No such thing as Inspiration & that any Man of a plain Understanding may by Thieving from Others. become a Mich Angelo" (Anno. Reynolds, 646); "Ages are All Equal. But Genius is Always Above The Age" (Anno. Reynolds, 649). Thus, "If Art was Progressive We should have had Mich Angelo's & Rafaels to Succeed & to Improve upon each other But it is not so. Genius dies with its Possessor & comes not again till Another is Born with It" (Anno. Reynolds, 656). Each genius, moreover, is not an exact repetition of the one before but a new eruption of genius into the mundane. Blake insists (repeatedly) on the difference of individual perspectives: "Every Eye Sees differently" (Anno. Reynolds, 645) and "Man varies from Man more than Animal from Animal of Different Species" (Anno. Reynolds, 656). Blake even extends his comments about genius being nonderivative to causation in general: "Identities or Things are Neither Cause nor Effect They are Eternal" (Anno. Reynolds, 656). When Blake does allow for the possibility of change or improvement, in nations and individuals, it is represented as an internal transformation rather than a reaction to an external agent: "The Increase of a State as of a Man is from Internal Improvement or Intellectual Acquirement. Man is not Improved by the hurt of another States are not Improved at the Expense of Foreigners" (Anno. Bacon, 625). As discussed in the previous chapter, Blake makes similar claims for the history of art, using an assemblage of values that intersect in his concept of genius to remove artistic objects from history and place them in a kind of ranking system that is, because its values are constant, ahistorical. Imagine a Cartesian graph, with *x* and *y* coordinates to signify time and space: Blake locates artists relative to the "degree zero" (to invoke Roland Barthes's phrase) of genius in a set of coordinates that is entirely independent of historical context. Blake thus retorts, "Never!" to Reynolds's claim that the "DEGREE of excellence [of] GENIUS is different, in different times and different places" (Anno. Reynolds, 656). And the proper nation also exists at this zero degree. Jerusalem is Jerusalem, whether it is the Jerusalem of the past ("was Jerusalem builded here" [*M*, 1.7]) or the future ("Till we have built Jerusalem" [*M*, 1.15]), the Jerusalem of Israel or the Jerusalem of England, or the personified Jerusalem of Blake's verse.

Conventional national narratives, however, require different premises. In "DissemiNation: Time, Narrative, and the Margins of the Modern Nation," Bhabha argues that nationalism, of the more expansionist variety, requires that the "scraps, patches, and rags of daily life must be repeatedly turned into the signs of a national culture, while the very act of the narrative performance interpellates a growing circle of national subjects."[21] The individual genius who exists and creates independently of his time or place can neither exemplify nor encourage participation in this mundane interpellative mechanism; according to Blake, he can only channel eternal truths into the mundane world that depends on and produces such ideologies. Blake situates genius, like the bard, outside of the communal perspective, outside of time, space, and other structures that distort perception, allowing only a few chinks in the cavern's walls—and he thus validates his own view of national truth and proper subjectivity. If the circulation of such narrative generates a sense of belonging to the nation that it constitutes, then controlling the narrative can entail control of the nation's identity and the community that it produces. Blake's resistance to certain national narratives operates in the context of the wider struggle to control such narrative. The "site of *writing the nation*"[22] during this period is a contested space—the hill of which national subjects fought to be king. Writing of *Jerusalem,* Rothenberg suggests that Blake creates

> an analytics of narrativity that reveals how narratives repress uncertainties about ends and origins by summoning up an ontologically transcendent "reality" to which the narrative supposedly "refers." At the same time, it shows how the vexed epistemological status of the subject in eighteenth-century moral philosophy receives an illusory grounding through the production of narratives that serve as "stable" or "coherent" memories of a "continuous" self-identity.[23]

There is a certain continuity between Rothenberg's observations and Bhabha's. Both critics posit a subject constituted by narratives that are implicated in traditional forms of authority: for Bhabha, the dominant form of modern nationalism and, for Rothenberg, "the phenomenalistically oriented self [that] exists in complicity with the oppressive metaphysics of absolute authority."[24] But Blake negotiates a path around this ideologically invested closure not only by subverting narrative, but by offering a kind of counternarration that, like the bard, operates outside of the linearity that governs telic narrative. Blake posits a discontinuous, heterogeneous, and unstable identity that is subject to instantaneous transformation, but he frames such transformations as the divestiture of the false ideologies that linearity supports.

Discussing Blake's representations of apocalypse, Goldsmith writes, "Truth displaces error as new heaven and new earth displace the old; apocalypse is internal, epistemological rather than phenomenal. This interior eschatology also binds apocalypse in a most explicit way to ideology. The Last Judgment is an attempt to close the battle among conflicting judgments; it involves a restructuring of the way one thinks one's world."[25] While Goldsmith proceeds to argue that Blake subverts the closure of the apocalyptic transformation in other texts, the very iterability of an "internal" apocalypse enacted with every displacement of error removes the apocalyptic transformation from the taint of the teleological. Blake's resistance to linear narrative, particularly in his more apocalyptic works, arises from this view that personal epiphanies, revolutions, and the resurrection of

Jerusalem must necessarily take place outside of history and chronology—outside of paradigms that organize shared perceptions and mitigate against individual realization or inspiration. This is consistent with the antiquarian model, in which history is plotted relative to the authenticity of the cultural elements that it delineates, rejecting the march of progress in favor of a decisive return to a national and natural essence that is latent in the individual but missing from the community. The unreliability of narrative, the illusion of causality, and a suspicion of closure give way to momentary eruptions of the latent eternal into the lapsarian temporal, eruptions that are coincident with the untaught genius of Blake's commentaries and the bards of his verse.

Poetical Sketches *and the Antique Nation*

Critics have generally viewed *Poetical Sketches* as an anthology of Blake's early writings that follows his development from juvenile imitation to the seeds of his mature works, and they have usually accepted the advertisement, which purports to have been written by someone other than Blake, more or less at face value. Peterfreund argues, however, that Blake wrote the advertisement, using that attribution as the basis for his discussion of originality in the collection.[26] Whether or not it was written by Blake, the advertisement introduces the volume as one concerned with recuperating the "primitive" past by classifying the texts as authentic juvenilia:

> The following Sketches were the production of untutored youth, commenced in his twelfth, and occasionally resumed by the author till his twentieth year; since which time, his talents having been wholly directed to the attainment of excellence in his profession, he has been deprived of the leisure requisite to such a revisal of these sheets, as might have rendered them less unfit to meet the public eye.
>
> Conscious of the irregularities and defects to be found in almost every page, his friends have still believed that they possessed a poetic originality, which merited some respite from oblivion. These their opinions remain, however, to be now reproved or confirmed by a less partial public. (846)

The *Sketches* are represented as a kind of personal antiquity, an authentic remnant of a poet's early cultural productions. The advertisement thus anticipates the verses' concern with the remnants of the nation's early cultural artifacts.

Attention to the *Poetical Sketches* has largely focused on the seasonal poems and songs, following Frye's curt evaluation that "*Poetical Sketches* falls into two parts, a group of lyrics of startling beauty and a less distinguished group of dramatic and rhapsodic experiments which are obviously the first attempts at the prophetic form."[27] The sequence of the poems in the volume follows Frye's model remarkably well, beginning with the seasonal lyrics and then proceeding to increasingly unconventional verse. Although the degree of control that Blake had over the arrangement of these poems is unknown, their order does strongly suggest a gradual disruption of the conventional poetic forms: the Gothic "Fair Elenor" interrupts the flow of conventional Renaissance genres, from sonnet to song, that begins the collection; the ballad "Gwin, King of Norway" mediates between the songs and the self-conscious "Imitation of Spenser"; "Blind-Man's Buff" closes the Renaissance imitations with the "style of the eighteenth century";[28] and the volume concludes with nonpoetic fragments, first in the style of Renaissance drama, then dramatic prologues, and finally Ossianic prose pieces. The volume's arrangement thus moves from sonnets and songs to the ballad, from poetry through drama to prose, and from pastoral scenes of nature to depictions of various northern European kings (Gwin, Edward III, Edward IV, and John) to meditations on suffering.

Generically, then, the *Sketches* plot the collapse of the pastoral ideal into political, earthy reality, simultaneously mapping that collapse onto the transition from "high" poetic forms to more popular genres and finally the supposed remnants of a lost primitivist culture. Moreover, this movement follows Blake's cultural ideals by shifting away from the Renaissance appropriation of classical elements to northern European and Hebraic features.[29] The incursion of popular, Gothic, and other elements foreign to Renaissance classicism is discernible even in the seasonal poems. Peterfreund finds Nordic references in the seasonal poems that tie them to the nativist tradition resurrected by Thomson, Gray, and Collins, while Lucas argues that the seasonal poems invoke stylistic elements from popular traditions that allow "an audience, also artisan and city dwelling, which had been excluded from the procedures of eighteenth-century literary orthodoxy, to feel at ease with this poetry, to take it as *their* poetry."[30] This ensemble of classical and anticlassical poems can thus be viewed as an early attempt to destabilize generic expectations, to lull the reader into a false sense of poetic security through highly conventional forms—forms that are familiar as part of a shared cultural tradition—and then gradually to disrupt those expectations. The destabilizing of generic expectations is, moreover, coincident with a political turn.

The pseudoantiquarian texts of *Sketches* reveal their participation in the nationalist implications of antiquarianism. In "Gwin, King of Norway," described by Harold Bloom "as Blake's first handling of the theme of political and social revolt,"[31] Blake uses the language and genre of antique texts to represent the overthrow of a tyrant:

> Come, Kings, and listen to my song,
> When Gwin, the son of Nore,
> Over the nations of the North
> His cruel sceptre bore:
> The Nobles of the land did feed
> Upon the hungry Poor . . .
> Arise, and pull the tyrant down;
> Let Gwin be humbled. (1–6, 11–12)

As Susan Wolfson has noted, "*Poetical Sketches* repeatedly relates its aesthetic forms to issues of power," and here "Blake works the ballad form into a dialectic, evoking its traditional status as cultural language, but also exploiting the recent emergence of the *literary* ballad to direct a reading of its forms toward ideological critique."[32] This poem, moreover, not only anticipates many of the images later used in descriptions of Orc—from "blazing comets" to recurring images of rolling clouds and fog to sound effects such as thunder and trumpets—but also involves constructions of the political dynamic that would later appear in *America* and elsewhere: the people's uprising against Gwin is framed as a revolt of "nations," led by the giant Gordred, against the "tyrant" and "Nobles." In the "Prologue to *King John*," whose title character is the quintessential tyrant, Blake again anticipates the poems of the 1790s: "Justice hath heaved a sword to plunge in Albion's breast; for Albion's sins are crimson dy'd, and the red scourge follows her desolate sons! Then Patriot rose; full oft did Patriot rise, when Tyranny hath stain'd fair Albion's breast with her own children's gore" (439). This definition of patriotism recalls the prolibertarian antiquarian nationalism of the late eighteenth century: it is the patriot, the true national subject, who rises up against the tyranny that has corrupted the land.

Similarly, the true nation of "Albion" is populist, inclusive, and peaceful rather than tyrannical and militaristic: "O yet may Albion smile again, and stretch her peaceful arms, and raise her golden head, exultingly! Her citizens shall throng about her gates, her mariners shall sing upon the sea, and myriads shall to her temples crowd!" (439–40).

In distinguishing the people from the ruling elite, Blake locates national identity in the former group, a group that is similar, in its love of liberty, to the nationalist representation of the Goths in Percy's preface to Mallet's *Northern Antiquities.* Robert Gleckner identifies "Gwin" and the "Prologue" as "effort[s] to incorporate prophecy into 'history' . . . mov[ing] immediately out of history, indeed out of all time, into an archetypal battle in the 'north'" where "the war is again both civil and internecine."[33] But this "internecine" battle is divided specifically: in both poems, Blake opposes the nationalist to the tyrant, and the people to the rulers, thus situating the heroes on the side of a morally justifiable revolution against the genealogical transmission of political power validated by the traditional nationalism espoused most famously by Burke.

"Blind-Man's Buff" seems to move in the other direction. Involving, as scholars have noted, a traditional game described in Chatterton's *Antiquity of Christmas Games,* the poem describes a delightful rustic scene in which various figures join to play blind-man's buff, only to have their game end in the injury of one child who, in the role of the blind man, is tripped by an unscrupulous player. Blake concludes, uncharacteristically, with a moral about the need for laws to guard against such dastardly behavior. Gleckner suggests that the poem, which has the same verse form as Gay's *Fables,*[34] might be a satiric subversion of the pastoral fantasy reflected in the poem's early lines (24–25), but its narrativization of national development is worth remark:

> Such are the fortunes of the game,
> And those who play should stop the same
> By wholesome laws; such as[:] all those
> Who on the blinded man impose,
> Stand in his stead; as long a-gone
> When men were first a nation grown;
> Lawless they liv'd—till wantonness
> And liberty began t' increase;
> And one man lay in another's way,
> Then laws were made to keep fair play. (61–70)

Blake thus not only identifies the origin of the "nation" in a moment of rustic play, reinforcing the positive view of the so-called noble savage, but also suggests that laws are the mark of a fallen society rather than a civilized one. The law is a restraint on liberty as well as a symptom of a nation that has fallen so far from the pastoral ideal that rules must be established to protect the vulnerable. Gleckner suggests that Blake "seems, rather, totally taken up with the fortunes and misfortunes of 'the game'" (24), but this is not necessarily a weakness—it is perhaps the point. The changing dynamics of the social relations depicted in the poem plot the fall from the pastoral scene of Susan, the shepherd, the "blushing bank" (3); and the verbal play of "laughing jest, the love-sick tale" and "chat" (10, 11); to flirting ("the game begins" [11]); to the decline of the game into violence. The game rapidly declines both as a form of play and as a rule-based means of coordinating personal relationships: moving at first from blind-man's buff without cheating to blind-man's buff with obvious but harmless cheating, it closes with undiscovered and dangerous cheating, which results in a serious injury that is treated medically by the other players and then morally by the narrator. In plotting the fall, in the literal and lapsarian sense, of the children from pastoral innocence to sexual play and then competitive games into which cheating intrudes, and in classifying their fall as one that nations experience, Blake identifies legislation not as the epitome of social organization but as the sign of its failure. This flies in the face of the prevailing ideology, the set of assumptions that justified imperialism in particular and hegemony in general. In "Civilians and Barbarians," Seamus Deane puts the English hegemony's position since the Renaissance succinctly: "Those who live under the law are civilians; those who live beyond it are barbarians."[35] Both colonization and the disempowerment of the greater part of the British population were justified as the propagation of civilization among the lawless, while the regulations that facilitated such control were presented as the embodiment of civilization. It is this view of civilization that Blake contradicts in his allegory of a nation's decay from affection to legislated protections against escalating malice.

In "Gwin," the "Prologue," and "Blind-Man's Buff," Blake polarizes the hegemonic and cultural field, placing at one extreme the popular nation and an original, unfallen state, and at the other the tyrant and the imposition of constraints, reflecting the same gulf that is mapped generically from the seasonal poems to the Ossianic prose pieces—the dissolution of newly familiar cultural paradigms in favor of a traditionally familiar and relatively uncoded originary form. Blake uses the elements of antiquity and antiquarianism, from "the iron helm of war" ("War Song," 1) to the assumption of an inherent, but corrupted, national identity, to posit and sanction a view of the original culture and the hegemony that corrupted it. He works within antiquarian conventions, in other words, to further the antiquarian agenda and subvert the Augustan, rationalist, "civilizing" agenda that prevailed at the time and emerged from Renaissance classicism.

It should be emphasized, however, that these are not recovered materials, like Gray's free translation of *Descent of Odin,* nor even just imitations of recently recovered material, but politically charged pseudoantiquarian materials that engage the ideological conflict in which antiquarian work was beginning to be implicated. The pseudoantiquarianism and popular nature of the Ossianic fragments with which the volume concludes, including the "Prologue to *King John,*" and of ballads such as "Gwin" and "Fair Elenor," insert the poems generically into a rising conflict about national identity and political order. The poems thus construct, while claiming to reconstruct, an original identity for northern Europe and England that is marked by pastoral harmony, liberty, and resistance to tyrannical constraints (whether political or generic). Blake is, in this sense, very much a part of the eighteenth century, in which "Liberty is the goddess of Britannia,"[36] positing freedom as the true basis of the original political organization from which society has strayed. The genres of the poems support this position by disrupting chronology and emphasizing instead the coincidence of different time periods, while moving generally toward the antique societies, and so challenging the premise of a genealogical development that leads society irrevocably away from its origin in a straight line. Beginning by moving through the annual cycle of seasons and then the diurnal cycle of night and day, after the advertisement's announcement that the anthology is the work of youth, Blake establishes at the outset overlapping cycles, not chronologies, of different scales and terms in which certain elements and tensions are iterated.

Epiphany and Apocalypse: Ruptures in the Line of History

Blake continued to produce pseudoantiquarian texts long after the *Sketches.* Written more than a decade after the material in *Poetical Sketches, The Song of Los* and *The [First] Book of Urizen* recall the pseudoantiquarian texts of the early anthology through their unusual verse forms and concern with pseudoantique characters and settings, as well as their manuscript-like appearance. Dealing with the familiar plots of power struggles, punishment, birth, and death, the poems insert themselves into a genre that encompasses Hesiod's *Theogony* and Gray's liberal translation of *Descent of Odin:* myth. This is, of course, stating the obvious, but I do so to redirect the discussion that follows that statement. Blake criticism was, until the 1980s, generally concerned with elucidating Blake's mythology, from identifying what element each figure personifies and mapping genealogies to tracing biographies among the different works in which a character appears, or with uncovering its elemental roots, tracking etymological or typological sources for the poems. At another end of the critical spectrum, the body of work involving Los has been used to construct theories regarding Blake's thought. But I am concerned here with the ways in which Blake presents the poems as early fragments of a lost culture, neither part of an emerging system nor an expression of Blake's poetic or general philosophy.

Blake's early mythological poems can productively be considered, I would suggest, as literary analogues to the ruins that the wealthy built on their estates during the eighteenth century, and as the literary siblings of the forgeries of Thomas Chatterton, James Macpherson, and Edward Williams. The Lambeth Books were not so much the precursors of a more fully developed system or derivatives of preexisting systems, or fanciful lines of regular print in a bound book, but handcrafted, illuminated manuscripts whose texts recall the flurry of antiquarian and mythological material being published and "discovered" in the latter years of the eighteenth century.[37] By working within this genre, Blake not only has license to present the unfamiliar in familiar terms. He can also supplement his texts with the antiquarian privileging of the exotic past as the site of uncontaminated cultural identity. Politically, Blake thus inscribes his texts into the discourse in which William Stukeley, Gray, and others were constructing northernness as fundamentally imbued with liberty in opposition to the tyrannical bent of contemporary British institutions. But Blake is also mapping what went wrong: he is rewriting history and formulating an exegesis of his own prophecies to assign blame where the prevailing nationalist ideology would assign kudos. Moreover, he continues to challenge the linearity and coherence on which historical narratives are predicated by locating transformation in the ruptures in temporality.

In these later pseudoantiquarian works, Blake offers history that is not history—neither thoroughly separating fact from fiction nor following a chronological narrative line. Through *The Song of Los,* he gathers the material of other histories and recombines it in a text that is founded on repetition and caesura. In *Fearful Symmetry,* Frye suggests that, among Blake's Lambeth Prophecies, "there are three poems which are evidently intended to form a single group: *America, Europe,* and *The Song of Los.*"[38] But *The Song of Los* (1795) is the work that binds the group together: Erdman, for example, notes that the first half of the *Song,* "Africa," ends with the first line of *America*'s prophecy, set in 1775, and that the second half, "Asia," begins in 1793, so that "the whole era 1775–1793 is passed over in *The Song of Los* without text, the era dealt with in the text and pictures of the two prophecies [*Europe* and *America*]."[39] Since "Africa" begins with Adam "in the garden of Eden" (*SL,* 3.6) and "Asia" ends with an apocalyptic raising of the dead (*SL,* 7.31–38), the use of *The Song of Los* as a frame for *Europe* and *America* duplicates the representation, within *Europe,* of history as the interruption of a song in which gathering, rather than chronology, is the governing operation by which elements are linked. *The [First] Book of Urizen* (1794), recalling both Genesis and Exodus, is Blake's first attempt at a prehistory of the main figures introduced in his prophetic material. These glosses on the prophecies operate by inserting the prophecies into a larger narrative that has the features of mythological, and often specifically biblical, texts. Their titles recall sections of the Bible: "The Song of Los" echoes "The Song of Songs" or "The Song of Solomon" (the first three letters of the name "Solomon" conveniently mirror the name "Los"); "The Book of Urizen" recalls the more conventional naming of biblical sections, such as "The Book of Job."

But there is a key difference between Blake's books, songs, and prophecies and those of the Bible: Blake's works remain fragments. Caught in an intertextual web of international religious texts and histories, the Lambeth Books assemble fragments without ever producing a complete history. Inscriptions of Blake's own mythological or historical narratives mimic this fractal organization: Blake's myth and history are present only as traces, describing certain characters at certain moments, but, like *Laocoön,* never obeying the Aristotelian imperative of a beginning, middle, and end. Characters' lives and political events begin and end in medias res. If *The Song of Los* frames *America* and *Europe* to seal them into a narrative line, where is the history of the years 1776 to 1792? Where are the shadowy females and Orc, major players in *America* and *Europe?* Rather than framing *America* and *Europe, The Song of Los* takes them out of history, slicing an intersecting plane right through the plane of historical chronologies to link them directly to the acausal realm of myth and song. The intersection marks the site of an irreducible tension between competing frames of reference, rather than the resolution of those two planes into a shared frame of reference.

In *Dangerous Enthusiasm,* Mee argues that mythography in Blake's time was "syncretic," "seeking to demonstrate the grand unity of all myths,"[40] or the "key to all mythologies" as George Eliot's Casaubon puts it—a shared frame of theological reference. The Koran, Bhagavad Gita, Bible, Ossianic pieces, and others are thus different descendants of unrecovered texts in which repetitions of the originary material can be traced, and Blake's own mythological works reflect this pattern of iteration. McGann has pointed out that the poems associated with the Bible of Hell—*The [First] Book of Urizen, The Book of Los,* and *The Book of Ahania*—repeat narratives from different perspectives or with different details, and Mee expands on this point to include *Europe* and *America* in the "reworkings of plot" that disallow "an authoritative version of a particular plot."[41] Williams suggests that Blake engages the genre of the progress poem in *The Song of Los* while dislocating the usual endpoints of those narratives, noting "his dual refusal to acknowledge Greece as the cradle of liberty and England as its final destination."[42]

We can go further than this, however. Beyond the repetitions of plots with different "reworkings," perspectives, or endpoints, there are formal repetitions:

> I will sing you a song of Los. the Eternal Prophet:
> He sung it to four harps at the tables of Eternity.
>   In heart-formed Africa.
> Urizen faded! Ariston shudderd!
>   And thus the Song began
> Adam stood in the garden of Eden . . .
> Adam shudderd! Noah faded! (*SL,* 3.1–6, 3.10)

There are two threads of iterations here. In the first, the speaker declares that he "will sing you a song," that it was "sung . . . to four harps," and that "thus the Song began," referring variously to what he will sing, the circumstances of its previous performance, and a repetition of the words of the first performance. As the tense changes from future, to past, to a blend of both through the anticipatory "thus" and the past form of "begin,"

Blake's choices of subject and object become increasingly indefinite: the poet progresses from first and second person ("I will sing you a song") to third person ("He sung it to four harps") and concludes with the passive voice, in which both singer and audience have disappeared ("And thus the Song began"). Through the staging and restaging of the song's performance, in the past of Los's singing and the present of a nameless singer's repetition, the usual narrative elements are obscured: speaker, place, and time are lost in the passive voice that subsumes both the past and the present performance in a repetition that is imperfect only insofar as it is marked as a repetition. The other thread of iteration mirrors the actions of Urizen and Ariston, fading and shuddering, in Adam and Noah. This repetition is, mirrorlike, inverted: not only are the latter characters valorized and the former demonized, but the order of the verbs is reversed ("faded . . . shudderd" becomes "shudderd . . . faded"). These two iterative strands create, as in *The Laocoön,* embedded, nonlinear associations, from the cross formation connecting the verbs to the involuted plotting of iterated performances.

Other formal iterations are scattered through the text: "Urizen wept" (*SL,* 4.17; 7.42) at two points of closure, when the "Philosophy of Five Senses was complete" (*SL,* 4.16) and again when "The SONG of LOS is Ended" (*SL,* 7.41); the last line of "Africa," as already noted, is the first line of *America;* the image of Adam in Eden and Noah on Ararat is given at the beginning of "Africa" and repeated in modified form at the end of "Asia." These kinds of repetitions are features of poetry that is close to an oral tradition.[43] But the iterations do not permeate the text as they would in that tradition. They are located at points of beginning and ending—in the prologue, the first and last lines of "Africa," and the last lines of the *Song,* as well as the completion of the materialist "Philosophy"—mapping the different telic points onto one another so that the texts no more have a stable beginning and ending than does *The Laocoön.*

At the same time, Blake disturbs received chronologies in ways that not only resonate with "prophetic practice," as described by Mee, but also recall Rajan's remark about "spectacular scenes" in the brief epic, a genre in which she includes the Lambeth Books: "Spectacle . . . subordinates event to rhetoric rather than allowing experience to complicate argument."[44] In *The Song of Los,* Blake "subordinates event to rhetoric" and, in doing so, not only "transposes the episode from diachronic and historical to synchronic and mythic time," as Rajan suggests,[45] but also breaks apart the historical narratives in which the events and characters originate and the temporal, spatial, and causal logics that underwrite them. By asserting that Adam "in the garden of Eden" and "Noah on the mountains of Ararat" "saw Urizen give his Laws to the Nations" (*SL*, 3.6, 3.7, 3.8), Blake goes beyond the typological equivalence of the two fathers of humanity in the Old Testament. He collapses the prelapsarian moment (before Adam knew of his procreative responsibility) with the end of the flood as well as an undefined time in which nations exist, and suggests the conflation of the globe by indicating that Urizen is visible from both Eden and Ararat. This geographical oddity can be overlooked, particularly since Eden's location is disputed (or, more absurdly, Urizen's height is not indicated), but Blake's next use of geographical license is harder to rationalize: "black grew the sunny African / When Rintrah gave Abstract Philosophy to Brama in the East" (*SL*, 3.10–11). This syntactical unit indicates a causal mechanism that physicists term "action at a distance," ascribing a change in Africa to a cause in India, as well as a corporeal event to a spiritual cause.[46] Similarly, the narrator claims that "Palamabron gave an abstract Law: / To Pythagoras Socrates & Plato" (*SL*, 3.18–19). As Williams notes, Blake rejects Greece as the origin of English liberty,[47] but he also casts aside the historical genealogy of ideas in which—according to Blake's contemporary, John Lemprière—Plato followed "the physics of Heraclitus, the metaphysical opinions of Pythagoras, and the morals of Socrates."[48] Instead, Blake collapses the three philosophers' development, and over a century of Greek thought, into one iteration of the Fall in which Palamabron gives a trio of human philosophers the apple of metaphysical discord, "abstract Law."

More disruptively, Blake takes different chronologies, including the Hebraic, classical, Christian, Islamic, and Norse, and weaves them into another chronology that is concerned not with the generation of thinkers but the fragmentation of humanity:

> black grew the sunny African
> When Rintrah gave Abstract Philosophy to Brama in the East:
> (Night spoke to the Cloud!
> Lo these Human form'd spirits in smiling hipocrisy. War
> Against one another; so let them War on; slaves to the eternal Elements)
> Noah shrunk, beneath the waters;
> Abram fled in fires from Chaldea;

Moses beheld upon Mount Sinai forms of dark delusion:
To Trismegistus. Palamabron gave an abstract Law:
To Pythagoras Socrates & Plato.
Times rolled on o'er all the sons of Har, time after time
Orc on Mount Atlas howld, chain'd down with the Chain of
Jealousy
Then Oothoon hoverd over Judah & Jerusalem
And Jesus heard her voice (a man of sorrows) he receivd
A Gospel from wretched Theotormon.
The human race began to wither, for the healthy built
Secluded places, fearing the joys of Love. (3.10–26)

This history follows a series of separations, as Blake narrates the division of humanity by race (3.10), war (3.13–14), the institution of laws (3.17–3.19), jealousy (3.21), and isolation (3.25–26). Moreover, Blake places the central figures of preexisting chronologies into this new chronology: Rintrah, Palamabron, and Theotormon are identified as origins prior to the ones that those chronologies identify, while Greek, Indian, African, and Blakean figures and events are mixed together in the same historical narrative.[49] Their removal from their own chronologies disrupts causal relationships, a disruption for which Blake's ascription of the first cause to his own mythological figures compensates. Instead of describing the development of Islamic thought by discussing its relationship to the Hebraic tradition and others, Blake need only write "Antamon call'd up Leutha from her valleys of delight: / And to Mahomet a loose Bible gave" (*SL,* 3.28–29). But Blake's causation does not merely allow him to avoid providing the other chronologies—it allows him to create a causation that operates outside of existing chronologies and chronology itself. In "Africa," Blake writes a history of the world in which a series of uncontextualized mythological figures initiate communal divisiveness through surrogates who are then idolized within other chronologies.[50] Blake thus not only represents the leading figures of various religions as the recipients of false, destructive doctrine—without offering a valid alternative—but also contradicts the chronologies that construct those figures as the catalysts for important and valued changes in thinking that define coherent (national) communities.

Blake's near-parody of Genesis, *The [First] Book of Urizen,* offers a further challenge to chronology. While *The Song of Los* disrupts the sequence of its narrative line through repetition and removes elements of other chronologies to insert them into a new chronology, *Urizen* offers an entirely new way of conceiving the flow of history. The ages of Urizen are not plotted in years, or epochs, but in the growth of parts of the body.

> A vast Spine writh'd in torment
> Upon the winds; shooting pain'd
> Ribs, like a bending cavern
> And bones of solidness, froze
> Over all his nerves of joy.
> And a first Age passed over. (*BU,* 10.37–42)
> From the caverns of his jointed Spine . . . Trembling
> Shooting out ten thousand branches
> Around his solid bones.
> And a second Age passed over. (*BU,* 11.1, 11.5–8)
> Two Ears in close volutions.
> From beneath his orbs of vision
> Shot spiring out and petrified
> As they grew. And a fourth Age passed. (*BU,* 12.21–24)
> He threw his right Arm to the north
> His left Arm to the south
> Shooting out in anguish deep,
> And his Feet stampd the nether Abyss . . .
> And a seventh Age passed over. (*BU,* 13.13–18)

The "changes of Urizen" (*BU,* 8.12) not only plot the growth of the body, from skeletal structure (first age), to nervous system (second), eyes (third), ears (fourth), nostrils (fifth), organs involved in eating (sixth), and limbs (seventh), but describe these extensions in nonlinear terms, as enclosed spaces (*BU,* 10.39–41, 11.3, 12.14, 13.5–7), a spectacularly multilinear net (*BU,* 12.6–7, 12.11–12), spiral formations (*BU,* 12.21–23), segmented lines (*BU,* 11.1), or, at least, bidirectional lines (*BU,* 13.13–14). This goes beyond Los's attempt to confine Urizen corporeally, and maps a series of ages onto the bodily form in a way that denies linearity and is identified with discontinuous transformation, with revolutionary change rather than evolutionary progress, in some sense anticipating Michel Foucault's model of a disjunctive corporeal history in "Nietzsche, Genealogy, History."[51] Bloom mentions that Los's work "to organize some definite outline for [Urizen], includ[es] the desperate invention of clock-time,"[52] as "the hammer / Incessant beat; forging chains new & new / Numb'ring with links. hours, days & years" (*BU,* 10.16–18). But that invention of a means of measuring linear time only emphasizes the unusual means used in the poem: "clock-time" is new and alien. The different Ages are also tied together through the iteration of the chorus, an "Age passed over, / And a state of dismal woe" (*BU,* 10.42–43), so that each age, while numbered, is equated with an identical "state of dismal woe," suggesting a history that is at once cyclical, because it moves through the same state periodically; sequential, because of its numbered epochs; and unteleologically organic, because of its corporeal emplotment of growth. Repetition and a nonsequential, organic collection of parts are used not only to identify the epochs of Urizen's changes, but also to contain their destructive potential: while Los's "Numb'ring" inventories Urizen as well as time, controlling them by dividing them into an assemblage of objects like a Petrarchan blazon,[53] iteration and other extralinear connections forge alternative alliances. Anatomically, the first age is connected to the sixth and seventh ages, and the second age links all seven periods together in ways that are unmappable in one dimension, or even two.

This challenge to conventional chronology is reiterated formally. The division of the poem into chapters and numbered sections not only parodies biblical organization, but breaks apart the narrative line, dividing it into discrete units rather than establishing it as a coherent, unbroken series. Moreover, the treelike branches that link the sections in Blake's designs suggest an alternative organic organization that mirrors the mapping of the ages onto the body. Like the convolutions of the Laocoön statue and the texts in which Blake wraps it, the organs of the body of Urizen and the pieces of the textual body of *Urizen* construct a space where conventional narrative would offer a line. The branching of the tree, or perhaps of a nervous system, that separates each piece of text on the page also links those pieces in a way that their cold enumeration cannot imagine.

Milton *and the Dissolution of National Narrative*

In *Milton,* Blake takes this *Laocoön*-like disruption of narrative linearity even further. He not only challenges conventional notions of temporality, but, as many critics have noted, also produces a text that is an assemblage of iterations. In his first completed, and printed, long poem, Blake not only returns again and again to the same events, images, and phrases, but also repeats passages from his earlier works and echoes Milton's writings.

As Betsy Bolton pithily puts it, "Milton's psychedelic plot baffles and bemuses."[54] Blake generates the same kind of complex intertextual affiliations as in *The Song of Los* and, through internal repetitions, turns the text back into itself, tying passages together in a complex filigree that recalls the patterning suggested by the treelike branches of *Urizen,* as well as the spatial orientations of words and scripts in *Laocoön.*

In *Poetic Form in Blake's* Milton, Fox writes, "Accruing definitions, simultaneity, multiple perspectives all are organized in *Milton* by the elaborate system of parallels that is the poem's basic framework" (24), arguing that the poem is the sum of different perspectives on a single event and that meaning is the sum of the definitions of a single term.[55] Andrew Cooper, however, takes issue with Fox's emphasis on parallelism, arguing that Blake's

> emphasis falls on their non-identicality and non-convertibility. . . . *Milton*'s "parallelism" is purely functional. It is the rehearsal of a single prophetic pattern on several different levels which serve, first, to expose the animating truth behind the pattern (the Logos of the conclusion), but then also serve to signal the falseness of reducing this truth to any of the vehicles that shadow it forth (the mythopoeic Bard, the mythological Los, the various spiritual figures of Milton, or the historical character William Blake in Felpham garden circa 1800).[56]

Albert J. Rivero, alternatively, suggests that "all these events are versions of the same event, viewed from different perspectives," but locates this in the context of typology rather than formal repetition.[57] All three critics argue that the "Truth" is, in *Milton,* revealed through a composite of "truths" that is formed through reference to a particular hermeneutic practice, whether typology (Rivero), "accruing" (Fox), or the deconstructive sum that shows the inadequacy of its constituent parts (Cooper). But this concern with what is repeated suppresses what is not: each recurrence of one entity entering the foot of another is described in different terms, is spoken by a different voice, is located in a different portion of the poem, and is affected by its membership in a set of repeated images. In other words, it is iterated in the sense that Derrida uses the term in "Signature Event Context": "Every sign, linguistic or non-linguistic, . . . can be *cited,* put between quotation marks; in so doing it can break with every given context, engendering an infinity of new contexts."[58] Each iteration, or citation, operates within a different context, creating not a rigid series to be summed or divided, but a dynamic of interrelationships. Moreover, given Blake's disruption of regular notions of time in *Milton,* this iterability needs to be placed outside of linearity.

Yvonne Carothers has argued that Blake's representations of time and space in *Milton* are Kantian, characterizing them as imaginative constructs rather than empirical standards.[59] Thus, for example, Blake suggests that space and time are constructs that distort truth:

> But in Eternity the Four Arts: Poetry, Painting, Music,
> And Architecture which is Science: are the Four Faces of Man.
> Not so in Time & Space: there Three are shut out, and only
> Science remains thro Mercy: & by means of Science, the Three
> Become apparent in Time & Space, in the Three Professions. (*M,* 27.55–59)

It is not time and space per se that are constructions of the imagination, but only their coding of the epistemological field. Space is thus "Limited / To those without but Infinite to those within" (*M,* 10.8–9). As with Dr. Who's TARDISS or Mary Poppins's carpetbag, standards of space are rendered specific to a particular vantage point, relativistic in senses that even Einstein would find far-fetched.

In *Milton,* Blake plays relentlessly with concepts of time and space that are at odds with the notions that inform historiography as well as the generic distinctions plotted by Lessing. Time becomes an elaborate architecture, as "the Sons of Los build Moments & Minutes & Hours / And Days & Months & Years & Ages & Periods; wondrous buildings" (*M,* 28.44–45), so that "every Minute has an azure Tent with silken Veils" (*M,* 28.50) and "every Year, invulnerable Barriers with high Towers" (*M,* 28.55). Every period of time that evades this taxonomical architecture has qualities that recall Enitharmon's song as well as that of Los:

> Every Time less than a pulsation of the artery
> Is equal in its period & value to Six Thousand Years.
> For in this Period the Poets Work is Done: and all the Great
> Events of Time start forth & are concievd in such a Period
> Within a Moment: a Pulsation of the Artery. (*M,* 28.62–29.3)

As in *Europe,* this timeless space—"the pulsation of the artery," like the interruption of Enitharmon's song, approaches the instantaneous—is bracketed by iterations that describe an indiscernible instant, and this space is the region from which decisive transformations of the historical domain originate. Moreover, as in *Europe,* the iterations that mark the temporal breach are not accurate citations. In *Europe,* "Enitharmon slept, / Eighteen hundred years" (*Eur,* 9.1–2), and "Then Enitharmon woke, nor knew that she had slept / And eighteen hundred years were fled" (*Eur,* 13.9–10): Blake repeats the period of the gap as well as the key words, "Enitharmon" and "slept," continuing to use the past tense but altering other parts of the wording.[60] In *Milton,* again, the period of the gap is repeated, but its capitalization is changed: "Every Time less than a pulsation of the artery" (*M,* 28.62) and "Within a Moment: a Pulsation of the Artery" (*M,* 29.3). The breach is never quite sealed, marking the seepage across the temporal divide. Social and political change do not arise from historical evolution, the slow steady march toward civilization, but from beyond such chronological constructions, in eruptions of the eternal domain via the conduit of genius:

> Come into my hand
> By your mild power; descending down the Nerves of my
> right arm
> From out the Portals of my Brain, where by your ministry
> The Eternal Great Humanity Divine. planted his Paradise.
> (*M,* 2.5–8)

These poems defamiliarize historiographical convention as well as historical touchstones, disrupting causal and linear constructions of history and relocating familiar historical persons and moments. The socio-political domain is transformed outside of such historical narratives and constituted in iterations rather than causalities and stable sequences. As Will McConnell proposes, the poem's own ending is an iteration, even a citation: "the repetition of apocalypse—traditionally, an end to time and a 'beginning' of eternity—in *Milton* suggests that the apocalypse with which the text closes, the liminal site between time and eternity, is no more than a production, and re-production of a desire for historical and textual closure that the text of *Milton* has already foreclosed."[61] Milton's movement through the lapsarian world of *Milton,* embodied in its commercial and industrial landscape as well as classical militarism (see chapter 5), traces the individual's release from a corrupt communal view of the nation, crossing through various closed spheres (*M,* 33). The decay of rigid literary structure traced through the pages of *Poetical Sketches* reaches a new limit in *Milton,* shattering the communal perspective in favor of individual epiphany. Just as *The Song of Los* opens the histories of *Europe* and *America* into a different frame of reference that is nominally personal (as the song of Los), just as Enitharmon's song to her children halts the flow of history, just as the pulsation of the artery brackets prophetic transformation, *Milton* locates the effects of narrative and antinarrative in the individual rather than in the collective that the former seeks to produce. Instead of national narratives generated by pseudoantiquarian mythologies that resurrect the Nordic elements of British culture, Blake writes a pseudobiography in which one national figure negotiates his way through corrupting and alien elements of the communal culture to emerge from their shackles.

Throughout these different works, Blake contests elements of the shared national culture and narrative, displacing the pastoral in favor of the Nordic, replacing the Christian myths with unique amalgams of various mythologies that are true to none of them, and transposing Milton from the milieu of the usual biographies of the poet to a space in which the nation is constituted quite differently. In *Milton,* the poet must evade the national narrative that he helped to produce—primarily, the paradigmatic tale of the national hero who dies for his nation—and so escape the communal economy of a nation bound by duty and self-sacrifice. Blake's critique of that particular brand of nationalism in *Milton* is the subject of chapter 5, but here it will suffice to say that Milton's release is, on a fundamental level, the poet's escape from the community into personal vision. It is a personal vision that is defined by Blake's personal vision, of course, and implicated in Blake's construction of Albion, but it is figured as such in the poem. The apocalypse is not the actual destruction of the nation, but the poet's epistemological release from it—his final alienation from the communal, temporally bound, perspective. Like other nationalists who appropriated antiquarian discourse for revolutionary political ends, Blake posits an inherent, latent identity that is discontinuous with the collective national identity but continuous with his notion of a culturally specific, ahistorical character. Renaissance genres such as seasonal poems, histories, and epic narratives, deriving from cultural exchanges with the classical past and contemporary Italy, are part of the false, collective culture. They are consequently cast off or subverted throughout Blake's corpus, along with the linearity that both valorizes and defines them.

"HOW DIFFERENT THE WORLD TO THEM"

Revolutionary Heterogeneity and Alienation

> What he then felt resembled that wild and delightful impression with which a traveller finds himself on a foreign shore, where all that he sees is alike strange—with one entire power subverts his previous associations, and violently, as it were, throws open his mind to a sense of new existence, and to the apprehension of a new world.
>
> *Anonymous*, "Of a National Character in Literature" (1818)

Los's declaration "I must Create a System, or be enslav'd by another Mans" (*J*, 10.20) contains both an imperative ("must") and a threat ("or be enslav'd"). The warning does more than establish Blake's belief that rational systems are limiting; it describes them as "enslav[ing]," a term that connotes institutionalized subjugation and abuses of power (particularly in the charged climate of the abolition debate of the early Romantic period), and it alienates the speaker from any preexisting system by defining it as "another Mans."[1] To function within a system that one has not created is to belong to someone else. Conversely, to create one's own system is to be isolated from all community, unless, of course, one creates a system that enslaves others—an option that Los does not seem to entertain. While the previous chapter addresses the formal, generic conventions that support such systems and Blake's subversion of them, the present is concerned with the means by which Blake plots the separation of the individual from interpellative social paradigms in prophecies that more clearly address contemporary politics. Nietzsche outlines the dynamic: "man . . . wants to live socially in the herd, [so] he needs a peace agreement," a "system" in Blake's terminology, so that "'truth' will be . . . fixed; a uniformly valid and binding terminology for things is invented."[2]

Various twentieth-century critics have elaborated on Nietzsche's point, emphasizing, like Nietzsche, the "invented" quality of the norms that members of society are taught to take for granted as unquestioned truths. Barthes calls them myths, arguing that they compose an attenuated repository of meaning, attenuated in that "myth is constituted by the loss of the historical quality of things: in it, things lose the memory that they once were made. The world enters language as a dialectical relation between activities, between human actions; it comes out of myth as a harmonious display of essences."[3] This "myth" or "Truth" is, moreover, a system that is homogeneous in the sense that Georges Bataille describes in his essay "The Psychological Structure of Fascism": "*Homogeneity* signifies here the commensurability of elements and the awareness of this commensurability: human relations are sustained by a reduction to fixed rules based on the consciousness of the possible identity of delineable persons and situations," so that "*Homogeneous* society is productive society, namely, useful society. Every useless element is excluded, not from all of society, but from its *homogeneous* part."[4] Foucault calls it "order," writing that

> "[a] system of elements"—a definition of segments by which the resemblances and differences can be shown, the types of variations by which those segments can be affected, and, lastly, the threshold above which there is a difference and below which there is a similitude—is indispensable for the establishment of even the simplest form of order. Order is, at one and the same time, that which is given in things as their inner law, the hidden network that determines the way they confront one another, and also that which has no existence except in the grid created by a glance, an examination, a language.[5]

A set of symbols is thus organized around principles that are held to be fundamental and common to all of its constituent elements, as well as different from that which is fundamental and common to all of the elements that do not belong to it. This principle of homogeneity—as myth, order, or "useful society"—arguably fosters conservatism (in the broadest sense of political inertia, rather than the ideology of the right), because to exile difference is to refuse change.[6] These are the systems of "Single vision & Newtons sleep" ("With Happiness," 88), in which rationalists "Reason & Compare" (*J*, 10.21), governed by the requirement of homogeneity, the rationalism of either/or, and the solace of membership.

As Ault notes, Blake's resistance to homogenizing forces was wide ranging, cutting across the interlaced domains of politics, subjectivity, and "language itself."[7] It is homogeneity that is promulgated to ensure the maintenance of an order like that described by Foucault. The corollary, however, is that heterogeneity can pry apart the grip of such an order. Discussing Paine's "analysis of the enslaving properties of customary power," Rothenberg suggests that by "advocating alienation, heterogeneity, and mobile alliances, Paine . . . establishes the conditions for the creation of new forms of political organization and social structures . . . that resist or dismantle the accretions of customary power."[8] To exceed the bounds of the homogeneous system, by being alienated from it, by exposing it as heterogeneous, or by moving from one system to another and so refuting its close hold on the elements that define it, is to reveal the possibility of change as well as the possibility of difference—to defamiliarize "customary power" and force the contemplation of alternatives external to the homogeneous system. The "unfamiliar" and the "alienating"—terms married in the various translations of Shklovsky's phrase *priem ostranenija* and extensions of it in Brecht's "alienation effect"[9]—associate the new perspective with an external position, estranged from the familiar perspective and those who share it, just as it is in Paine's writings as analyzed by Rothenberg. Defamiliarization alienates the percipient from the semiological systems that guarantee a homogeneous society and so makes possible the critique of that society and the contemplation of alternatives—it divides "my system" from "another Mans."

It is this nebulous division that Blake explores in three poems of the early 1790s: *America; a Prophecy* (1793), *Europe; a Prophecy* (1794), and *Visions of the Daughters of Albion* (1793). The conflicts between different discursive systems in those texts produce the alienation and heterogeneity that each system, by itself, cannot admit: within the military, the political structure, notions of sexual propriety, or any other system that constructs itself as homogeneous, that which does not fit cannot be accommodated except by the strategy of exclusion that Bataille describes. In *Europe* and *Visions,* mutually exclusive systems are brought into contact so that the borders by which they divide are revealed, but their homogeneity, though briefly challenged in each text, is finally sustained. In *America,* however, those borders are not marked by unyielding battlements, but exposed as they are transgressed.

Rather than marking the divide, *America* deals with the eddies in the boundary as seepage across the divide takes place: Angels descend from heaven and become historical heroes, George III changes names and shapes, and even God is exposed as ambivalent. It is in this flux within a boundary that is failing to bound that revolution is possible: it is the only "outside" that is not another homogeneous "inside," a heterogeneous space in which assumptions can mingle with their alternatives. David L. Clark describes a similar space: "Irreducibly divided from itself, the field of contraries ideally defers the emergence of a fixed center, a singularity or

'Negation' (as Blake would come to call it) which would assimilate that field to an outlying or underlying unity."[10] In these poems, however, the space in which this is possible is not a separate field but a marginal space in which various systems mix, the intersection of a set of interlocking fields like that depicted in the illustration on plate 33 of *Milton*. Such a space is still implicated in the systems that intersect in it: as Derrida argues, "all destructive discourses . . . must inhabit the structures they demolish,"[11] and Blake still operates within the terms of the systems that he critiques. David Gross suggests that Blake "create[s] a poetic practice which limits the inevitable hegemonic effects of his own discourse by the very newness and unfamiliarity of his imaginative projections. What he retains from the existing mythos—Jesus, Jerusalem—are those aspects of human vision which he feels have survived hegemony's distortion."[12] But it is not always easy to separate the new from the uncontaminated in Blake's texts. By plotting the intersection of different systems rather than the center of a homogeneous space, however, he helps to constitute a dynamic space in which choices can be made. This hybrid space appears briefly in *Europe*, as myth and history meet only to be separated by rationality in the form of Newton's trumpet blast, but it is in *America*, the narrative of a successful revolution, that the liberating force of the flux at the margins is realized. At the end of *America*, "the five gates of their law-built heaven . . . were consum'd, & their bolts and hinges melted" (*Am*, 16.19, 16.22).

Visions of the Daughters of Albion *and the Alienation of Oothoon*

Visions of the Daughters of Albion is one of Blake's most explicit attacks on existing institutions. In comments on institutions from slavery to marriage, conventional assumptions about property and propriety, rights and needs, and love and power are raised to be challenged in the conflict between the protagonists. Its central event, described in the opening lines of the poem, is controversial:

> Then Oothoon pluck'd the flower saying, I pluck thee from thy bed
> Sweet flower. and put thee here to glow between my breasts
> And thus I turn my face to where my whole soul seeks.
> Over the waves she went in wing'd exulting swift delight;
> And over Theotormons reign, took her impetuous course.

Bromion rent her with his thunders. on his stormy bed
Lay the faint maid, and soon her woes appalld his thunders
hoarse. (*VDA*, 1.11–17)

Frye suggests that "Blake may have been protesting against" "that very conventional story of a romantic heroine's preference of death to dishonor [in Ossian's *Oithona*]."[13] But, despite the value of this protest, critics have still been troubled by Blake's handling of the rape. Fox suggests that Blake chose a female protagonist because "he needed a chief character who could be raped and tied down and suppressed without recourse," while Rajan notes,

> By figuring the Blakean paradigm through the story of a rape, the poem calls into question the very making of figures, crossing aesthetics with ethics and asking us whether it is right to use rape as a figure of something else. Blake's own complicity in this displacement is marked by the curious fact that Oothoon's rape is not simply refigured; it is never actually named in the poem. It enters the poem not only as a figure for other violations that are similarly named, but also through a figure: the figure of Bromion's thunders.[14]

These two different views of the rape meet within the context of alienation: rape, according to contemporary understanding, could happen only to women. No man could enter the world of the rape victim except figuratively, by likening it to something else; the victim's feelings could only be described through vague and indirect clichés, such as "the fate worse than death." It is exclusively the Daughters of Albion, the only other women in the poem, who "hear her woes. & eccho back her sighs" (*VDA*, 2.20): "Theotormon hears [her] not" (*VDA*, 2.37), and only Bromion can "hear [her] lamentations" (*VDA*, 3.1). The rape thus not only places Oothoon beyond the pale of patriarchy's paradigms of social acceptability but also beyond the experience of those with whom she is concerned, Bromion and Theotormon. Conversely, Oothoon cannot place herself outside of her experience to understand their inability to comprehend her position, the inability with which she tries to come to terms in her speeches.[15] The rape, as something that is, according to cultural codes, unavailable to male experience and inadmissible to the public space of patriarchal ideology (that is, as something not to be spoken of, as well as a stigma that excludes victims from society), drives an alienating wedge between the characters, leaving them to grapple with tropes in their attempts to comprehend the communal implications of the event.

Even classifying the act as a "rape" is an interpretive leap that cannot necessarily be made, by the characters or by many of Blake's contemporaries.[16] If slavery is the "master trope" of *Visions,*[17] then sex is the master signified. Damrosch writes, "[O]ne can argue that the problem lies in their attitude toward sex rather than in sex itself, but I think that Blake wants us to consider both possibilities."[18] I would suggest, however, that Blake's notion of what "sex itself" might be is not represented in this poem. Instead, Blake offers only a clash of perspectives on the social realities of sex (rape, prostitution, so-called conjugal rights), none of which are granted any authenticity outside of social institutions. *Visions* does not ask what sex means in any absolute or intrinsic sense but explores the different significations that can be attached to it. A crucial question raised by the poem, consequently, is to what extent licit sex and rape are interchangeable: Oothoon is assaulted, but she is labeled a "harlot" and "adulterate," while wives "turn the wheel of false desire" (*VDA,* 5.27), suggesting that they are no more willing than Oothoon. If women's desires are invisible to the paradigms through which sex is discussed, then distinguishing rape and licit sex becomes difficult except by means of the factors that those paradigms do recognize, such as territorial or proprietorial claims.[19]

Each character interprets the act differently. Bromion views it as a sign of conquest that indelibly marks Oothoon and her children as possessions (*VDA,* 1.20–23); Theotormon views it as a personal loss that nature, through the pathetic fallacy, reflects (*VDA,* 3.22–4.11); and Oothoon first regards it as an event that has defiled her in the view of others.[20] Although Bromion declares that she is a "harlot" (*VDA,* 1.18, 2.1), Theotormon's own declarations do not support that view. Oothoon dismisses the characterization:

> And does my Theotormon seek this hypocrite modesty!
> This knowing, artful, secret, fearful, cautious, trembling hypocrite.
> Then is Oothoon a whore indeed! and all the virgin joys
> Of life are harlots: and Theotormon is a sick mans dream
> And Oothoon is the crafty slave of selfish holiness.
> *But Oothoon is not so.* (*VDA,* 6.16–21; my emphasis)

Having been "brand[ed] . . . with the name of whore" (*VDA,* 6.12) by Bromion and by the values that she ascribes to Theotormon, Oothoon now declares that she "is not so" but is "Open to joy and to delight where ever beauty appears / If in the morning sun [she] find[s] it" (*VDA*, 6.22–23). Oothoon contrasts her view of herself with the Urizenic view that she associates with Theotormon and Bromion—"How different their eye and ear! how different the world to them!" (*VDA*, 5.16). Oothoon thus describes the construction of the fallen woman in various discourses and then places herself outside of those paradigms. She does not allow the sexual act to which she did not consent to inscribe her into the patriarchal paradigms by which sex is comprehended, to classify her as either wife or whore and, in either case, as the property of a man to whom her desires are irrelevant.[21] Instead, Oothoon places herself outside of those systems by declaring that "Oothoon is not so" and identifying herself as the subject, rather than the object, of desire, a classification that cannot be recognized within the patriarchal systems that she critiques. Given the prevalence of those systems in Blake's England and the only recent radical rethinking of them in Wollstonecraft's *A Vindication of the Rights of Woman*, Oothoon's perspective is defamiliarizing: through her, Blake not only takes the unusual step of giving a voice to the rape victim who affronts expectations by choosing to live, but also articulates views of imperialism, marriage, and female sexuality that are not coincident with the prevailing ideologies. Placed "on the margin of non-entity" (*VDA*, 7.15) by patriarchy, she is alienated from cultural systems and therefore in a position to offer another view of them. She is not in the utopian space of future salvation, but the uncharted space that lies beyond known identities—what ideology recognizes as "entities."[22]

The scene of Oothoon's alienation from the men that concludes *Visions* is often seen as a failure, as the consequence of the men's inability to convert to Oothoon's views or Oothoon's inability to convert them.[23] Such readings assume that the desirable conclusion is a successful conversion and, at least implicitly, the romantic ending of a reconciliation between Theotormon and Oothoon.[24] This is one of the two conventional endings addressed by Rachel Blau DuPlessis—heroines must marry or die.[25] What Erdman calls a "three-sided soliloquy,"[26] however, is not necessarily a failure. Bracher argues that each of the three figures "represents a metaphysical perspective," where Bromion is an empiricist, Theotormon an idealist, and Oothoon an "avatar of that intrinsic dynamism . . . of organic existence itself."[27] These perspectives are fundamentally incommensurable, but this is not necessarily tragic, or counterproductive. This incommensurability of perspectives liberates one from the other in a manner suggested by Rothenberg's comments on Paine's notion of alienation:

> Paine's analysis of the enslaving properties of customary power uncovers three successive sites of alienation. First, he shows that each individual is alienated from his or her natural rights and true interests by the veil of custom. Second, in order to see through that veil, the rhetor must be alienated from the community. Finally, and most critically, the return of each individual to a perfect civil liberty requires that each be alienated from the others, since the "right of self-interest" of each member of the populace . . . must be held as inalienable property, a wedge rather than a link between individuals.[28]

Quite apart from its utility as a description of Paine's work, this passage is useful for redirecting analysis of *Visions* away from the failure of the three protagonists to resolve their differences and toward the positive implications of their mutual alienation, particularly their liberation from the bonds of the shared lies that Nietzsche mocks.

Rothenberg's "three successive sites of alienation" coincide with the plot of *Visions*. Bromion's actions and speech, legitimizing conquest, the enslavement of children, and the rape victim's status as a "harlot," reveal the denial of Oothoon's rights, as well as the rights of those for whom she is a figure (particularly indigenous Americans of both sexes and British women), within colonial and patriarchal ideologies. Theotormon's subscription to patriarchy, insofar as he clearly views her victimization as his loss and, if Oothoon is correct, as her defilement too, leads to Oothoon's alienation from the one social relationship with which she identifies, her bond with Theotormon. Dramatically shown that her rights are not a concern and alienated from her beloved, Oothoon is able to escape and so analyze the ideologies that deny her rights, to find an answer to her request—"tell me the thoughts of man, that have been hid of old" (*VDA*, 3.13).

In turning from her analysis in which "Theotormon is a sick mans dream" (*VDA*, 6.19) to Theotormon's misery, however, Oothoon reinserts herself into Theotormon's community.[29] In the first two-thirds of her speech, Oothoon does not envision herself with Theotormon but stands aside to describe the limitations of others:

> With what sense does the parson claim the labour of the farmer?

> What are his nets & gins & traps. & how does he surround him
> With cold floods of abstraction, and with forests of solitude,
> To build him castles and high spires. where kings & priests may dwell.
> Till she who burns with youth. and knows no fixed lot; is bound
> In spells of law to one she loaths: and must she drag the chain
> Of life, in weary lust! must chilling murderous thoughts. obscure
> The clear heaven of her eternal spring? to bear the wintry rage
> Of a harsh terror driv'n to madness, bound to hold a rod
> Over her shrinking shoulders all the day . . . (*VDA*, 5.17–26)
> Who taught thee modesty, subtil modesty! child of night & sleep
> When thou awakest. wilt thou dissemble all thy secret joys
> Or wert thou not awake when all this mystery was disclos'd!
> Then com'st thou forth a modest virgin knowing to dissemble
> With nets found under thy night pillow, to catch virgin joy,
> And brand it with the name of whore; & sell it in the night.
> (*VDA*, 6.7–12)

Oothoon's position as knowing spectator distances her from the social norms that she represents. Her alienation from the ideology in which those she observes are interpellated is positively expressed in her declaration "But Oothoon is not so, a virgin fill'd with virgin fancies / Open to joy" (*VDA*, 6.21–22), as she explicitly differentiates herself from the "modest virgin knowing to dissemble." She then acknowledges her alienation and derides it: "Why hast thou taught my Theotormon this accursed thing? / Till beauty fades from off my shoulders darken'd and cast out. / A solitary shadow wailing on the margin of non-entity" (*VDA*, 7.13–15). But by this point she regards Theotormon with sympathy rather than sarcasm, viewing him as a victim rather than an agent of victimization. Instead of asking ironically, "And does my Theotormon seek this hypocrite modesty!" (*VDA*, 6.16), she asks sympathetically, "Can that be Love . . . That clouds with jealousy his nights, with weepings all the day" (*VDA*, 17.18). In effect, Oothoon returns to the desire that she articulates in her early speech to Theotormon: "Silent I hover all the night, and all day could be silent. / If Theotormon once would turn his loved eyes upon me" (*VDA*, 3.14–15). After moving through the three stages of alienation charted by Rothenberg, Oothoon regresses so that, instead of achieving "perfect civil liberty," she turns from her condemnation of the ideologies that deny her that liberty to reaffirm her dependence on Theotormon; "Thus every morning wails Oothoon" (*VDA*, 8.11).[30]

There is, however, a fourth player in this drama: the Daughters of Albion, to whom these visions belong. The Daughters are separated from the community that they observe, geographically but also perceptually. Oothoon is either unaware of them or does not acknowledge their presence as significant: the narrator repeats, "The Daughters of Albion hear her woes" (*VDA,* 2.20), but Oothoon asserts, "And none but Bromion can hear my lamentations" (*VDA,* 3.1). The Daughters, however, align themselves with Oothoon, anticipating her enslavement and lamentation (*VDA,* 1.1–2) as well as repeating her "sighs" (*VDA,* 2.20, 5.2, 8.13). It is not clear even whose voice is being transcribed in the poem. Oothoon's speeches after her rape are preceded by the statement "The Daughters of Albion hear her woes, & eccho back her sighs" (*VDA,* 2.20, 5.2), and not by a statement of the form "Oothoon then said," thus leaving it unclear whether it is the original or the echo that is cited in the following lines. (There is no such ambiguity in Oothoon's speech before her rape: "Then Oothoon pluck'd the flower saying, I pluck thee from thy bed" [*VDA,* 1.11].) Pointing to oddities in the Daughters' responses to Oothoon's speeches, Behrendt aligns the Daughters with uncertain vision but excepts Oothoon from that failure: "the attendant daughters see and hear what their own condition has led them to expect to see and hear: recorded through corrupted senses, their perceptions are unreliable."[31] But we cannot, to invoke W. B. Yeats's famous phrase, separate the dancer from the dance—or, in this case, the original from the echo.

Leaving aside the question of the relative merits of the women's perceptions, I wish to emphasize the negotiation of communal divisions that the Daughters' lament represents. While Oothoon "wails on the margins," as a fallen woman, the Daughters, who carry no such stigma, affirm community with Oothoon and thereby join her in her alienated perspective; they "eccho" Oothoon's sighs, suggesting an attempt to duplicate Oothoon's position rather than to maintain an allied but distinct position. But Oothoon does not hear or return that affirmation. There is a scission in the world of the *Visions,* between the enslaving, hierarchical world of Bromion and Theotormon and the sympathetic one of the Daughters of Albion, and Oothoon lies between them—and outside of both. As David Blake and Elliott Gruner suggest, "The poem depends on an increasingly complex metaphysical calculus in which the captive [Oothoon] is ironically and paradoxically situated between liberation and captivity, between spiritual vision and political reality, and finally between the language of resistance and the fettered, physical body."[32] This hybrid world of mutually exclusive perspectives splices together irreconcilable views of the rape, sustaining the coherence of those perspectives while revealing them as choices from a range of options and, more to the point, alienating the reader from the prevailing ideologies, which Bromion and Theotormon represent, by inviting identification with Oothoon. Oothoon's ability to move between the different perspectives marks the possibility of transgressing a powerful ideology, even though her reversal at the poem's conclusion suggests that escape from social bonds and the institutions that structure them can be only partial and temporary.

Europe *and the Alienation of the Narrator*

A similar scission appears in *Europe.* Such scissions remind us that Blake's multiperspectivism not only offers an assemblage of perspectives that dissipates the authority of any single view, but also calls attention to the ruptures between those perspectives. The inescapable incommensurability submerged in the prefix "multi" characterizes the space in which the percipient cannot rest, even for a moment, in another's perspective: the interstitial domain has neither ideology, nor ruler, nor constitution, and this has implications for the production of shared perspectives in general. In *Europe,* as in *Visions,* there are different perspectives that are closely identified with characters within the poem, in this case Enitharmon and Urizen. In the prophecy,[33] however, the border between systems is not marked by a character within the poem who turns from one to the other, but by the narrator. The narrative perspective switches from Enitharmon's domain to that of Urizen, marking their alienation from each other through oppositions that include myth/history, speech/writing, private/public, family/society, and union/division, as well as linear/circular.[34] The prophecy begins with the end of the Urizenic conflict (*Eur,* 3.4), then it turns to Enitharmon's family reunion; but Enitharmon falls asleep and Urizenic strife returns, and then that conflict ends as Enitharmon awakes, only to be resurrected when Enitharmon again stops singing. The realm of Enitharmon and Los is one of singing, reunion, rejoicing, and family, but the world of Urizen is roughly a radical's view of late-eighteenth-century Europe, ruled by written texts, divisive conflict, howling, and relationships founded on power rather than affection. The mythic section thus begins by noting, "Enitharmon saw her sons & daughters rise around. / Like pearly clouds they meet together . . . And Los . . . joy'd in the peaceful night" (*Eur,*

3.5–7), while the historic section opens, "Shadows of men in fleeting bands upon the winds: / Divide the heavens of Europe / Till Albions Angel smitten with his own plagues fled" (*Eur,* 9.6–8). In *Theory of Religion,* Bataille argues that the distinction between body and spirit leads to the positing of two distinct worlds: "The unreal world of sovereign spirits or gods establishes reality, which it is not, as its contrary. The reality of a profane world, of a world of things and bodies, is established opposite a holy and mythical world."[35] *Europe* neatly follows this division, but there are limited incursions across the boundary between myth and history as Orc moves between the two worlds, and there are crucial interruptions by the excluded domain in the mythological and historical sections.

The text divides oral from written language, myth from history, centripetal from centrifugal social forces, a parent from an anonymous and absent authority, and rejoicing from oppression, sustaining what Foucault calls the "sympathy-antipathy pair."[36] The opposition between the mythic and historic sections, in which the former is associated with "sport" (*Eur,* 14.32) and the latter with "strife" (*Eur,* 15.11), is reinforced by the visual components of the engravings. Plates 12 and 14, spoken by the historical voice and Enitharmon respectively, have the same spatial organization, with a design about six lines deep halfway through the text, and substantial designs along the right-hand margin and the bottom of the page. The historical text of plate 12 (see fig. 2), however, is darkly surrounded by spiders, spiders' webs, flies, and a figure praying, while the ahistorical text of plate 14 (see fig. 3) is almost cheerfully bordered by plants, vines, birds, butterflies, caterpillars, and snakes. The snakes, moreover, are separated from the rest of the images and confined to the borders around the passage at the bottom of the plate, in which the cessation of Enitharmon's song is described (*Eur,* 14.32–37). The illustrations thus reinforce the celebratory nature of Enitharmon's song and the text's envisioning of history as a trap, while visually inviting a comparison of the two plates in those terms.

There is no direct communication between these two worlds. For those who inhabit history, the mythic is always mediated, whether through a copy of Urizen's book (*Eur,* 11.3–5), "the clouds of Urizen" (*Eur,* 12.32), the "flames of Orc" (*Eur,* 12.32), or Albion's Angel, who alone can both see Urizen and be seen by the Europeans (*Eur,* 11.1–2, 12.5–6). Similarly, for those who inhabit myth, history is always indistinct, and perceived rather than engaged, as Orc can only "hear the howling shadows" (*Eur,* 12.22), and Enitharmon can only dream history. Prescriptive, secondary discourse is the only element common to both, but in both instances it appears as an

Fig. 2 Plate 12 of ***Europe*** (copy E), Lessing J. Rosenwald Collection, Library of Congress. Copyright © 1998 the William Blake Archive. Used with permission.

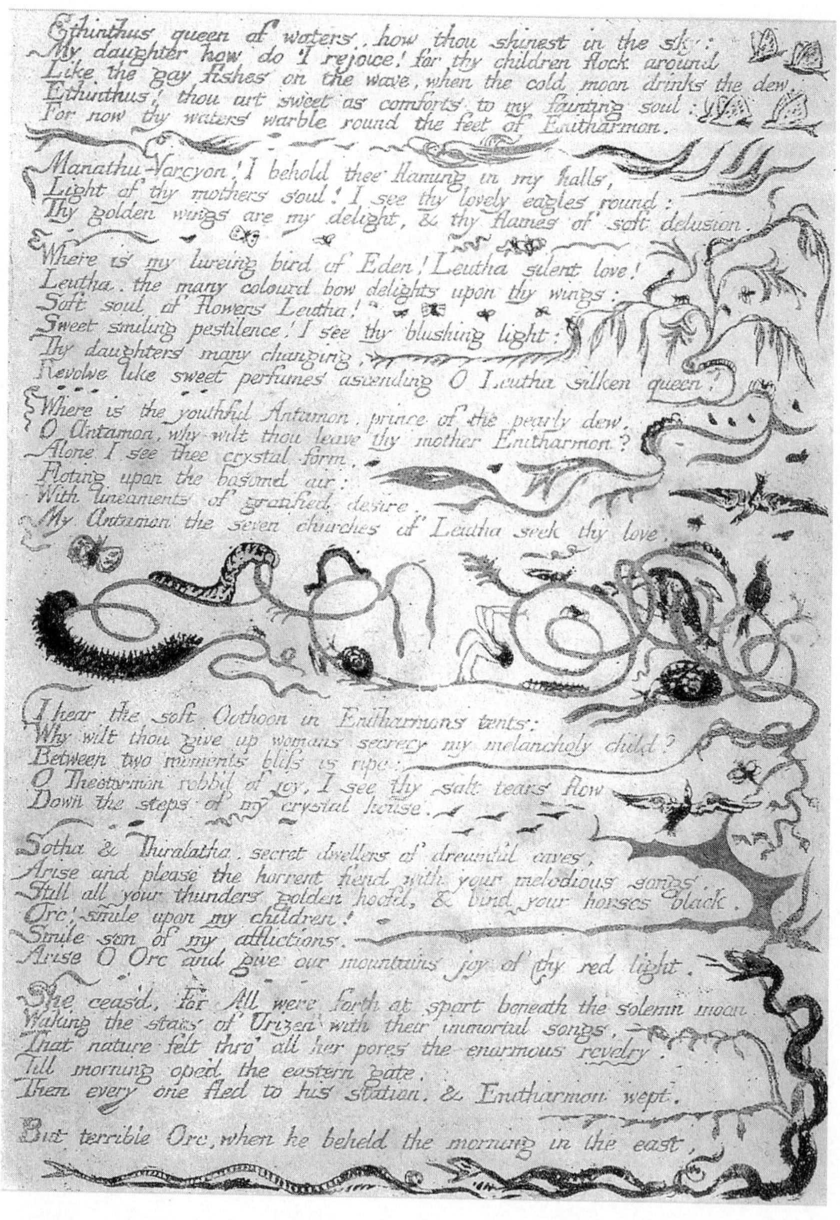

Ethinthus queen of waters, how thou shinest in the sky:
My daughter how do I rejoice! for thy children flock around
Like the gay fishes on the wave, when the cold moon drinks the dew.
Ethinthus! thou art sweet as comforts to my fainting soul:
For now thy waters warble round the feet of Enitharmon.

Manathu-Varcyon! I behold thee flaming in my halls,
Light of thy mothers soul! I see thy lovely eagles round;
Thy golden wings are my delight, & thy flames of soft delusion.

Where is my lureing bird of Eden! Leutha silent love!
Leutha, the many colourd bow delights upon thy wings:
Soft soul of flowers Leutha!
Sweet smiling pestilence! I see thy blushing light:
Thy daughters many changing,
Revolve like sweet perfumes ascending O Leutha silken queen!

Where is the youthful Antamon, prince of the pearly dew,
O Antamon, why wilt thou leave thy mother Enitharmon?
Alone I see thee crystal form,
Floting upon the bosomd air:
With lineaments of gratified desire.
My Antamon the seven churches of Leutha seek thy love.

I hear the soft Oothoon in Enitharmons tents:
Why wilt thou give up womans secrecy my melancholy child?
Between two moments bliss is ripe:
O Theotormon robb'd of joy, I see thy salt tears flow
Down the steps of my crystal house.

Sotha & Thiralatha, secret dwellers of dreamful caves,
Arise and please the horrent fiend with your melodious songs.
Still all your thunders golden hoofd, & bind your horses black.
Orc! smile upon my children!
Smile son of my afflictions.
Arise O Orc and give our mountains joy of thy red light.

She ceas'd, for All were forth at sport beneath the solemn moon
Waking the stars of Urizen with their immortal songs,
That nature felt thro' all her pores the enormous revelry,
Till morning ope'd the eastern gate.
Then every one fled to his station, & Enitharmon wept.

But terrible Orc, when he beheld the morning in the east,

Fig. 3 Plate 14 of ***Europe*** (copy E), Lessing J. Rosenwald Collection, Library of Congress. Copyright © 1998 the William Blake Archive. Used with permission.

interruption of mythic song, and it is when Enitharmon stops singing that history supersedes myth (*Eur,* 9.4, 14.32). The mythic is sustained discursively, by Enitharmon's song, and it falls into history when Enitharmon is silenced. While it has been argued that Enitharmon is responsible for the historical interlude of *Europe,* that history constitutes the "corrupt centuries of Enitharmon's reign,"[37] Enitharmon is asleep during and unaware of that history: for her, "eighteen hundred years were fled / As if they had not been" (*Eur,* 13.10–11). By beginning with history falling into myth and ending with the myth's fall into history, Blake denies either category the power to bound the other, and frames the narrative with points of flux that are dramatized in Orc's movement between the two domains.

Their distinctness is reinforced by the distribution of spoken and written texts within the poem. All of the speeches in *Europe*'s prophecy are contained in the parts in which Enitharmon is awake, taking place after she is introduced into the scene, if not spoken by Enitharmon herself, while the preludium is addressed to her. Conversely, utterances in the historic section are inarticulate and supplanted by written texts, as the speeches of the mythic characters are replaced by "Howlings & hissings, shrieks & groans, & voices of despair" (*Eur,* 12.34), and the people are prescribed by inscriptions: "Shut up" (*Eur,* 10.22) by Urizen's "brazen Book" (*Eur,* 11.3), "volumes of grey mist" (*Eur,* 12.3), "secret codes" (*Eur,* 12.15), "windows wove over with curses" (*Eur,* 12.27), and other figures of textual barriers. The only prescriptive passage in the part in which Enitharmon is awake is the heavens' reply, which calls for the establishment of Christian religion and its cult of chastity (*Eur,* 5.2–9); and it, like Urizen's book, is what "Kings & Priests had copied on Earth" (*Eur,* 11.4), as the king Rintrah and the priest Palamabron are sent to repeat the heavens' command (*Eur,* 5.5). The prescriptive language of negatives, "Thou shalt not" (*Eur,* 12.28) and "Forbid" (*Eur,* 5.8), is associated with secondary texts and the silence of Enitharmon, occupying the breaks in Enitharmon's calls to her children and involving the repetition of the heavens' reply or the copying of the Urizenic text (*Eur,* 11.3–4). The indeterminate multivocality of the mythic section is thus juxtaposed with the univocal Urizenic commands of the historical section, and the orality of the mythic part with the writings of the historical part. These writings are cited only when they are employed as limitations placed on the masses by the literate—the ruling classes with access to "secret codes"—so that they work to establish an oppressive hierarchy, a divisive structure that stands in stark contrast to the celebratory reunion in the mythic section. The opposition characterized by Bataille in *Theory of*

Religion is thus maintained with the homogeneity that he describes in his essay on fascism, sustaining the coherence of the two domains—except on plate 5 and plate 12.

On plate 5, Enitharmon's celebratory invitation to her children is interrupted by the prescriptive passage:

> Arise O Orc from thy deep den,
> First born of Enitharmon rise!
> And we will crown thy head with garlands of the ruddy vine;
> For now thou art bound;
> And I may see thee in the hour of bliss, my eldest born.
> The horrent Demon rose, surrounded with red stars of fire,
> Whirling about in furious circles round the immortal fiend.
> Then Enitharmon down descended into his red light,
> And thus her voice rose to her children, *the distant heavens reply.*
> Now comes the night of Enitharmons joy!
> Who shall I call? Who shall I send?
> That Woman, lovely Woman! may have dominion?
> Arise O Rintrah thee I call! & Palamabron thee!
> Go! tell the human race that Womans love is Sin!
> That an Eternal life awaits the worms of sixty winters
> In an allegorical abode where existence hath never come:
> Forbid all Joy, & from her childhood shall the little female
> Spread nets in every secret path. (*Eur,* 4.10–5.9; my emphasis)

Arguments that blame Enitharmon for the oppression of history and other evils—Suzanne Araas Vesely even calls her "Blake's first truly malevolent female figure"—rest on assigning this speech to her.[38] But the evidence for this reading is ambiguous, given the absence of quotation marks, as a controversy about earlier lines attests.[39] Moreover, the speech on plate 5 is inconsistent with the other speeches that can be ascribed to Enitharmon with greater certainty.[40] There are also contradictions between the prescriptive speech (*Eur,* 5.1–9) and the speeches that frame it (*Eur,* 4.10–14, 8.1–12). The prescriptive voice refers to Enitharmon in the third person (*Eur,* 5.1), a form that Enitharmon uses only when naming Orc with the phrase "First born of Enitharmon" (4.11). This prescriptive voice also does not refer to its children, although that is the convention of all the other calls to arise, before as well as after the historical interlude. In the other calls to arise, the caller is clearly identified as the parent of the addressee:

> Arise O Orc from thy deep den,
> First born of Enitharmon rise! . . .
> And I may see thee in the hour of bliss, my eldest born.
> (*Eur,* 4.10–11, 4.14)
> Arise O Rintrah eldest born: second to none but Orc: . . .
> Arise my son! (*Eur,* 8.1, 8.8)
> My daughter how do I rejoice! (*Eur,* 14.2)
> O Antamon, why wilt thou leave thy mother Enitharmon?
> (*Eur,* 14.16)

Moreover, if both speeches are Enitharmon's, then Enitharmon calls Rintrah and Palamabron twice (*Eur,* 5.4, 8.1, 8.2), and gives them two different sets of orders: the prescriptive voice orders them, "Go . . . Forbid all Joy" (*Eur,* 5.5, 5.8), and the other tells Rintrah to bring others for rejoicing (*Eur,* 8.3, 8.7, 8.8). In the second mythic section, Enitharmon even complains when one of her children leaves, asking "O Antamon, why wilt thou leave thy mother Enitharmon?" (*Eur,* 14.16). The speech that is cited to condemn Enitharmon is thus subverted and contradicted by the two speeches that frame it, as well as other statements by Enitharmon, and those speeches are clearly ascribed to the parent of Orc. The verb tenses of the line in which the narrator introduces the passage, moreover, implicitly assign the speech that precedes it to Enitharmon and the speech that follows it to the heavens: "thus rose her voice to her children, the distant heavens reply" (*Eur,* 4.18). The past tense "thus rose" is followed by the present tense "reply."

These contradictions are resolved if it is the heavens that command Rintrah and Palamabron to "Go! tell the human race that Womans love is Sin" (*Eur,* 5.5) and "Forbid all Joy" (*Eur,* 5.8), in reply to Enitharmon, and it is Rintrah's parent (*Eur,* 8.8) who asks Rintrah to "bring all [his] brethren" (*Eur,* 8.8) and envisions Rintrah as his "eyes rejoice" (*Eur,* 8.12). In this division of lines, it is the Urizenic heavens that interrupt and disrupt "the night of Enitharmons joy" (*Eur,* 5.1) through prescription, just as, after Enitharmon has collected all of her children for "enormous revelry" (*Eur,* 14.34), the children's songs "Wak[e] the stars of Urizen" (*Eur,* 14.33), so that song is transformed into weeping (*Eur,* 14.36), night is transformed into day (*Eur,* 14.35), the gathered children are dispersed (*Eur,* 14.34), and again the text slips into history. Enitharmon brings her children together while the Urizenic heavens and stars tell them to go and utter divisive commands; Enitharmon calls for songs and revelry while the heavens transmit prescriptive texts that "Forbid all Joy." History is represented as an interruption and dispersal of the mythic, implying that the two cannot coexist.

This prescriptive passage, spoken by the heavens rather than Enitharmon and apparently ignored by her, since her own contradictory invitation to Rintrah and Palamabron does not mention it, is arguably the first intrusion of the historic into the mythic. It introduces the Urizenic heavens, prescription from above, division, the scattering of Enitharmon's children rather than their collection—all the features of the historical interlude in Enitharmon's dream and the fall into history at the poem's close. The distinction is reinforced by Blake's designs for the plates: plate 4 (see fig. 4), with the speech clearly identified as Enitharmon's, has a generally joyous design, with human figures embracing, floating, and reclining on clouds, divided by a cloudy blanket from the weeping figure along the bottom edge of the design; plate 5 (see fig. 5), with the speech that I ascribe to the heavens, is dominated by a reptilian representation of Lucifer, a martial Lucifer whose scales look like chain mail and who carries a sword, and the two pious angels that stand behind and look toward him. One is filled with floating, frolicking human figures, and the other with immobile, imposing, supernatural figures—fallen and unfallen angels, the heavens' residents.[41]

In plate 12, the border between the two domains is transgressed from the other direction: "Albions Angel howl[s] in flames of Orc" (*Eur,* 12.12), "The Guardian of the secret codes forsook his ancient mansion, / Driven out by the flames of Orc" (*Eur,* 12.15–16), and "Between the clouds of Urizen the flames of Orc roll heavy / Around the limbs of Albions Guardian" (*Eur,* 12.32–33). In the middle of the plate, the scene turns from Albion to the mythic figures:

> Thus was the howl thro Europe!
> For Orc rejoic'd to hear the howling shadows
> But Palamabron shot his lightnings trenching down his wide back
> And Rintrah hung with all his legions in the nether deep
> Enitharmon laugh'd in her sleep to see. (*Eur,* 12.21–25)

Again, the mythic is associated with rejoicing rather than prescription, as the mythic characters intrude on the historical narrative.[42] Orc then finds the "trump of the last doom," which he had been "Seeking" (*Eur,* 12.13). He is, however, unable to "blow the iron tube" (*Eur,* 13.2)—it is silent. Newton "blow'd the enormous blast" (*Eur,* 13.5), and instead of an apocalypse that will "awake the dead to Judgment" (*Eur,* 13.3), the cycle begins again, as

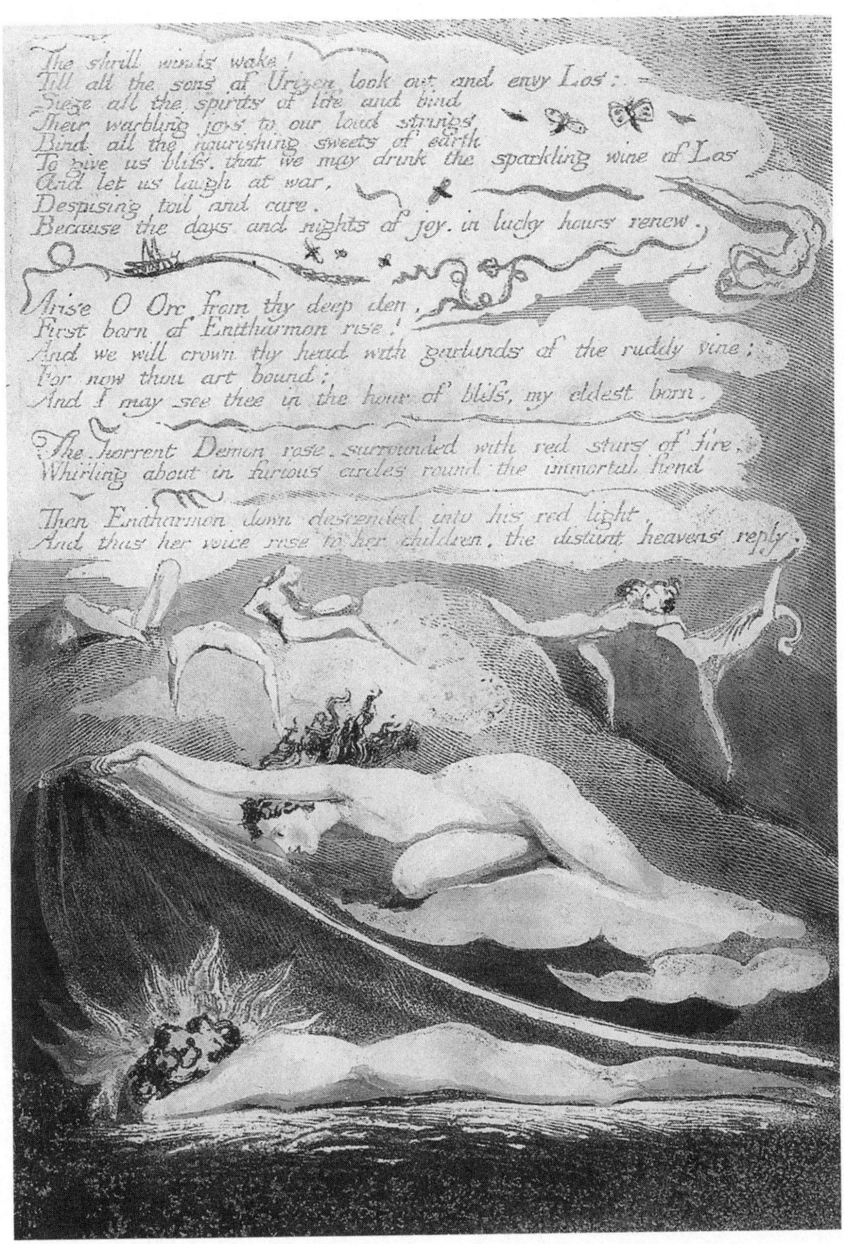

The shrill winds wake!
Till all the sons of Urizen look out and envy Los:
Sieze all the spirits of life and bind
Their warbling joys to our loud strings
Bind all the nourishing sweets of earth
To give us bliss, that we may drink the sparkling wine of Los
And let us laugh at war,
Despising toil and care.
Because the days and nights of joy, in lucky hours renew.
Arise O Orc from thy deep den,
First born of Enitharmon rise!
And we will crown thy head with garlands of the ruddy vine;
For now thou art bound;
And I may see thee in the hour of bliss, my eldest born.
The horrent Demon rose, surrounded with red stars of fire,
Whirling about in furious circles round the immortal fiend
Then Enitharmon down descended into his red light,
And thus her voice rose to her children, the distant heavens reply.

Fig. 4 Plate 4 of *Europe* (copy E), Lessing J. Rosenwald Collection, Library of Congress. Copyright © 1998 the William Blake Archive. Used with permission.

Fig. 5 Plate 5 of *Europe* (copy E), Lessing J. Rosenwald Collection, Library of Congress. Copyright © 1998 the William Blake Archive. Used with permission.

Enitharmon continues her call to her children. The mingling of the mythic and the historic that marks the collapse of the latter's boundaries presages the possibility of apocalypse, the potential to end history. After the completion of Enitharmon's song, the two domains again meet as "in the vineyards of red France appear'd the light of [Orc's] fury" (*Eur,* 15.2) and the "strife of blood" (*Eur,* 15.11) (which again promises the possibility of apocalypse). While Orc is never fully able to engage the historical world—he is inarticulate throughout the poem as well as unable to blow the trumpet—he is able to move physically between the two domains. He rises to Enitharmon during the mythic section (*Eur,* 4.11), his flames surround the lower world of Europe during the historical section, and he descends again at the end of *Europe:* "terrible Orc . . . Shot from the heights of Enitharmon; / And in the vineyards of red France appear'd the light of his fury" (*Eur,* 14.37–15.2).

The text thus grafts the two worlds together, but constructs no homogeneous, unhybridized space that can contain them both or allow them both to be vocal, commenting on their inability to accommodate the other without compromising their presumed self-contained completeness and homogeneity. Like Oothoon, readers are left at the border of either/or. But unlike Oothoon, readers do not move through these systems but around them. History and myth, as well as their respective rulers, are, by the poem's definition, unaware of each other. There is, however, the apocalyptic promise that contact between the two domains creates the conditions in which the boundaries that separate them can be destroyed. By associating the transgression of the boundary between myth and history with Orc—the figure of revolution, as well as the end of war (*Eur,* 3.4), the conditions for apocalypse (*Eur,* 12.13), and the French Revolution (*Eur,* 15.2)—Blake identifies the compromise of the boundary with radical, and potentially liberating, social change, the change that, as discussed in the previous chapter, erupts in the instant between temporal divisions.

America *and the Alienation of the Reader*

It is in *America,* however, that such divisions are radically compromised. *America,* which focuses on the circumstances in which a successful revolution is possible, takes place in a context in which the borders between myth and history are repeatedly crossed rather than, as in *Europe,* being represented as indiscernibly opaque. Orc not only enters the historical world in

America, but is able to speak in it, an achievement unique to *America* among the poems of the early 1790s. If "Urizen's willful silence is a form of suppressed or concealed speech," Orc's articulateness is a sign that he has escaped containment.[43] But Orc is not, as in *Europe,* the only figure able to cross the divide between myth and history. Blake moves figures across the boundaries of discursively constructed systems through what Rothenberg terms "mobile alliances" and so questions the inevitability of those systems. These transgressions, moreover, are manifested through changes in appearances and names that implicate them in spectacles of power. In *Shakespearean Negotiations,* Stephen Greenblatt contrasts a "power that dreams of a panopticon in which the most intimate secrets are open to the view of an invisible authority," described by Foucault in *Discipline and Punish,* with an "Elizabethan power [that] depends upon its privileged visibility."[44] At a critical moment in the prophecy, authority is exposed to public view in a manner that it does not control, and the rebelling population stages a counterspectacle that dramatizes the change in the configuration of power, manipulating the two types of theatrical power described by Foucault and Greenblatt to unmask traditional authorities and establish new ones.

Informing this manipulation of visibility is the masquerade, a site of spectacular disguises that popularized the crucial innovation that appearance is not a reliable marker of identity, an innovation that threatened contemporary hegemonic practices and assumptions. As Terry Castle's study of eighteenth-century masquerade shows, the masquerade not only involved assuming a different identity but required the assumption of an identity opposite, in hierarchical terms, to one's own: "Costume ideally represented an inversion of one's nature. At its most piquant it expressed a violation of cultural categories. If one may speak of the rhetoric of masquerade, a tropology of costume, the controlling figure was the antithesis: one was obliged to impersonate a being opposite, in some essential figure, to oneself."[45] This was clearly threatening to the status quo, and opponents "unanimously castigated its disorienting anti-taxonomic force": "Without the principle of opposition, the ordering principle of civilization itself, the classification of entities became impossible," and so the masquerade made possible "a convulsive negation of every form of ideological discrimination."[46] Identity could be assumed with the evening's costume, leaving no residual trace of the sumptuary laws to mark class, occupation, gender, or distinctions of birth.[47] Each masquer began as an equal cipher, as a ticket holder unencumbered by marks of social status, revealing the arbitrariness of the hierarchy that critics of the masquerade sought to establish as natural and rational. As Blake's contemporary Mary Brunton wrote in a novel, "At a subscription masquerade, indeed, one might meet with low people," and "the very use of masks is to banish the privileges and the restraints of personal respectability."[48] This is a challenge not only to social order but to linguistic order: William Keach argues that the Romantics tried to come to terms with the distinction between arbitrary and motivated language through the trope of apparel, where arbitrary language is to thought what clothing is to the body, and motivated language is to thought what the body is to the soul.[49] The masquerade foregrounds the arbitrariness of signs, as language or clothing—or titles.

Part of Paine's attack on customary power involves "attacking aristocratic titles as dangerous abstractions" or constructions that are falsely naturalized.[50] In *Common Sense* (1776), Paine begins his discussion of hereditary titles with the statement "Mankind being originally equals in the order of creation, the equality could only be destroyed by some subsequent circumstance"; later, in *Rights of Man* (1791–1792), he argues, "That . . . which is called aristocracy in some countries, and nobility in others, arose out of the governments founded upon conquest."[51] The latter remark, published two years before *Europe,* economically raises crucial questions about the natural authority claimed by the ruling class. The arbitrariness of the name of the class under consideration is emphasized by the initial phrasing, "That . . . which is called aristocracy," and by Paine's offer of a culturally dependent synonym, "nobility." Moreover, the hierarchy that the aristocracy presumes is inverted by the identification of the aristocracy, in this passage and throughout Paine's writings on the subject, with what might be termed "inhumanity": he identifies them with conquest rather than heredity, brutality rather than civilization, incompetence rather than superiority, and arbitrary power rather than natural right. In Paine's rhetoric, even the symbols of power are arbitrary and, by implication, deceptive. (Paine depends heavily on the notion of an originary, natural state that precedes and is superior to contemporary political organization.)[52] For example, the figure of "the sword assum[ing] the name of sceptre" emblematizes the rise to power and subsequent legitimization of "a race of conquerors."[53] Later, Paine asks, "[A]fter all, what is this metaphor called a crown, or rather what is a monarchy? Is it a thing, or is it a name, or is it a fraud? . . . Doth the virtue consist in the metaphor, or in the man? Doth the goldsmith that makes the crown, make the virtue also? Doth it operate like Fortunatus's wishing-cap, or Harlequin's wooden sword? Doth it make a man a conjuror?"[54] Paine thus challenges the authority of the ruling class by classifying its power, and its signs of power, as arbitrary while challenging, through inversion, the portrayal of its power as natural. These are defamiliarizing devices that offer a new view of the distribution of power in British society, disrupting the expectations founded by the prevailing political rhetoric through the mechanisms that conservatives feared in the masquerade, especially inversion, the exposure of arbitrary naming, and radical equality.

Blake puts such devices to similar uses in *America.* In his discussion of *Europe,* Bloom suggests that the figure of "Albion has much to do with [George III and Pitt]; in the historical allegory he is to be identified with them, or very nearly. But in Blake as in Spenser the political allegory and the moral allegory or mythic meaning tend to exist on intersecting but quite distinct levels."[55] There is not one Albion in *Europe* and *America,* however, but a series of related figures that includes Albion's Angel, Albion's Guardian, Albion's Prince, "Angel voice" (*Am,* 10.1), the "King of England" (*Am,* 4.12), and even Albion's Angels (*Eur,* 9.12, 9.14). These avatars coexist without merging into a single identity, sustaining the dependence of identity on context: the martial king is a guardian, the religious dogmatist is an angel, and the thwarted hierarch is a prince, as Blake provides different avatars (or perhaps masks) for the historical figures of the king and prime minister to suit the role specific to the context. This fracturing of identity to enable quick, fluid transitions from Prince to Guardian to Angel suggests that names and identities are context dependent, related to function and circumstance rather than inherent qualities.[56] In a cancelled plate to *America,* a longer version of plate 4, Blake describes the metamorphosis of one Albion figure into another:

> on his cliffs stood Albions wrathful Prince
> A dragon form clashing his scales at midnight he arose,
> And flam'd red meteors round the land of Albion beneath[.]
> His voice, his locks, his awful shoulders, and his glowing eyes,
> Reveal the dragon thro' the human; coursing swift as fire
> To the close hall of counsel, where his Angel form renews.
> (*Am,* 3.14–17, b.1–2)

While plate b is primarily concerned with George III's consultation with his "Lords & Commons" (*Am,* b.9), recalling Satan's consultation with the rest of the fallen in *Paradise Lost,* the first two lines of the plate also indicate a connection between Albion's Angel and Albion's Prince that is not made in the uncancelled version. In the prophecy proper, Albion's Angel,

Albion's Guardian, and Albion's Prince operate in their own spheres of activity, but in the cancelled plate Albion's Angel, Albion's Prince, and George III intersect: in moving from the "cliffs" to the "hall of counsel" this figure metamorphoses from "dragon form" to "Angel form" and arrives at the place "[w]here George the third holds council" (*Am,* b.9). The engraving for plate 4 retains the implication by depicting a figure in trailing robes that visually echoes the neighboring figure of a dragon, graphically introducing the metamorphosis that was described verbally in the cancelled lines. As the figure moves from context to context, and geographically from the "cliffs" to the "hall of counsel," its form, its outward appearance, as well as its name, changes.

These transformations disrupt not only the determinacy of identity, but also the relationship between body and spirit, which, according to Bataille, informs the construction of myth and reality. If one figure can have the form of a dragon, an angel, and a man, then the absolute distinction between body and spirit as well as myth and reality collapses in that figure. Such distinctions are also compromised when the "thirteen Angels" descend from heaven to stand beside "Washington & Paine & Warren" (*Am,* 12.2, 12.7), recalling the myth, described in Paul Henri Mallet's *Northern Antiquities,* that Odin would join the fray during battle to "inflame the fury of the combatants," and also recalling Orc's participation in the conflict.[57] There are similar destabilizations of identity and taxonomy elsewhere in the text, such as the parallelism on plate 11, which suggests that God, the "pitying Angel," and the "crawling villain" are the same figure (*Am,* 11.13, 11.14). Similarly, Orc's speeches are composed of a series of reversals and paradoxes, from the freeing of captives and the rebirth of the dead, to the temporally problematic assertion that "[t]he Sun has left his blackness . . . And the fair Moon rejoices in the clear & cloudless night" (*Am,* 6.13–14), to his claim that "letchery" "May find [Virginity] in a harlot, and in coarse-clad honesty / The undefil'd tho' ravish'd" (*Am,* 8.10, 8.11–12).

Familiar classificatory binaries, from myth/history and spirit/body to virgin/harlot and day/night, as well as key assumptions that are derived from aligning such oppositions, such as "God is good" and "the King is the rightful ruler," are complicated and then peeled away, challenged in such a way that the reader must reevaluate her identification of the figure and the semiological systems that are being employed. If the statement "God is good" is not necessarily true, then the Angel's condemnation of Orc as "transgressor of Gods Law" (*Am,* 7.6) can be read as praise. Sceptres, uniforms, and animal shapes that are assumed "Sometimes" (*Am,* 1.13) are all arbitrary, and therefore subject to change, just as the classifications regarding myth and history or virginity and harlotry are. Consequently, when power is revealed to depend on such signs it too becomes subject to change—no longer rooted in the essentials of the "divine right of kings" or the natural nobility, it can be transferred. If the scepter is not an expression of an inherent regality but an arbitrary sign that grants significance within a political power structure, then the scepter can be passed from one person to another. If God is not necessarily the ultimate authority, then the divine right of kings can be replaced by another method for selecting rulers.

The use of superficial symbols to determine a role within a system rather than to express an essential identity is fundamental to an important turning point in the narrative of *America:* the passage in which Boston's Angel exposes God as a masquer, the Angels disrobe, and then descend "from out their heav'nly heights" (*Am,* 12.5). Colley notes that uniforms became particularly important toward the end of the eighteenth century because they served two functions, operating as a kind of masquerade dress that turned the less-than-imposing body of a soldier into a martial spectacle and as an inscription of the wearer into a position of authority.[58] This twofold project informs this pivotal passage in Blake's *America,* as Boston's Angel asks,

> What God is he, writes laws of peace, & clothes him in a tempest
> What pitying Angel lusts for tears, and fans himself with sighs
> What crawling villain preaches abstinence & wraps himself
> In fat of lambs? no more I follow, no more obedience pay.
> So cried he, rending off his robe & throwing down his scepter.
> In sight of Albions Guardian, and all the thirteen Angels
> Rent off their robes to the hungry wind, & threw their golden
>   scepters
> Down on the land of America. indignant they descended
> Headlong from out their heav'nly heights, descending swift as fires
> Over the land; naked & flaming are their lineaments seen.
>   (*Am,* 11.12–12.6)

Boston's Angel begins with an argument that exposes the discrepancies between the apparent identity of authority figures (their rhetoric, their names, their clothing) and the actual actions of those figures. The response of Boston's Angel to these hypocrisies is to revolt by "rending off" the symbols of his authority. Similarly, the "British soldiers" "threw their swords & muskets to the earth . . . in sight / Of Albions Angel" (*Am,* 13.6, 13.7, 13.9–10). The authorities are punished not by the troops' arms but by the disarming of the troops, as "The millions . . . threw off their hammerd mail, / And cast their swords & spears to earth, & stood a naked multitude. / Albions Guardian writhed in torment" (*Am,* 15.4–6). Casting off marks of power—scepters, robes, swords, and so forth—constitutes a refusal to be oppression's delegate, a refusal to empower the Guardian by following his orders and wearing his uniforms, and it follows a revisionary characterization of the oppressor's attire.

As symbols of power, uniforms, titles, and formal orders inscribe the bearers into a chain of command in which they are both oppressed and oppressing, marking their complicity in "another Mans" "System," but they do not, as Paine argues, indicate an essential power. The description of God marks the disjunction between clothing and identity as a contradiction between words and actions. By casting off the marks of power that were granted to them by rulers, the Thirteen Angels deny the power of Albion's Angel over and through them, becoming something other than the rulers' delegates and altering their appearance to reflect their new allegiances. The disrobing is thus not only an act that reflects identity, but an act that constitutes it, recalling Judith Butler's notion of performative identity: to cast off their clothes is to reject the authority in which that clothing is implicated and redefine themselves as rebels.[59] Moreover, as they seize control over their own representation, they stage a counterspectacle that contradicts the authority of Albion's Angel by placing the Angel in the position of the spectator of a scene in which his military power dissolves. They seize power, in other words, by seizing control of spectacle.

Orc reverses the actions of the soldiers, while employing the same assumptions. He tries to transcend his shackled body by clothing himself in various figures of regal power: "Sometimes an eagle screaming in the sky, sometimes a lion, / Stalking upon the mountains, & sometimes a whale I lash / The raging fathomless abyss, anon a serpent folding" (*Am,* 1.13–15). Orc's unapparelled self, however, is not associated with such power in the preludium: "feeble my spirit folds. / For chaind beneath I rend these caverns" (*Am,* 1.17–18). More is going on here than the assertion of animal power over the domains of the earth.[60] Like the uniforms of the British troops, the robes of the Angels, and the aristocratic costume worn by a lower-class masquer, Orc's animal shapes are powerful to those who accept their importance but are not continuous with his naked self. The female figure of the preludium attempts to prescribe Orc's power through language by limiting the shapes to specific regions and to her own field of perception: "I see a serpent in Canada, who courts me to his love; / In Mexico an Eagle, and a Lion in Peru; / I see a Whale in the South-sea, drinking my soul away" (*Am,* 2.12–14). The female defines Orc in terms of her own world, characterizing him as what she sees—as her suitor and as "the image of God . . . fall'n to give [her] life" (*Am,* 2.8–9). Against Orc's empowering definition of himself, the female offers a definition of Orc that empowers her at least as the one in relation to whom he is defined in a conflict of "System." Albion's Angel offers a third series of types to describe Orc, a series that demonizes Orc and so legitimates the Angel's opposition to him, declaring, "Art thou not Orc . . . Blasphemous Demon, Antichrist, hater of Dignities; / Lover of wild rebellion, and transgresser of Gods Law" (*Am,* 7.3–7). Each figure characterizes Orc in terms that empower the one who is characterizing: representation is a vehicle for appropriating power, and specifically for taking it from the one being represented. The female, Orc, Albion's Angel, Boston's Angel, and others are all trying to empower themselves or disempower another by manipulating the symbols—uniforms, robes, scepters, names—that determine identity in England and its colonial possessions. Further, Albion's Angel fails to control the new kind of spectacular power, the panopticonic power of the surveying authority of the post-Enlightenment: he laments, "America is darkned; and my punishing Demons terrified" and "clouds obscure my aged sight" (*Am,* 9.3, 9.12). He can see only "The terror," Orc, and the rebellion of Boston's Angel and his soldiers. The Angel sees only the spectacles that establish the failure of his control.

Amidst this swirl of changing names, modified forms, and layers of disguise are figures battling for power by trying to control the spectacular representation of power in titles, uniforms, and other signs. A value system is implicit here: the rebels generally disrobe, suggesting the casting off of the artificial power structure, as Paine proposed, while hegemonic figures are associated with clouds and shadows that conceal. After the soldiers throw down their weapons "in sight / Of Albions Angel" (*Am,* 13.9–10), for instance, the Angel regains some control after he "enrag'd his secret clouds open'd . . . and burnt outstretchd on wings of wrath cov'ring / The eastern sky, spreading his awful wings across the heavens" (*Am,* 13.10–12). The revolutionaries control both kinds of spectacular power: seeing and being seen, they are threatened only when their enemies are shrouded and thus invisible to their sight. The description of Urizen on the final plate of the poem is a catalogue of shrouds, as the figure that took "fiery joy" and "perverted [it] to ten commands" (*Am,* 8.3) is "in thunders wrap'd," "flag'd with grey-brow'd snows," and "clothed in tears & trembling shudd'ring cold" as he "Hid[es] the Demon red with clouds & cold mists" (*Am,* 16.3, 16.5, 16.8, 16.13) until the French Revolution. Blake thus echoes those who condemned the masquerade by identifying costume and masks with deceit and the abuse of power—though such conservatives would have certainly hesitated to suggest that nakedness is the best demonstration of honesty—and he uses conventional assumptions about appearance to inculcate through the poem a clear sense of which side we are supposed to favor.

But by staging the battle for power as a struggle over names and appearances, Blake exposes the terms of the conflict in an unconventional way. Despite the references to soldiers and arms, Blake's battles are not martial: the central figure for the battle here sets the diseases of the hegemony against the sterilizing fires of Orc and the rebels, characterizing hegemony as the force that compromises boundaries by invading the body politic. The viral figure for battle thus produces a negative hybridity that subverts that which Blake valorizes, rather than the positive variety that subverts that which Blake opposes (see chapter 6). Apart from this figure, the battle's direction is plotted in the ongoing reversals and inversions, from the liberation of slaves to the builder who drops his hammer (*Am,* 6.6, 14.16). In *America,* opposing ideologies collide, while hierarchies imposed on a wide range of subjects, from political and religious authority to chastity and slavery, shatter and are overturned. Blake does not address the establishment of a government in the United States, nor in France, but retains as his focus the dynamic that results from the collision of two fundamentally incompatible ideological camps, which nevertheless share the recognition that the terms of battle are semiological.

Locating the Alienated Reader

By including different systems in these poems, Blake produces a text that is radically different from the Urizenic model. The examples of Urizenic texts offered in *Europe* involve commands that are addressed directly to the reader: "Thou shalt not" and "Fear" (*Eur,* 12.28). Such dictates seek to bring the reader under the text's control, not only by seeking to alter the reader's behavior, but also by making the reader an implied one, already anticipated within the text and contained by its pre(in)scription. In *Visions* and *Europe,* however, the reader is placed in an alienated position, from which it can be seen that the assumptions that govern the homogeneous societies that are represented do not operate naturally or totalize the field; the reader is a spectator of mutually exclusive systems and, in being able to see the different systems that are fundamentally unable to recognize each other, is placed on the edges of them all. The reader has access to the *Visions*' "three-sided soliloquy," eavesdropping on the speeches unheard by characters within the text, while the reader of *Europe* is placed outside of the mythological and historical domains that the narrative perspective tries to separate.[61] In *America*, the reader is even more alienated by the constantly marked, but never limiting, boundaries between myth and history, as well as the reversals of power that reveal the symbolic, rather than essential, nature of authority. This alienation does not create a new system, but it does mark that crucial first step toward the recognition that the prevailing system is "another Mans."

In this context, the sympathetic construction of Oothoon is something of a trick. Fox suggests, "It is certainly true that Oothoon speaks for Blake in this poem, that she is as noble in its context as ever Los is in the final poems (more noble: she does not make mistakes)," and Ostriker declares that Oothoon is "a heroine unequalled in English poetry before or since."[62] These qualities (nobility, the apparent coincidence of views with the author, heroism, intelligence, courage, and so forth), particularly when juxtaposed with those of an unrepentant rapist like Bromion and a self-indulgent whiner like Theotormon, invite the reader who is looking for a figure with whom to identify to take Oothoon's part. The reader, like the Daughters, is thus placed in a position outside of all three systems, as well as nudged toward sympathizing with Oothoon as she moves through different, mutually exclusive perspectives, so that the reader can follow at once the narrator's and Oothoon's unfamiliar perspectives on fundamental social institutions. But then Oothoon declares, in a line that has long troubled Blake scholars, that she will "catch for thee girls of mild silver, or of furious gold" (*VDA*, 7.24). Where is the reader now? While Oothoon speaks of Theotormon in the third person and herself (usually) in the first person, it is easy for the reader to follow conventional literary practice by searching for a figure with whom to identify and select the most sympathetic character, Oothoon. But in turning to the second-person form of address, Oothoon not only implicates the reader—just as commandments of the form "thou shalt not" or gestures such as "gentle reader" do—but locates the reader elsewhere. On plate 7, she asks, "Why dost thou seek religion" and "Why hast thou taught my Theotormon this accursed thing," as well as declares, "thou seekest solitude," "be thou accursed from the earth," and "I'll lie beside thee on a bank" (*VDA,* 7.9, 7.13, 7.10, 7.12, 7.25), before closing with a return to Theotormon's proper name (*VDA,* 7.26). This referent, "thou"/"thee," is characterized, in series, as one who seeks confining structures, one who criminally imposes confining structures, and one who accepts the avails of Oothoon's confining structures, "silken nets and traps of adamant" (*VDA,* 7.23). If Blake is positing a (heterosexual) male reader, if only implicitly (as well as practically, given the rarity of his manuscripts and the select distribution of them), Oothoon's offer to "catch for thee girls" and "lie beside thee" is at once a compromise of her heroic status, because she is serving Theotormon's desires and denying her own, and an inscription of the reader into Theotormon's Bromion-like position in her fantasy. (Theotormon's position is like Bromion's because of Oothoon's use of the commodification of women that marks Bromion's speech about his proprietorial rights.) Our identification with Oothoon, already problematic because of the different perspectives that she expresses, from her plea to Theotormon that she is "pure" (*VDA,* 2.28) to her critique of marriage and other social institutions that define purity to her offer to trap women for him, is thus further compromised by her use of pronouns that implicitly include the reader in the male positions that she decries. It is here that Blake comes closest to Brecht's "alienation effect," prohibiting the audience's easy identification with characters and, in doing so, subverting the pervasive, familiar practice of identification.[63]

In *Europe,* there is no figure with whom to identify. The indefinite assignment of the speeches in the first mythic section, the overwhelming violence of the historic section, the quick descriptions of Enitharmon's children in the final mythic section, and the inarticulateness of Orc prohibit the identification of a clear protagonist or hero. The reader is instead faced with an alternation between extremes of familiar dichotomies, as the narratorial perspective switches abruptly from one set of characters to another. The reader is thus shown that each system is self-contained and unaware of its alternative, functioning as a homogeneous society like that defined by Bataille. But the reader, aware of the alternative, is also shown that neither totalizes the field, as it believes it does. The reader, moreover, in being aware of both, is placed outside of both, and occupies a liminal space in which she is aware of myth and history but is part of neither. This is crucial, because it is at the points at which revolution approaches that the boundary between the two domains is compromised and the reader is placed in the position of always seeing those domains as compromised. In *America,* this liminal space is all-inclusive, as there is no homogeneous space in which the reader can rest except briefly. The rape depicted in the preludium also unsettles any alignment with Orc, particularly since he appears to be as hypocritical as the God of which Boston's Angel complains, because Orc seizes the female in the preludium and condemns bonds in the prophecy. (And his assertion in the prophecy that a woman is "undefil'd tho' ravish'd in her cradle night and morn" [8.12] looks uncomfortably like a denial that his rape could have detrimental effects on his victim.) The marginality of the reader places the reader in a potentially liberating place, as long as the reader is not drawn to the center through an identification that incorporates the reader into a single ideological perspective.

Blake's reader thus sees and is alienated from both halves of the "sympathy-antipathy pair." The strange language and names, the revision of history, and the articulation of radical viewpoints are defamiliarizing and estranging, placing the reader, like all spectators, on the margins of the domains being represented. This is finally what we can take from Blake's description of *A Vision of The Last Judgment:* "I have represented it as I saw it[.] to different People it appears differently . . . every thing else does" (*VLJ*, 555). Besides referring to fallen vision as fractured and fallible, Blake sets apart his vision, and the vision of every other individual, denying, in a fundamentally alienating way, the possibility of a shared vision. This is not, as I have argued with reference to alienation in *Visions of the Daughters of Albion,* necessarily negative, because it also operates as a liberation from the perspective of others. Blake's discomfort with simple equality is noted by Ferber, who suggests, "Perhaps equality bore connotations offensive to his love of uniqueness, the minute particularity, of each individual."[64] Pluralism is, in one sense, a condition of the fallen world, but it is also a diversity worth celebrating and engaging. By dramatizing this plurality of vision and perspective in *Visions, Europe,* and *America,* Blake places the reader not only outside of one system, but outside of a set of systems, disrupting any simple binaries. The reader necessarily occupies the intersection of the different systems represented in Blake's poems, at the margins of all and included in none. Blake's work retains its unfamiliarity, its strangeness, and its estranging effect, leaving the reader in the space in which revolutionary transgressions of homogeneous societies are possible.

"AND NONE SHALL GATHER THE LEAVES"

Unbinding the Voice in *America* and *Europe*

Fós ní ghéillfinn, caoch mar a bhí mé
Do ghlór gan éifeacht aon a mhaígh é,
Ach magadh nó greim gan feidhm, gan chéill.
Gur aithris a broinn dom deimhin gach scéil.
Níor chomhrá leamhais ná dúrtam bréige é,
Ná dúirt-bean-liom-go-ndúirt-bean-léi é,
Ach labhair an bheart i gceart 'is in éifeacht.

Brian Merriman, CÚIRT AN MHEAN-OÍCHE (1780)[1]

In the preludiums to *America* and *Europe,* Blake ties his critique of gender paradigms to his subversion of bibliographical practices through the childbirth metaphor, a trope in which art meets the politics of gender and the body meets the book. The production of texts that totalize the field of social relations and the convention of linearity that totalizes the narrative are thus mapped onto the females' assimilation into the dominant gender codes and the unified identity that those codes presume. On the verge of being incorporated into a system that views them only as fecund wombs, the females of the preludiums resist that assimilation by complicating their identities through the addition of a voice that is productive in ways that exceed, and are alien to, gender codes, generating the same kind of destabilizing hybridity as that discussed in the previous chapter. The voice not only articulates their alienation from those codes, but marks that alienation by its very existence. As in *Visions of the Daughters of Albion,* Blake produces a female character who defamiliarizes prevailing assumptions about gender from a position on the margins of that totalizing system. Through the childbirth metaphor, moreover, the implications of such resistance are extended to the reader's assimilation into the totalizing paradigms that govern the hegemonic text. Blake aligns mass-produced texts with the alienated uterus through which the women are reduced to silent fecundity. Just as the women resist their reduction to reproductive receptacles by rendering their identity self-alienated—representing themselves as an assemblage of parts with varying interests—Blake resists his works' implication in the production of readers as reproductive receptacles, passively repeating what they are told, by splitting his texts into an assemblage of textual and visual parts with varying significatory interests. The preludiums to *America* and *Europe,* through the childbirth metaphor, establish a crucial link between the discursive incorporation of individuals into an ideologically invested norm and the normalizing effects of ideologically invested discourses on individuals.

The Childbirth Metaphor and Blake: Defamiliarizing Gender and Reading

Western discourse about creativity is pervaded, and partially determined, by the construction of a homology between intellectual and biological creation: the mind conceives a work, is pregnant with it, or gives birth to it, while biological conception is described as the materialization of an idea.[2] The field of these analogies is complicated by fluctuations in the discursive domains of which it is the intersection, by differences in notions of maternity, paternity, the mechanics of reproduction from conception to childbirth, the mechanics of nonbiological creativity from inspiration to public reception, the relationship between the creator and the work at each of those stages, and numerous others. In her essay "Lab'ring Bards: Birth *Topoi* and English Poetics, 1660–1820," Castle shows that women's procreative role was held to be a passive one in the eighteenth century and that the use of the procreative function as a metaphor for artistic production altered profoundly as poetic theories changed. Enlightenment writers, defining the "good poet" as one who is "free from physical constraint, free to construct rational worlds of discourse," use the metaphor in pejorative contexts to describe the work of failed poets, while Romantic authors, favoring an "organic theory of art," use the metaphor positively to describe their own work.[3] When these poetic theories collided with eighteenth-century models of gender as well as related assumptions about procreation, the similitude between biological and intellectual creativity was subordinated to the imperative to differentiate male from female creativities, "divid[ing] *labor,*" as Susan Stanford Friedman notes, "into men's *production* and women's *reproduction.*"[4] In the words of Blake's contemporary Mary Whateley, "But hark!—my darling infant cries, / And each poetic fancy flies."[5] The homology was thus fractured into a divisive paradigm by which women were denied access to a textual power that (male) authors could monopolize, recursively defining the terms of that textual power. Blake, at the leading edge of the transformation described by Castle, accepts the devaluation of maternity, but in terms that are not fully consistent with contemporary models of gender and also serve to challenge the distribution of textual power.

Blake complicates the childbirth metaphor by representing women who are named only "female" yet resist biological reproduction and articulate their resistance through an alternative mode of creativity: the females speak, supplementing their uterine identities by appropriating a nonbiological mode of production from which they are excluded by the paradigm that genders creative labor. Blake thus renders them too complex to be comprehended within the absolute terms of the law "Verses are only writ by men: / I know a woman cannot write."[6] Moreover, the females' role in procreation is disparaged not because it is coarsely corporeal, but because it functions as a figure for a model of reading that Blake opposes, one in which the reader is the passive receptacle of a text that is disseminated by the author. To read passively is to follow the text, to copy it, and thus for the reader to become aligned with "women's *reproduction*" rather than "men's *production*." To reinforce this emphasis on copying, the sexual violence of the preludiums is described in terms that recall the technical language of printing, implicating it in the mass (re)production of texts that facilitates the exercise of authoritarian control through the dissemination of prescriptive texts to a wide readership.[7]

Blake goes still further in contesting the passive receptivity of the reader, as well as its corollary, the hermeneutic control of the author. He fragments his text visually in ways that contradict conventional logical groupings, rendering it too complex to be comprehended definitively and therefore resistant to passive reading. Heterogeneity offers an avenue through which enforced homogeneity, the rule of paradigms that are defined by absolutes such as "women cannot" and propagated by the replicated text, can be transgressed. Heterogeneity repudiates the universality, absoluteness, and coherence on which prescriptive models depend and so questions their authority. In *America* and *Europe,* females do not necessarily wish to be mothers; women can be intellectually creative; printing is akin to sexual violence; the author can relinquish, at least in part, his authority; the text need not be a coherent expression of the author's position; and the reader need not yield to the author's dictates. Blake's advocacy of heterogeneity and active reception unsettles the conventional distribution of power on the level of politics by proposing an engaging, untotalizable population that generates ideas of its own rather than bowing to those of an elite, a proposal that has much to do with the radical politics of Paine. But my concern here is with the ways in which this mechanism is played out on the level of reading. While I addressed, in the previous chapter, the representation of alienated perspectives and its impact on the reader, I now wish to turn to Blake's renegotiation of the configuration of power in the relationship between reader, author, and text, focusing in particular on the ways in which he combines the childbirth metaphor with a critique of the reduction of women to fecund beings that is indebted to another member of the Johnson circle, Wollstonecraft. Repeatedly transgressing the conventions of the childbirth metaphor, as well as related constructs that govern the introduction of the text into the public domain, Blake folds the metaphor back upon itself to challenge the assumptions about creativity and reading that inform it.

Voice against Body: Mapping Alienation through Differentiation

In the preludiums to *America* and *Europe,* Blake depicts females who are subjected to sexual violence. The female of *America* is raped by Orc and the female of *Europe* is forced to give birth repeatedly against her will. Blake studies has traditionally averted its critical gaze before the violence of Blake's texts, neutralizing gore by folding it into allegory.[8] It is thus a critical commonplace to identify these females with Nature, so that the sexual violence of *America*'s preludium is transformed into the farming of land, while the travail of *Europe*'s female is seen as her defining function.[9] Such readings emphasize the fecundity of the females' bodies and identify the figures according to that fecundity. This approach is consistent with the conventional gendering of creative labor, but it fails to account adequately for the females' resistance to being "farmed": these women are more than the sum of their reproductive parts. If the female of *Europe* is "a kind of personified womb" and that of *America* "personifies the physical earth," then the females must have nonuterine characteristics that are recognized as indicators of personhood.[10] To recognize these markers of personhood is to see that the females are enchained by their reduction to sexual utility, rather than necessarily equated with that utility. It is to these characteristics, alien to the definitions of femaleness that inform the preceding characterizations of the females, that I wish to draw attention in order to disentangle the females' involvement with different types of creativity and Blake's configuration of those creativities.

In *A Vindication of the Rights of Woman* (1792), Wollstonecraft maintains that women are naturally weaker than men physically, but that they are educated to be intellectually weaker by men who, "considering females rather as women than human creatures, have been anxious to make them alluring mistresses than affectionate wives and rational mothers."[11] In the *Vindication,* Wollstonecraft complicates female identity to include an asexual intellect: as physical beings females are women, inferior, and potential victims, while as thinking beings females are human, equal, and potentially unoppressed, or at least able to excel at prized social roles.[12] In *Europe* and *America,* the doubled status of females as both women and human beings is articulated through the distinction between the womb and the voice, where the latter is potentially a means of liberation from reduction to the former, because it operates outside of the assumptions under which such reductions are made. This distinction is implicated in the separation of the corporeal and the incorporeal, and the hierarchization of those terms that allows the privileging of noncorporeal creativity and the gendering of creative labor noted by Friedman. Blake, however, disrupts such Cartesian dualism. As in *The Marriage of Heaven and Hell,* in which Blake argues, "Man has no Body distinct from his Soul for that calld Body is a portion of Soul discernd by the five Senses" (4), the body/spirit opposition does not describe an antagonism between two wholes. Orc complains, "I fold, feeble my spirit folds. / For chaind beneath I rend these caverns" (*Am,* 1.17–18), indicating that the "I" can refer to the body as well as the spirit, and that the two terms operate synergically. The distinction between the corporeal and incorporeal is a discursive vehicle for articulating incommensurable aspects of the self rather than an ontologically valid stratification, much as the paradoxical definition of light as both a massless wave and a waveless mass provides a paradigm through which to divide incompatible evidence into two coherent sets of data.[13] The coercion of the body is not merely the manipulation of an object, like the womb, but an appropriation of a subject's body, "a portion of Soul," with implications for that subject.

Because of the situation of the figures' identity in their sexual features, it has generally been assumed that the female speakers in the preludiums to *America* and *Europe* are the same character. While the speakers are both "nameless" (*Eur,* 1.1; *Am,* 1.4), "shadowy" (*Eur,* 1.1; *Am,* 1.1), and "female" (*Eur,* 1.1; *Am,* 1.4), the male speaker of the preludium to *The [First] Book of Urizen* is also nameless and "shadowy" (*BU,* 2.4). Being nameless and "shadowy" is a feature of all three preludiums' protagonists, rather than of the females in particular, and it is an at best tenuous basis for equating the two figures, rather like assuming that "the dark-haired man" in two separate works is the same character.[14] The females are identical only in their sexual utility. To view them as the same figure is to fail to see beyond their reduction to their sex, to characterize them "rather as women than human creatures," in Wollstonecraft's words. While equating the two figures, James E. Swearingen argues, "The 'nameless female' represents nature not as it might be in itself, but nature as already interpreted and available to human agency. . . . Patriarchal intentions have already determined the female as nameless, a shadowy indeterminate something."[15] Both characters have been hermeneutically reduced to beings that are definite, from the narrator's perspective, only in their sex, but this interpretation of the characters as nameless and shadowy female bodies is challenged within the texts by the females' speeches.

In *Europe,* Blake apparently authorizes the reductive interpretation by providing only the noun "female" for the speaker's naming, but this reduction of her to "female" is presented as neither a politically neutral act nor an adequate representation of her identity. In arguing for her release from childbirth, the female describes childbirth as painful for her (*Eur,* 1.15) and a contravention of her will (*Eur,* 2.1), but she begins by associating labor with the effacement of her identity and of her name in particular. The closing lines of the preludium demonstrate the validity of her concerns:

> And thus her voice arose.
> O mother Enitharmon wilt thou bring forth other sons?
> *To cause my name to vanish,* that my place may not be found.
> For I am faint with travel [travail]! (*Eur,* 1.3–6; my emphasis)
> I see it smile & I roll inward & my voice is past.
> She ceast & rolld her shady clouds
> Into the secret place. (*Eur,* 2.16–18)

In "the secret place," her "place may not be found," and so the preludium's conclusion fulfills the female's prophecy regarding what will happen if she gives birth again—the "I" becomes "faint with travel" (*Eur,* 1.6). The female's plea, and the evidence of its failure, recalls *Visions of the Daughters of Albion,* in which Oothoon is "[a] solitary shadow wailing on the margin of non-entity" (*VDA,* 7.14–15). Ferber suggests that the female's fear of losing her name is "an odd fear in one who had no name to begin with,"[16] but this argument reverses the chronology of the passage: the narrative tense places the female's speech in the past ("And thus her voice arose" [*Eur,* 1.3]). In the narrative present, from the narrator's perspective, she is "nameless," but in the narrative past, from her perspective, she did have a name, and one that she valued. To revise Swearingen's comment, "The 'nameless female' represents [the female] not as [she] might be in [her]self, but [the female] as already interpreted" by a system that understands, and uses, her only as a uterus.

The female's disappearance, moreover, is simultaneous with the passing of her voice. The "I" that speaks actively seeks to overturn the effacement of her name and identity by articulating a cogent argument that maps the oppressive nature of the female's physical fecundity on a personal and a social level: "the overflowing stars rain down prolific pains. . . . I sieze their burning power / And bring forth howling terrors, all devouring fiery kings. / Devouring & devoured" (*Eur,* 1.15, 2.3–5). The speaker also issues an imperative to Enitharmon, declaring, "Ah mother Enitharmon! / Stamp not with solid form this vig'rous progeny of fires" (*Eur,* 2.7–8). Far from being "passive" or merely "lamenting . . . mortality,"[17] the speaking "I" seeks to gain control over the female's identity, particularly in the form of the body's release from maternity, and it attempts to do so through the power of language. In the conventional alignment of the mind/body duality with word/womb, speech becomes a means for contesting the character's confinement on one side of the binary oppositions; by producing words, she puts her foot in the door of masculine power, as well as outside of the confines of feminine disempowerment. She even appropriates the childbirth metaphor's displacement of fecundity from the (feminine) uterus to the (masculine) mind by referring to her "lab'ring head" (*Eur,* 1.12). Ultimately, however, the opposition between womb and voice is not a vehicle for transcending the division of labor implicit in the childbirth trope, but an articulation of the dependence of each term on its antithetical stance toward the other term: labor erases the female's name, her speech seeks to end her labor, and, at the end of the preludium, her labor ends her speech (recalling the movement of *Europe* between myth and history). Her predicament exposes the gendering of creative labor by representing a fecund womb and an articulate voice as mutually exclusive terms; yet, at the point at which the preludium is set, the female is capable of both types of activity. This ambivalence is reflected in contradictions within the speech itself, as the female's complaint is punctuated by suggestions of complicity and compensation: "Unwilling I look up to heaven! unwilling count the stars . . . I sieze their burning power" (*Eur*, 2.1, 2.3); "I am drown'd in shady woe, and visionary joy" (*Eur*, 2.12). The female is still in possession of her name, and her synergetic heterogeneity has not yet been reduced to a passive, unipartite anonym.

The fragmentation of a woman into voice and womb is more explicitly marked in the preludium to *America*, in which Orc "siez[es] the panting struggling womb" (*Am*, 2.3), not even the female body in its entirety. Allegorical readings of the preludium have elided the female's subjectivity, particularly by inscribing her rape into a ritual with a wider compensatory significance, and by maintaining the heroic status of Orc through the naturalization of Orc's seizure of her as "the expression of desire fulfilling itself."[18] The distinction between whole and part is, however, emphasized by Blake's use of pronouns. It is neither "he," nor "she," nor "they" enjoying the sexual seizure, but only the objectified womb—"It joy'd" (*Am*, 2.4). The female's voice is explicitly differentiated from the seized womb in the introductory phrase, "then burst the virgin cry" (*Am*, 2.6), which depends on the same distinction that Orc employs in the prophecy—"find . . . in coarse-clad honesty / The undefil'd tho' ravish'd in her cradle night and morn . . . Because the soul of sweet delight can never be defil'd" (*Am*, 8.11–14)—but transforms that principle by applying the "undefil'd" to voice rather than soul, to "the virgin cry." In both the preludium and the prophecy, the seized body is distinguished from an unwilling incorporeal aspect of the self, the "cry" and the "soul," that can transcend the treatment of the body with which it is connected while retaining an investment in how that body is treated. This division is not absolute: like the Orc of the preludium, whose spirit is "feeble" (*Am*, 1.17) because of his physical chaining, and the female of *Europe*, whose identity is erased by her own physical subjugation, the female of *America*'s preludium is also spiritually disempowered by her physical seizure, as one of Orc's avatars, she complains, "drink[s] [her] soul away" (*Am*, 2.14). The "soul" may not be stained, according to Orc, but it is still being weakened. As in *Europe*'s preludium, the emphasis is on a process of disenfranchisement rather than a cataclysmic loss of identity or a state prior to subjectivity—the females are never entirely soulless or purely corporeal.

This weakening is reflected in the trajectory of the female's speech in *America*. She begins by verbally seizing Orc and defining him in terms of her own desires: "I know thee, I have found thee, & I will not let thee go . . . And thou art fall'n to give me life in regions of dark death" (*Am,* 2.7, 2.9). She inverts Orc's Petrarchan assertions of desire (*Am,* 1.19–20), in which he is the desiring subject and she is the desired object, by expressing her own wants.[19] While Minna Doskow complains of the "perversity of the female's images" and suggests that they indicate "sexual possessiveness,"[20] the female is only turning the tables, so to speak, on Orc, but with a difference: he seizes "It" (*Am,* 2.4), and she seizes "thee" or "thou" (*Am,* 2.7–9). Failing to objectify Orc fully, the female slides back into Orc's system, in which she is object and he is subject—just as Oothoon is drawn back into Theotormon's system in *Visions.* Although the female revises Orc's spiritual transformations into figures of power by confining those figures' sovereignty to specific regions (*Am,* 2.12–14), she readmits Orc's Petrarchan justification for his seizure of her by changing their activities from "screaming" and "Stalking" to "court[ing] [her] to his love" (*Am,* 1.13, 1.14, 2.12). While the role of suitor is conventionally servile, the concern of the courtship is "his love" and overturning her resistance to it. By reconstructing Orc as the desiring subject and herself as the desired object, she falls back into his discursive model and discards her characterization of him as her self-sacrificing captive (*Am,* 2.7–9). It is after this abandonment of her first exclamations, foreshadowed by her continued recognition of his status as a person ("thee"), that she asserts that one of her suitor's avatars is "drinking [her] soul away" (*Am,* 2.14).

By tracing her use of pronouns, the disappearance of her "soul" can be mapped:

> I know thee, I have found thee, & I will not let thee go;
> Thou art the image of God who dwells in darkness of Africa;
> And thou art fall'n to give me life in regions of dark death.
> On my American plains I feel the struggling afflictions
> Endur'd by roots that writhe their arms into the nether deep:
> I see a serpent in Canada, who courts me to his love;
> In Mexico an Eagle, and a Lion in Peru;
> I see a Whale in the South-sea, drinking my soul away.
> O what limb rending pains I feel. thy fire & my frost
> Mingle in howling pains, in furrows by thy lightnings rent;
> This is eternal death; and this the torment long foretold.
> (*Am,* 2.7–17)

Her last use of "I" appears in the line after she laments the draining of her soul, as she exclaims, "O what limb rending pains I feel" (*Am,* 2.15), but the only pronoun in the next line is "thy" (*Am,* 2.16), indicating Orc's possession, and in the last line the suffering of which she complains is divorced from her "I" entirely: "This is eternal death; and this the torment" (*Am,* 2.17). As when the narrator writes, "It joy'd" (*Am,* 2.4), her physical condition is pointed to as an object rather than as a set of feelings that belong to a subject. From saying "I" three times in one line, as well as expressing knowledge and agency (*Am,* 2.7), to referring to her pain as an object (*Am,* 2.17), from verbally seizing Orc "to give [her] life" (*Am,* 2.9) to submitting fatalistically to death and suffering (*Am,* 2.17), from constructing Orc as desired object (*Am,* 2.7–9) to readmitting his construction of himself as desiring subject (*Am,* 2.12), the female's speech simultaneously plots the failure of her effort to control the situation through language and the effacement of the subjectivity that she expresses at the beginning of her attempt. While Bloom suggests that Orc's seizure is sanctioned by the fact that it makes her speak, since she was "dumb till that dread day" (*Am,* 1.10),[21] her voice erupts in an endeavor to reassert verbally the control that she once had physically. As long as Orc was chained she was "Invulnerable tho' naked" (*Am,* 1.7), but her voice proves unable to reclaim that degree of protection, and the final lines of her speech describe her exceptional vulnerability and loss of identity. Again, the "I" has become "faint" and "ceast" (*Eur,* 1.6, 2.17), after "wailing on the margin of non-entity" (*VDA,* 7.15).

In the preludiums, each female is discursively divided into a womb and a voice, into two parts with agendas—biological reproduction and verbal production—that are mutually exclusive within the terms of the gendering of creative labor, yet that coexist in a single individual. This discontinuity between sex and speaker is affiliated with other oppositions that are similarly fundamental to patriarchy, such as passive/active, desired/desiring, reproducing/producing, body/spirit, object/subject, and disempowered/empowering.[22] The females, having both a womb and a voice, as well as other features, do not exist at one extreme or another but move along the spectrums whose endpoints these oppositions define. Speaking from positions of bodily, specifically uterine, devaluation, the females express resistance to that reductive coding through speech, and employ the synergy between body and subjectivity to counter a reduction of their selves to their sex.[23] But since neither female succeeds in overturning her victimization or escaping the structure of discursive control, it is not clear if the voice can rescue the subject from a system of victimization that depends on the vulnerability and desirability of the female body (or if it is possible to render the females purely uterine or purely vocal). Moreover, as Blake and Gruner note, "Oothoon's stasis points to the dangers of treating the voice as a consequence of the body's confinement," and, further, "In the process of remaking the world, of re-investing the self with a radicalized voice, the heroine's body becomes the site of an almost forgotten captivity."[24] To read the subjugation of the females as generative—in the sense of Victor Brombert's "happy prison," in which the incarcerated male subject transcends confinement through the imagination[25]—is to deny the significance of their bodily pain.

It is not clear, however, whether such a denial is quite Blake's object. By opposing uterine and verbal creativity, Blake sustains their conventional separation and supports the traditional hierarchization of those creativities. But by aligning that opposition with sexual violence and rebellion against it, Blake deflects part of the devaluation of women's reproduction onto the devaluers and supports the females' resistance through the valorization of verbal creativity. The voice, by expressing dissent and articulating suffering, even during the brief moments represented in the preludiums, denies oppression the concealing cloak of homogeneous acquiescence and demonstrates the illegitimacy of the reduction of women to essentially identical female bodies. By speaking, the females create themselves as heterogeneous entities over which physical force cannot exert complete control, discursively naming and constructing alienated aspects of their selves from which they can criticize their confinement to their sexual category.

The Childbirth Metaphor in the Industrial Age: The Mass Reproduction of Books

The females, however, are not just entangled in discursive constructions of verbal production and biological reproduction. They are also implicated in an intersection of those two types of creativity: textual reproduction. In the preludiums to *Europe* and *America,* the discourse in which biological and nonbiological creativity are rendered homologous is applied to a critique of publishing rather than writing: biological reproduction is aligned with the copying, the re-production, of a prior text, and, as the vehicle of prescriptive hegemony, it is opposed to free expression. As Mitchell argues, an "iconographic code" operates in Blake's texts, a code that is articulated by a series of aligned binary oppositions, which include "mechanical" and "hand-crafted," "Book" and "Scroll," "law" and "prophecy," as well as "writing" and "speech/song."[26] The discussion of the Europeans' textual imprisonment begins with a reference to Urizen's "brazen Book, / That Kings & Priests had copied" (*Eur,* 11.3–4), while Orc describes his destruction of the "stony law" as the tearing of a book (*Am,* 8.5–6). The copied book homogenizes the social discursive field through material and intellectual mechanisms of replication—the mass reproduction of texts and the promotion of learning by rote—that are fundamentally silent and silencing.[27] Speech, however, diversifies that field merely by allowing discourse to operate outside of the aphasic book. Blake submerges this position in the preludiums: the violence that the females condemn in their speeches is described in terms that suggest the printing process, the mechanical copying of texts. The narrator's description of the female's seizure in the preludium to *America* as well as her spoken response to it suggest the engraving of a plate, while the description of childbirth in *Europe* suggests printing, so that each female resists a stage of textual reproduction as well as the corresponding stage of biological reproduction. The Latin term for womb, *matrix,* denotes, in English, the mold for casting printer's type, providing a technical term through which Blake can displace the childbirth metaphor from private inspiration to public indoctrination. The females' vocal resistance to their reduction to their reproductive capacity operates simultaneously as a critique of the replication of the silent and silencing book.

In the preludium to *Europe,* the female's description of her children recalls Blake's association of engraved books with fire, as in the Printing House of *The Marriage of Heaven and Hell.* Erdman suggests that Los's reference to his sons' "bright fiery wings" (*Eur,* 3.8) is such an association, noting, "Blake consistently calls his works children. Winged thoughts are thoughts put on paper. The pages (wings) are illuminated (bright) and etched with acid (fiery)."[28] The "shadowy female" uses similar language, as well as the jargon of printing, with reference to her children:

> I am faint with travel!
> Like the dark cloud disburdend in the day of dismal thunder.
> My roots are brandishd in the heavens. my fruits in earth beneath
> Surge, foam, and labour into life, first born & first consum'd!
> Consumed and consuming!
> Then why shouldst thou accursed mother bring me into life?
> I wrap my turban of thick clouds around my lab'ring head;
> And fold the sheety waters as a mantle round my limbs.

> Yet the red sun and moon,
> And all the overflowing stars rain down prolific pains.
> Unwilling I look up to heaven! unwilling count the stars!
> Sitting in fathomless abyss of my immortal shrine.
> I sieze their burning power
> And bring forth howling terrors, all devouring fiery kings. . . .
> Ah mother Enitharmon!
> Stamp not with solid form this vig'rous progeny of fires.
> I bring forth from my teeming bosom myriads of flames.
> And thou dost stamp them with a signet, then they roam abroad
> And leave me void as death:
> Ah! I am drown'd in shady woe, and visionary joy. (*Eur,* 1.6–2.12)

The female recalls Erdman's recognition of fire's association with etching in her references to the "burning power" from which she "bring[s] forth . . . fiery kings" (*Eur,* 2.3–4), the "progeny of fires" and "myriads of flames" (*Eur,* 2.8, 2.9), as well as the "red sun" (*Eur,* 1.14). She also invokes the image of paper when she mentions "fold[ing] the sheety waters" (*Eur,* 1.13) and she specifically associates her children with impressed paper: "Stamp not with solid form this vig'rous progeny of fires. . . . [T]hou dost stamp them with a signet, then they roam abroad" (*Eur,* 2.8, 2.10). "Stamp[ing] with solid form" suggests the printing process, particularly since "forme" is a typesetter's term for type locked in a chase for printing. Further, "stamp[ing] . . . with a signet," in order that the text can "roam abroad," recalls the licensing of texts for publication in the latter part of the eighteenth century: the Stamp Act of 1765 required texts to be stamped to indicate that taxes had been paid before they could be circulated to the public.[29] Thus, stamping with a solid form and stamping with a signet, printing and then paying the tax that permits regulated circulation, are paralleled, connecting the printer's stamping of the plates with the state's certification of the book. By associating the female's children with books, and with state-sanctioned books in particular, the preludium anticipates the prescriptive and authoritarian writings of the prophecy: Urizen's "brazen Book," the Guardian's "secret codes," and the commandments (*Eur,* 11.3, 12.15, 12.28). Imaged as mass-reproduced books, these children are "howling terrors, all devouring fiery kings" (*Eur,* 2.4). The female's forced reproductive activity propagates both tyrants and the tyrannical texts that empower them.

The seizure of *America*'s female also recalls the mechanical reproduction of texts. While the preludium to *Europe* describes printing, the preludium to *America* suggests a method of etching that involves coating the plate in acid-resistant wax, scoring the design into the plate through the wax, immersing it in acid to eat away the exposed metal, then removing the wax and covering the plate with ink, filling the grooves left by the acid:[30]

> free are the wrists of fire;
> Round the terrific loins he siez'd the panting struggling womb;
> It joy'd: she put aside her clouds & smiled her first-born smile;
> As when a black cloud shews its light'nings to the silent deep . . .
> On my American plains I feel the struggling afflictions
> Endur'd by roots that writhe their arms into the nether deep . . .
> O what limb rending pains I feel. thy fire & my frost
> Mingle in howling pains, in furrows by thy lightnings rent.
> (*Am,* 2.2–5, 2.10–11, 2.15–16)

The female recalls the corrosive scoring of cold metal by acid, and the language with which that process is described in the *Marriage of Heaven and Hell,* in her complaint, "thy fire & my frost / Mingle in howling pains, in furrows by thy lightnings rent" (*Am,* 2.15–16). The etching process is described allegorically in the rape itself, in which Orc's "wrists of fire" (*Am,* 2.2) penetrate a clouded figure; the Orc-resistant clouds are removed (*Am,* 1.20, 2.4); and then the "first-born smile" (*Am,* 2.4) is produced, "As when a black cloud shews its light'nings to the silent deep" (*Am,* 2.5). This description of the "first-born" suggests the practice of filling the plate's furrows with black ink for printing and also recalls one of the images of childbirth in the preludium to *Europe,* "the dark cloud disburdend in the day of dismal thunder" (*Eur,* 1.7). The female, moreover, refers to "roots that writhe their arms into the nether deep" (*Am,* 2.11), suggesting the scoring of the design onto the plate through the wax, and perhaps a pun on "writhe" and "write." The oppressiveness of her engraving is semantically reinforced by the prophecy: the female is "in furrows by [Orc's] lightnings rent" (*Am,* 2.16), and Washington, just a few lines later, complains about "the furrows of the whip" (*Am,* 3.11), "the opressors scourge" (*Am,* 6.11) to which Orc refers. The final line of the preludium, "This is eternal death; and this the torment long foretold" (*Am,* 2.17), can thus refer to the character's physical anguish and/or the text that follows, since "foretold" is the literal meaning of "prophecy," the title attached to the next section. The suffering of the shadowy female thus foreshadows the sufferings of the prophecy, and is connected to those sufferings through engraving: her engraving, as her ongoing "eternal death" (*Am,* 2.17), is the type of the suffering that appears on subsequent pages.

The females' reduction to silenced wombs that are allusively connected to printing plates enacts the oppression of the individual voice through the replication of the authoritarian text. The authoritarian text, like "curses of iron" (*Eur,* 12.27), confines and silences the reader, forcing compliance to its dictums. The male of *Urizen*'s preludium embodies the implications of such a text: receptive, passive, and an auditor, the shadowy male uses language only, for three lines, to identify himself as a submissive copyist and encourage the violence of authority rather than condemn it. While the male implores, "fear not / To unfold your dark visions of torment" (*BU,* 2.6–7), and then falls silent, the females defer their silencing and contextualize it. The association of stages in the printing process with the sexual utilization of the females over their vocal protests implies that, at its inception, the mass reproduction of texts is implicated in reductive and confining structures of power. These structures include not just those that limit women's role in creativity to that of identical vessels that receive another's "idea" passively, but also those that view the populace as a collection of identical vessels that are, like *Urizen*'s copyist, to receive the hegemony's Word passively.[31]

Tearing Up the Replicated Text: The Reader against the Book

By examining images of reproduction within the context of the childbirth metaphor, I do not wish to counter the equation of the females with Nature by equating them with Reproductive Mechanisms. At issue here is not an allegory, in which "the shadowy female" can simply substitute for different concepts, but a tension between competing discursive forces—including constructions of gender, maternity, writing, reading, individuality, and nationality—that struggle to control the definition of the females and the different forms of creativity with which they are connected. To stretch a metaphor, just as the printing press "stamp[s] . . . with solid form" to produce essentially identical texts, patriarchal discourse stamps women with uterine form to produce essentially identical beings. Similarly, if those identical texts are read passively rather than creatively, so that the reader, like the fecund female in contemporary medical discourse, merely receives the disseminated text rather than engages it, then the reader is also being "stamp[ed] . . . with solid form," parroting the text and subscribing to its dictates in the same way as every other compliant reader. Such duplication would be anathematic to Blake because of its repetition of dogma and silencing of difference on terms to which he objected, particularly through the figure of the Book of Urizen. The Book of Urizen represents that which initiates and sustains prescription by constraining readers to replicate certain dictums, overtly through legislation and covertly through indoctrinating reading, and thus generates the coherent and uniform discursive space that Blake resists. As Edward Larrissy notes, "Education" is, for Blake, "the subjection of youthful inspiration to dead, systematic book-learning"; moreover, in *There is No Natural Religion* [a], Blake's condemnation of education articulates a congruence between the senses and the book—"they are both obstructions to Imagination."[32] The body and the book are both vehicles of restraint, facilitating the binding of what Blake privileges as the legitimate core of human activity, the imagination. In the preludiums, Blake conjoins these two sets of constraints, rather than permitting one system to represent the other: the book is not an analogue for the body, or vice versa, but both are prescribed within a discourse that suppresses creativity in favor of the passive reception that was held to define the female role in reproduction.

In *Areopagitica,* Milton employs a homology between the body and the book to argue that there is no authoritative Truth, but only partial truths that cannot be authoritatively evaluated. In condemning censorship, Milton rejects the notion that authorities have special access to the Truth by maintaining that Truth was fragmented at the ascension of Christ and will not be pieced together until Christ's return:

> when He ascended . . . then straight arose a wicked race of deceivers, who, as that story goes of the Egyptian Typhoon with his conspirators, how they dealt with the good Osiris, took the virgin Truth, hewed her lovely form into a thousand pieces, and *scattered them to the four winds.* From that time ever since, the sad friends of Truth . . . imitating the careful search that Isis made for the mangled body of Osiris, went up and down *gathering* up limb by limb.[33]

In *America,* Orc repeats the imagery, and language, of *Areopagitica* in declaring that he will "scatter religion . . . To the four winds as a torn book,

& none shall gather the leaves" (*Am,* 8.5–6). But while Milton anticipates the eventual reconstitution of Truth as a positive event, Orc depicts its ultimate destruction as positive and denies anyone the opportunity of regathering its torn fragments—the leaves "shall rot on desart sands . . . To make the desarts blossom" (*Am,* 8.7–8). Bloom draws a parallel between Orc's speech and the distribution of the poet's words in P. B. Shelley's "Ode to the West Wind": "Scatter . . . my words among mankind! / Be through my lips to unawakened Earth / The trumpet of a prophecy."[34] The emphasis on "mak[ing] the desarts blossom" and overturning tyranny, however, more closely recalls an earlier text to which Blake would have had access at the time of engraving the prophecies, Wollstonecraft's *Vindication:* "Men of abilities scatter seeds that grow up and have a great influence on the forming opinion; and when once the public opinion preponderates, through the exertion of reason, the overthrow of arbitrary power is not very distant."[35] Orc, however, makes an important departure from models such as P. B. Shelley's and Wollstonecraft's. Shelley's poet employs the didactic mode, in which the writer persuades his readers to accede to his viewpoint by distributing copies of a text that retain his intended meaning. Wollstonecraft's version, while placing more emphasis on the role of the public, still retains the primacy of texts by "Men of abilities." But Orc repudiates the aims of that hermeneutic project by scattering the "torn book." For Orc, and arguably for Blake, the fecundity of the text lies not in its ability to replicate the progenitor's perspective but in the destruction of its power to limit others' perspectives.

While noting the same premise as Milton, the impossibility of special access to Truth, Blake valorizes the pluralism that freedom from a unified and fixed Truth offers rather than lamenting it as a condition of the fallen world. Orc's utopia does not depend on the reproductive fecundity of the womb or the printer's matrix, but on the innate productivity of a world that is not stultified by the book:

> The fiery joy, that Urizen perverted to ten commands,
> What night he led the starry hosts thro' the wide wilderness:
> That stony law I stamp to dust: and scatter religion abroad
> To the four winds as a torn book, & none shall gather the leaves;
> But they shall rot on desart sands, & consume in bottomless deeps;
> To make the desarts blossom, & the deeps shrink to their fountains,
> And to renew the fiery joy, and burst the stony roof. (*Am,* 8.3–9)

Orc's utopia is heterotextual, and it is the scattered body of Osiris that provides a figure for a radically different model of proliferation, a model that is based on the pluralism that is allowed by fragmentation rather than the dissemination of a single, uniform, "stony" textual Truth. Like Paine, he favors "the production of heterogeneities in a strategy to dissolve consolidated forms of power,"[36] fragmenting the text so that the legibility of the author's message is compromised and, with it, the requirement that the reader recover that message rather than generate a new one.

Blake, of course, presents this position in a book. This contradiction pervades Blake's work and is variously accommodated in Blake criticism: Mitchell, for example, argues that Blake "does not single out his own books for unique authority," while Gross suggests that Blake's "awareness of language's power can only aid his counter-hegemonic purpose."[37] But self-consciousness about employing an authoritarian medium, whether the book or language itself, does not exculpate the texts from the charge of authoritarianism. To accept a text's claim to be nonauthoritative is to accept the authority of that claim. In *Europe* and *America,* however, Blake goes beyond self-consciousness about his media by following Orc's commands and tearing up his own texts, thus subverting the authority of the medium that he cannot entirely escape. Orc insists that "none shall gather the leaves" (*Am,* 8.6), suggesting the technical term, "a gathering," for the collection of printed sheets into book form, and recalling the many references to binding in these two works. Rajan suggests that by not binding the leaves of his texts, Blake "makes his parts movable" and allows for a variety of arrangements rather than a single, authoritative sequence.[38] Moreover, addressing the division of Blake's texts into prefaces, preludiums, and mottoes, she argues that "Segmentation . . . creat[es] spaces between texts that act as frames," so that "the preludium is stopped from functioning as the major premise in the poem's argument because its voice is placed outside the text of the prophecy."[39]

In *Europe* and *America,* this textual compartmentalization and decentralization extends beyond generic classifications. Blake not only fails to gather the leaves of *Europe* and *America* and divides the texts into prefatory and core material: he divides the lines of those parts with spaces that are filled with designs, from trailing ivies to figures six or more lines deep; he divides speeches by printing them on separate pages; and he divides pages of texts by interposing full-plate designs. Blake's illuminated works in general subvert the conventions of the book by making them obviously visual artifacts as well as verbal ones, but these two prophecies are visibly different, more emphatically disrupting the characterization of the text as a unified verbal entity. The text of *America* is visually broken into at least thirty sections: more than half of those interruptions are within a plate, including four in which a major figure is drawn (3, 4, 11, 14), and five plates have twelve lines or fewer (4, 5, 7, 10, 12). Although the designs that divide it are typically less pronounced than those in *America, Europe* is even more fragmented, being visually broken into approximately forty-five sections. Visually, particularly when compared to that of the contemporaneous *Visions of the Daughters of Albion,* the texts of these poems appear to be torn apart, challenging their reduction to a verbal entity without a physical component, just as the females' speeches challenge their reduction to a corporeal entity without a verbal component.

This fragmentation of the book also marks the dissolution of the text. In these two prophecies, Blake often breaks apart passages that would be grouped together in a conventional, uninterrupted, narrative line. *The [First] Book of Urizen* is divided only when chapter and verse dictate, mirroring the submissiveness and unobtrusiveness of its shadowy male in its use of those typographical markers that are too conventional to be noticeable. But the divisions in *America* and *Europe* resist such a Urizenically controlled pattern, just as their shadowy speakers do. For instance, in *America,* a figure riding a swan flies between the assertion that "Bostons Angel cried aloud" (*Am,* 11.3) and the Angel's speech (*Am,* 11.4–15), while the description of what Boston's Angel does as he speaks appears on the next plate (*Am,* 12.1–12), separating the identity of the speaker, the speech, and the speaker's actions, with the latter two being "movable," as Rajan puts it, because Boston's Angel is not mentioned by name in either segment. Similarly, in *Europe,* while logic might group together the lines that describe the torment and howling in Europe (*Eur,* 12.1–21), those that describe the mythic figures' reactions (*Eur,* 12.22–25), and those that describe the textual imprisonment of the Europeans (*Eur,* 12.26–31), the breaks are staggered so that the last line of each logical grouping is attached to the next group (see fig. 2):

> Above the rest the howl was heard from Westminster louder &
> louder:
> The Guardian of the secret codes forsook his ancient mansion . . .
> he fled
> Groveling along Great George Street thro' the Park gate; all the
> soldiers

> Fled from his sight; he drag'd his torments to the wilderness.
> [a spider's web, three spiders, and various flies]
> Thus was the howl thro Europe!
> For Orc rejoic'd to hear the howling shadows
> But Palamabron shot his lightnings trenching down his wide back
> And Rintrah hung with all his legions in the nether deep
> [numerous flies and a trailing ivy-like line]
> Enitharmon laugh'd in her sleep to see (O womans triumph)
> Every house a den, every man bound. (*Eur*, 12.14–15, 12.18–26)

The line "Thus was the howl thro Europe" (*Eur*, 12.21) is divided from the rest of the description of Europe (*Eur*, 12.1–20) by a design about six lines deep, and grouped with the description of the spectatorship of Orc, Palamabron, and Rintrah (*Eur*, 12.22–24); the description of Enitharmon's viewing of the conflagration (*Eur*, 12.25) is divided by insects from the lines that describe the responses of her sons (*Eur*, 12.22–24), but connected with the description of the Europeans' imprisonment. This visual division of the lines has guided interpretation of the poem, as many have taken for granted that Enitharmon "laugh'd in her sleep to see" (*Eur*, 12.25) the suffering of the Europeans,[40] but Orc, the ostensible hero of the piece, "rejoic'd to hear the howling shadows" (*Eur*, 12.22). By grouping Enitharmon's response with the suffering of the Europeans, instead of the mythic figures' reactions to the expulsion of Albion's Angel and Guardian, the engraving invites a reading of Enitharmon's laughter that is different from that which would be offered by a continuous text, a text in which Enitharmon's reaction could be more readily grouped with the reactions of her sons:

> Above the rest the howl was heard from Westminster louder & louder:
> The Guardian of the secret codes forsook his ancient mansion . . . he fled
> Groveling along Great George Street thro' the Park gate; all the soldiers
> Fled from his sight; he drag'd his torments to the wilderness.
> Thus was the howl thro Europe!
>
> For Orc rejoic'd to hear the howling shadows
> But Palamabron shot his lightnings trenching down his wide back

> And Rintrah hung with all his legions in the nether deep
> Enitharmon laugh'd in her sleep to see (O womans triumph)
>
> Every house a den, every man bound; the shadows are filld
> With spectres, and the windows wove over with curses of iron:
> Over the doors Thou shalt not; & over the chimneys Fear is
> written. (*Eur*, 12.14–15, 12.18–28)

The visual organization of plate 12 deflects the division of the lines according to the status of its characters as mythic or historic but does not disallow it, offering instead contradictory readings, one guided by visual groupings and one guided by verbal content.

A similar contradiction is contained in the generic classifications of the texts: both *Europe* and *America* are subtitled, "a Prophecy," yet are divided into two parts titled "Preludium" and "A Prophecy," placing the preludiums inside as well as outside of a "prophecy" and calling into question the point at which prophecy begins. Such radical segmentation disrupts attempts to authorize one reading over another by breaking the text into various, overlapping collections of parts in which no one part dominates, collections that are governed by contradictory keys. The texts can be divided into mythic and historic action, passages spoken by the narrator and those spoken by actors, visually delineated sections, preludiums and prophecies, as well as visual and verbal components. Readers are denied authorial sanction not only for a specific reading, but for the very existence of a reading in which all of the pieces can be combined into a seamless whole that is not a collation of parts, in which each part has its own coherence. As Blake writes in "On Homers Poetry," "when a Work has Unity it is as much in a Part as in the Whole." To read *Europe* and *America* as whole poems is to elide the seams in the works, to skip over the swans, ivies, insects, and spiders' webs that fill, and draw attention to, the gulfs that separate parts of the texts. These gulfs tear the book up not only physically, but conceptually, distinguishing the mythic from the historic, and the womb from the voice. Blake, in effect, hews apart the corpus of his own text, so that, rather than "dead, systematic book-learning," in Larrissy's phrase, readers are offered opportunities "To make the desarts blossom" (*Am*, 8.8).

Blake thus employs the homology between biological and nonbiological creativity to address the politics of the copied text, offering, for both the self and the book, heterogeneity as a means by which hegemonic prescription can be undermined. Heterogeneity proliferates centers of identity—as the definition of the self or as the meaning of the text—so that no one part can dominate the whole and no part can be discarded as incompatible with, or irrelevant to, the governing meaning or the paradigm that determines priority within a communal culture. Through references such as "limb rending pains" (*Am,* 2.15), "my soul" (*Am,* 2.14), "my lab'ring head" (*Eur,* 1.12), "my limbs" (*Eur,* 1.13), and "my voice" (*Eur,* 2.16), each female discursively constructs a nonuterine body and a nonuterine subjectivity while articulating the investment of her nonsexual aspects in the treatment of her sexual features. When they speak of their nonuterine position(s), the females scatter their words as well as aspects of their identities and so evade the gathering, the interpretive binding, of those portions into a stifled self that is creative and significant only sexually. When Blake visually scatters his words within the space of his book, he produces a textual model that provides an alternative to that of the gathered and binding Urizenic book, a model that is decentralized rather than hegemonic, both in the fragmentation of its text and in its relinquishment of the author's hermeneutic control. There are complications, of course: Blake retains the construction of the female sex as passive and powerless even as he turns that construction against the enforcement of passivity and powerlessness, he retains bookish conventions even as he contests the power of the conventional book, and he uses his artistic control to subvert the power of authors and authorities. But the designs, the unorthodox textual divisions, the unbound leaves, and the contesting voices disrupt the univocality and the requirement of passive reception that characterize the authoritarian book, compromising the power of the dominant paradigms in which Blake's works remain implicated. While the aphasic book is countered by the unbound voice, the "Singing" (*Am,* 6.13) of freed captives, it is also undermined by the torn book. The scattered text is unbound, and unbinding, and it contributes to the generation of meaning through the dissolution and defamiliarization of univocality and unity rather than their dissemination.

"A STATE ABOUT TO BE CREATED"

Modeling the Nation in *Milton*

Self is the medium least refined of all
Through which opinion's searching beam can fall;
And, passing there, the clearest, steadiest ray
Will tinge its light and turn its line astray. . . .
But 'tis not only individual minds
That habit tinctures, or that interest blinds;
Whole nations, fooled by falsehood, fear, or pride,
Their ostrich-heads in self-illusion hide.

Thomas Moore, THE SCEPTIC (1809)

Blake's first published epic, *Milton,* is usually read as a formally interesting spiritual autobiography, representing Blake's relationship with his bardic and mystic precursor, Milton,[1] as well as his vision of spiritual, if not apocalyptic, renovation or apotheosis,[2] in a fragmented, multiperspectival text.[3] Blake's personal identification with the poem is such that it is common in Blake criticism to find one of the poem's narrators referred to as Blake himself.[4] Such readings provide valuable insights into the main plot—or, rather, the central incident—of the poem, but they necessarily marginalize the political context of Milton's quest for self-annihilation and reunion with his emanation, a context energized by Milton's recent recuperation as a national bard. In *Milton,* Blake not only subverts the prevailing national narrative formally, as discussed in chapters 1 and 2, but explicitly critiques the cultural roots that inform it. These cultural origins are, like the bookish tyrants of *Europe,* propagated textually through the printing press. But it is not books generally, or the Book of Urizen symbolically, that Blake condemns in *Milton.* Instead, Blake singles out, in the preface, "The Stolen and Perverted Writings of Homer & Ovid: of Plato & Cicero" (*M,* 1)—classical texts.[5] Blake contends that classical texts infect English culture with classical paradigms and values, particularly false gods, imperialist militarism, and sacrifice: "Shakspeare & Milton were both curbd by the general malady & infection from the silly Greek & Latin slaves of the Sword" (*M,* 1). By doing so, Blake shows a sensitivity to hegemony's dependence on classical models in the promotion of duty and self-sacrificing heroism during the domestic and military conflicts of the Romantic period. In *Milton,* the protagonist thus not only functions as a representation of a poet, but as a symbol for the neoclassical national culture to which Milton was iconically related. Milton's purification at the climax of the poem is thus the cultural purification of England anticipated by the preface:

> This is a false Body: an Incrustation over my Immortal
> Spirit; a Selfhood, which must be put off & annihilated alway
> To cleanse the Face of my Spirit by Self-examination.
> To bathe in the Waters of Life; to wash off the Not Human
> I come in Self-annihilation & the grandeur of Inspiration
> To cast off Rational Demonstration by Faith in the Saviour
> To cast off the rotten rags of Memory by Inspiration
> To cast off Bacon, Locke & Newton from Albions covering
> To take off his filthy garments, & clothe him with Imagination
> To cast aside from Poetry, all that is not Inspiration
> That it no longer shall dare to mock with the aspersion of
> Madness
> Cast on the Inspired. (*M,* 40.35–41.9)

> when the New Age is at leisure to Pronounce; all will be set right: & those Grand Works of the more ancient & consciously & professedly Inspired Men, will hold their proper rank, & the Daughters of Memory shall become the Daughters of Inspiration. Shakspeare & Milton were both curbd by the general malady & infection from the silly Greek & Latin slaves of the Sword. . . . We do not want either Greek or Roman Models if we are but just & true to our own Imaginations. (*M,* 1)

Milton, the new national martyr and the author of the quintessential national epic, is an ideal figure to enact Blake's own nationalist solution: to cast off that which is not, in Blake's view, English.

Milton and Nationalist Martyrdom

While there are many references to British geography, Albion, British historical figures, commerce, and political issues in the poem, they have often been marginalized or elided in Blake criticism as the scale of the poem is limited to the poet and extended to a mythological metareality. But, as Wittreich argues,

> Milton . . . provides Blake with a precedent for celebrating the English as the second chosen people and the poet as their deliverer. He began *Paradise Lost* by equating England with Israel and himself with Moses. Blake, therefore, introduces *Milton* with a lyric that makes similar claims. England, he promises, will be the great agent in the apocalypse and the poet—a new and more successful Moses—will be the nation's awakener and guide.[6]

While Bloom suggests that "[t]he poem *Milton* is not written to correct *Paradise Lost* so much as to invoke Milton as a savior for Blake and for England, and therefore for mankind,"[7] this final step—"therefore for mankind"—is not so clear and is very much at odds with contemporary representations of Milton.

Milton was often figured as a savior for England in the limited national sense. In Wordsworth's sonnet "London, 1802" Milton appears as a Christlike national savior who, like Arthur, Merlin, and other British heroes, should rise in the nation's hour of need:

> Milton! thou should'st be living at this hour:
> England hath need of thee: she is a fen
> Of stagnant waters: altar, sword, and pen,
> Fireside, the heroic wealth of hall and bower
> Have forfeited their ancient English dower
> Of inward happiness. We are selfish men;
> Oh! raise us up, return to us again;
> And give us manners, virtue, freedom, power.
> Thy soul was like a Star and dwelt apart:
> Thou hadst a voice whose sound was like the sea;
> Pure as the naked heavens, majestic, free,
> So didst thou travel on life's common way,
> In cheerful godliness; and yet thy heart
> The lowliest duties on itself did lay.[8]

This view of Milton as an important player in a specifically national epic was developed in the latter years of the eighteenth century. Milton was "more or less anathematised" in Johnson's *Lives of the Poets*,[9] as well as characterized as a regicide apologist; his authorship of *Paradise Lost* was omitted in Bayle's *A General Dictionary* (1697)[10]; and he makes no appearance in Warton's copious *History of English Poetry* (1774). Milton's work remained in print and retained an audience throughout the century, of course, but Milton's literary star rose primarily with his representation as the hero of Protestantism and English liberty in the wake of the conflict that damaged England's sense of itself as the Protestant center of liberty—the American Revolution.

It is the additional cultural resonance offered by the American Revolution that arguably helps to explain not only Milton's rapid recuperation, but also the pervasiveness of references to the poet in political contexts, as various writers sought to contest or use Milton's cultural weight in support of their own arguments. The extent of such appropriations was pronounced enough to warrant comment in Hazlitt's essay on Shakespeare and Milton. Referring to a passage in *Paradise Lost,* Hazlitt claims that

> when any interest of a practical kind takes a shape that can be at all turned into this, (and there is little doubt that Milton had some such in his eye in writing it), each party converts it to its own purposes, feels the absolute identity of these abstracted and high speculations; and that, in fact, a noted political writer of the present day has exhausted nearly the whole account of Satan in the *Paradise Lost,* by applying it to a character whom he considered as after the devil (though I do not know whether he would make even that exception) the greatest enemy of the human race.[11]

This engagement with Milton's texts led to the poet's canonization, completely in the literary sense and very nearly in the sacred sense. Thus, Francis Jeffrey refers to passages on Milton in a critical essay by Thomas Campbell as "offerings not unworthy of the shrine."[12]

Milton, however, is not a generic national savior. A figure of rebellion for some and the hero of a more imperial nationalism for others, Milton was exploited by various competing definitions of nationalism. Milton's function as Blake's savior is particularly entangled with the nationalism that perhaps did the most to lift Milton from the literary and ideological margins that he inhabited in the decades that followed his death, the nationalism that restores England's status as the seat of Protestant liberty and values sacrifice for the national good. At the end of the eighteenth century, Milton was appropriated to serve an English, Protestant iconography that was disseminated and promoted to support a nationalist agenda that included militarist expansion and commercial exploitation. This agenda was validated by the belief, supported through reference to Milton's writings, that England had a divinely sanctioned mission. In *Milton,* however, Blake separates the prophetic Milton from the Milton amenable to such a political agenda without denying that those elements are present. While Frye argues that "though [Blake] symbolizes humanity by the name of his own nation, his 'Albion' has nothing to do with the frantic jingoism which a confused idea of the same symbolism might easily develop, and has developed in our day,"[13] the poem, I would argue, has everything to do with "frantic jingoism"—or rather, in more moderate language, everything to do with discarding one brand of patriotism in favor of another.

In the eighteenth century, Milton, as a figure for English national identity, was caught between two irreconcilable views of the nation. First, there was "royal national government" that "taught English people to look to the central government rather than to lord and priest."[14] In this system, most prominent during the Renaissance, the monarch was the focus of nationalist sentiment and political power. The royal system was later subverted, however, most dramatically in the execution of Charles I, by a view that defined the nation as a relationship between its populace and its institutions, arguably in recognition of the shift of power (both economic and intellectual) toward a broader demographic base. This revised view of the subject's fealty facilitated the generation of a nationalism that transcends class differences—or at least appears to do so—through the unifying ideologies of Protestantism, cultural supremacy, and commercialism. In a sense, the Protestant dimension of English national identity was extended to the secular: rather than defining the monarch as the bodily representative of the nation and the mediator through whom each subject expresses nationalism, each subject of the state could have a personal, unmediated relationship to the nation by embodying on a personal level a commitment to nationalist ideologies and a national identity that were ostensibly equally available to all. As Colley argues convincingly in *Britons,* the promotion of a Protestant national identity facilitated a kind of "mass patriotism" and a renovation of the monarchy's position as ideological rather than divinely granted to the person of the king.[15] The elite still set the agenda, but they did so under the guise of an allegiance to institutions—the Anglican church, Parliament, and the commercial infrastructure—that they revered as much as those outside of the aristocratic oligarchy. It is this brand of nationalism that became more powerful during Blake's lifetime, particularly after the French Revolution and during the wars that ensued.[16] And it is a brand of nationalism that was particularly amenable to nonaristocratic heroes who displayed great devotion to fundamental institutions. Thus, instead of being rejected as a regicide apologist, Milton could be rehabilitated as a national martyr, described by Behrendt as "the preeminent exemplar of the visionary bard who sacrificed comfort, health (and eyesight), and contemporary fame in service to his country."[17] A self-sacrificing, decidedly Protestant parliamentarian such as Milton could be a powerful figure in popular nationalist discourse—just as a sacrificed, decidedly aristocratic, Protestant king had been a powerful figure in the elitist nationalist discourse in which Milton had been represented very differently.

This view of Milton as a self-sacrificing patriot is particularly important to emergent nationalism because of the emphasis on national martyrs in its iconography, an iconography that was communicated through a medium important to both Blake and *Milton*—painting. Behrendt identifies Blake's *Milton* not as a spiritual (auto)biography, but as a form of history painting within the "apotheosis tradition" "that fuses topical and biblical allusion [in] an apocalyptic view of war."[18] Such paintings were not, however, just produced to generate transcendence, but were used to generate political consensus through visual propaganda.[19] This propaganda was effective because it employed compelling iconography and could be reproduced for the masses in cheap engravings. It promoted duty, sacrifice for the national good, and other qualities that served particular political aims, such as facilitating the elite's self-representation as dutifully laboring to support key national institutions. Colley argues that Benjamin West's *Death of Wolfe* "caused a sensation" because it "took classical and Biblical poses of sacrifice and brought them into the British here and now," "start[ing] a vogue for paintings of members of the British officer class defying the world, or directing it, or dying in battle at the moment of victory."[20] Blake resists the assimilation of the individual into the self-sacrificing posture of the national subject, complaining in his Annotations to Reynolds's *Discourses,* "A History Painter Paints The Hero, & not Man in General" (Anno. Reynolds, 652).[21] Colley, moreover, demonstrates that the notion of the dutiful British subject who sacrifices all for the good of the nation was developed at the same time that Protestantism became a crucial divine validation for Britain's commercial and military power. Classicism became the conduit for such lessons: "patriotism of a kind was embedded in the classical curriculum. The emphasis on Greek and Roman authors and ancient history meant a constant diet of stories of war, empire, bravery and sacrifice for the state."[22] It was the classical model of self-sacrificing aristocrats that informed the "paintings of members of the British officer class . . . dying at the moment of victory."[23]

The elite in Britain thus, at least in part, justified its existence in an age of radicalism and revolution through this nation-producing cult of self-sacrifice.[24] The view of the ruling classes as dutiful servants of the nation was so well-established in this period that it became a powerful rubric in the Victorian era, giving rise to Rudyard Kipling's notorious phrase "the White Man's burden" in the poem of that name. In *Tom Brown's Schooldays,* Thomas Hughes articulates it concisely in Arthur's description of his near-death epiphany: "I was beginning to see my way to many things, and to feel that I might be a man and do a man's work. To die without having fought, and worked, and given one's life away, was too hard to bear."[25] As early as 1784, however, the paradigm was being parodied. In John Boyne's *General Blackbeard Wounded at the Battle of Leadenhall* (3 January 1784), a clear parody of West's painting of Wolfe, the artist "lampoon[s] the very concept of a heroic death scene" and the model of duty which it underwrites.[26] Even Keats's "Ode on a Grecian Urn" echoes this reaction against classically inspired representations of sacrifice: the figures are "coming to the sacrifice" in a "Cold Pastoral" of unfulfilled desire ("never canst thou kiss, / Though winning near the goal"), trapped in the "slow time" of the "Sylvan historian," suggesting the stultification of a society that cannot escape the models of the distant, classical past it too readily valorizes aesthetically.[27] Blake's *Milton* participates in this subversion of the contemporary mythologizing of the aristocracy and martial elite through the rhetoric of the classics.

But Blake goes further, interrogating the operation of sacrifice within that mythologizing dynamic.[28] Sacrifice, including self-sacrifice, is not an isolatable construct within the poem: it is intimately linked, through the neoclassical ideology in which it is an important mechanism, to a violent economy in which, in the most general terms, destruction empowers the destroyer's clique, not least by establishing a network of sacrificial debt that traps all of the nation's subjects. Self-sacrifice raises the stakes, uniting the population behind its martyrs and the ideology in whose service they are enlisted. A few decades after Blake composed *Milton,* Ernest Renan remarked on the importance of shared sacrifice in the production of nationalist conviction:

> More valuable by far than common customs posts and frontiers conforming to strategic ideas is the fact of sharing, in the past, a

> glorious heritage and regrets, and of having, in the future, [a shared] programme to put into effect, or the fact of having suffered, enjoyed, and hoped together. . . . [S]uffering in common unifies more than joy does. Where national memories are concerned, griefs are of more value than triumphs, for they impose duties, and require a common effort. A nation is therefore a large-scale solidarity, constituted by the feeling of the sacrifices that one has made in the past and of those that one is prepared to make in the future.[29]

But self-annihilation removes individual destruction from a public economy, and ends the communal suffering that validates that suffering in the name of the national agenda. Milton's own *Paradise Regain'd* can shed some light on this economy. In that poem, the Son delivers a condemnation of imperialism that is also a condemnation of earthly glory and the sacrifice it demands:

> They err who count it glorious to subdue
> By Conquest far and wide . . . what do these Worthies,
> But rob and spoil, burn, slaughter, and enslave
> Peaceable Nations, neighbouring, or remote,
> Made Captive, yet deserving freedom more
> Then those thir Conquerours, who leave behind
> Nothing but ruin wheresoe're they rove,
> And all the flourishing works of peace destroy,
> Then swell with pride, and must be titl'd Gods,
> Great Benefactors of mankind, Deliverers,
> Worship't with Temple, Priest and Sacrifice;
> One is the Son of *Jove,* of *Mars* the other.[30]

In his rejection of secular glory, Milton links imperial conquest with the pursuit of that glory, destruction, self-aggrandizement, sacrifice, and Roman gods. In other words, he maps the same economy in which destruction empowers the destroying social group under a classical rubric, and so links it intimately to nationalism and imperialism.[31] This is crucial to Blake's *Milton*—and Blake's Milton.

Self-Sacrifice and the Annihilation of Nationalist Selfhood

As Milton moves toward self-annihilation in *Milton,* Blake describes a nation—in geographic, economic, historical, mythological, and political detail—that is being undermined and oppressed by particular constructs, especially classical gods, "Moral Law," "Milton's Religion," commerce, Satanic tyranny, and the glorification of war. In *Milton,* all of these oppressive constructs are related to, but not contained by, the selfhood that Milton seeks to overcome. In this context, "Selfhood" functions as a sign for nationalism, as it does in Moore's poem *The Sceptic.*[32] It is the nexus of ideological constructs that inhabit and distort identity, generating a British landscape of "Satanic mills" and sacrifice rather than a pastoral Jerusalem. Milton's rejection of selfhood in Blake's poem is thus, on one level, the national bard's repudiation of the nationalist ideology in which he was implicated. By producing an alternative narrative of Milton that critiques this version of nationalism in favor of the precapitalist pastoral ideal, Blake defamiliarizes a central nationalist icon and renders the prevailing nationalist narrative alien and alienating in terms of content as well as form.

Shortly after the conclusion of the Bard's song, "Milton rose up from the heavens of Albion," "And Milton said, I go to Eternal Death! The Nations still / Follow after the detestable Gods of Priam; in pomp / Of warlike selfhood, contradicting and blaspheming" (*M,* 14.10, 14.14–16). Blake's Milton, however, is himself implicated in this "warlike selfhood":

> I will go down to self annihilation and eternal death,
> Lest the Last Judgment come & find me unannihilate
> And I be siez'd & giv'n into the hands of my own Selfhood. . . .
> I in my Selfhood am that Satan. (*M,* 14.22–24, 14.30)

Satan, earlier, is linked to the cult of sacrifice and self-sacrifice:

> Satans Druid Sons
> Offer the Human Victims throughout all the Earth, and Albions
> Dread Tomb immortal on his Rock, overshadowd the whole
> Earth:
> Where Satan making to himself Laws from his own identity.

Compell'd others to serve him in moral gratitude & submission
Being call'd God. . . .
And it was enquir'd: Why in a Great Solemn Assembly
The Innocent should be condemn'd for the Guilty? Then an
 Eternal rose
Saying. If the Guilty should be condemn'd, he must be an
 Eternal Death
And *one must die for another* throughout all Eternity.
Satan is fall'n from his station & never can be redeem'd
But must be new Created continually moment by moment
And therefore the Class of Satan shall be calld the Elect.
 (*M*, 11.7–12, 11.15–21; my emphasis)

With Druidic and Nordic associations,[33] as well as classical ones, Satan is aligned with various repressive and imperialist regimes as well as the "pomp / Of warlike selfhood" (*M*, 14.15–16), the Elect, the repressive portion of Milton, and the charge of "making to himself Laws from his own identity / Compell[ing] others to serve him in moral gratitude & submission" (*M*, 11.10–11). The Satanic position that Christ articulates in *Paradise Regain'd* is thus extended and ascribed to Milton's "Selfhood," a selfhood that he must annihilate.

Blake draws a clear distinction between self-annihilation and self-sacrifice. Self-annihilation is entirely personal; it is the individual's destruction of selfhood for the good of that individual. Conversely, self-sacrifice posits a social system of exchange in which "one must die for another," demanding the destruction of the self for a good that the sacrificed individual cannot realize but someone who has not abnegated selfhood can realize through a national economy. Crucially, self-annihilation operates in a limited, closed system, while self-sacrifice functions in an open, social one—hence Blake's references to a never-ending chain of sacrifices, "throughout all Eternity," so that Satan can "be new Created continually" (*M*, 11.18, 11.20).[34] Self-sacrifice, in other words, binds individuals into an aggregate, linking them, as Renan's remarks suggest, through bonds of duty and obligation rather than affection. Self-sacrifice, moreover, posits a power structure in which self-abnegation draws benefits from a higher authority and, as crucially, operates in propagandist discourse as an example to be followed by others for the greater good, implicating the members of the group in a rigid hierarchy as well as a duty-bound unit. It is the classical "cult of heroism" of the period, populated by men of rank "who had been indoctrinated . . . with Greek and Roman classics in which heroes sternly sacrificed their lives for the sake of honour and country,"[35] that Blake critiques at length in *Milton.* Daniel J. O'Neil also implicates such modes of self-sacrifice in Romantic organicism, arguing that it offers "a rejection of Lockean individualism. . . . They appealed back to an older Greco-Medieval tradition that perceived man as a link in a chain or a cell in a body. Accordingly, such thinking emphasized the common good and man's duties in contrast to natural and individual rights."[36] As O'Neil notes, "The implication of organismic thinking is that the sacrifice of an individual or one generation for the collective well-being is not an unreasonable request; the organism survives"[37]—a model with clear investments in the kinds of national narratives discussed in chapters 1 and 2. In *Milton,* however, the individual's well-being supersedes the collective, as Milton's self-annihilation corrects, at least for the poet, the self-sacrificing model in which "one must die for another throughout all Eternity" (*M,* 11.18), a "Human Harvest" (*M,* 42.33).

The broader social implications of everlasting Satanic sacrifice are elucidated further in related passages. The outline of the sacrificial system immediately precedes Leutha's self-sacrifice, and that offering is emphasized by the Bard's refrain:

> when Leutha . . . beheld Satans condemnation
> She down descended into the midst of the Great Solemn
> Assembly
> Offering herself a Ransom for Satan, taking on her, his Sin.
> Mark well my words. they are of your eternal salvation!
> (*M,* 11.28–31)

Repetitions of key phrases and images—"created continually," the Bard's refrain, and the three classes—link these passages, nonlinearly, to an earlier discussion of sacrifice:

> So Los spoke! Satan trembling obeyd weeping along the way.
> Mark well my words, they are of your eternal Salvation
> Between South Molton Street & Stratford Place: Calvarys foot
> Where the Victims were preparing for Sacrifice . . .
> Christ took on Sin in the Virgins Womb, & put it off on the Cross
> All pitied the piteous & was wrath with the wrathful & Los
> heard it. (*M,* 4.19–22, 5.3–4)

> For the Elect cannot be Redeemd, but Created continually
> By Offering & Atonement in the crue[l]ties of Moral Law
> Hence the three Classes of Men take their fix'd destinations
> They are the Two Contraries & the Reasoning Negative.
> While the Females prepare the Victims. the Males at Furnaces
> And Anvils dance the dance of tears & pain. (*M,* 5.11–16)

"Offering & Atonement in the crue[l]ties of Moral Law": in this chain of affiliated references to sacrifice, and particularly self-sacrifice, Satan is "Created continually" through the sacrifice of innocents and the circulation of sin—as if it were a transferable debt, like the obligation of Wordsworth's Michael, which forces the sacrifice of Luke—and that sacrifice of innocents is linked to British imperialism.

This interpenetration of capitalism, imperialism, and self-sacrifice in Blake's characterization of nationalism can be further comprehended through Colley's analysis of the constitution of British national identity via industrial and commercial power as well as military and imperial strength. Colley argues that commercial interests, and more generally individuals' concerns for their own prosperity, often determined political loyalties; "there was a real sense in which this commercial bonanza was dependent on government investment in naval power and imperialism. . . . [W]ar and empire indisputably played a vital part in breaking into and securing markets."[38] The arts were also encouraged through the market for engravings. Eaves notes the pattern in the promotion of engraving: "Since the commercial spirit . . . is also the national spirit, the English merchant helps English art clarify its own identity. In the new Rome the improved Maecenas is commercial. . . . Boydell realized that engraving was more than another department of the arts. It was the missing link with commerce: engraving, as it reproduces painting, makes painting commercial."[39] These three values—imperial success, military power, and a strong commercial sector, particularly in the international domain—are inseparably intertwined in the constitution of British identity at the turn of the century. The many references in *Milton* to the commercial sector, especially its industrial component, can usefully be viewed in this context.

Constituting the Neoclassical Nation

In *Milton,* moreover, Satan is identified as a state: "We are not Individuals but States: Combinations of Individuals. . . . Distinguish therefore States from Individuals in those States. . . . Satan & Adam are States Created" (*M*, 32.10, 32.22, 32.25). It is fairly common, in discussions of this passage and others on the same subject, to limit the significance of "state" to the nonpolitical. States are thus identified as "states of existence" or "states of mind," often in an evolutionary context, so that one passes from one state to the other as one moves toward Eden.[40] While Blake does associate states with embodiment (*M*, 32.10–29) and identifies four states—Beulah, Alla, Al-Ulro, and Or-Ulro—that are located in different regions of the body, the so-called doctrine of states is complicated by Blake's use of the term in political contexts. As Esterhammer notes, "Throughout Blake's work, the term 'state' seems more strongly influenced than has been realized by the notion of a state as a political entity and, secondly, the state(ment) as a linguistic entity. An expanded sociopolitical context can reveal profound connections among Blake's states, political states, and the speech acts on which both depend."[41] Blake is using clearly polysemic language here and generating a complex framework that is both ontologically and politically implicated. Damrosch writes of the doctrine, "[T]he invention of states represents a decisive change in Blake's myth, and I think an unfortunate one. Instead of showing that all parts of the self must be rehabilitated and harmonized, he now defines the qualities that he dislikes . . . as illusory and external to the self."[42] But this is precisely what interests me about it: Blake represents characters under the sway of external, cultural forces throughout his work, from the female characters in *Visions, America,* and *Europe* to the pestilential errors of *Jerusalem,* but the doctrine of the states attempts to define and organize those forces into an intracultural topography. They are not simply "external to the self," but map systems that the self inhabits, including political systems (sometimes embodied in the constitutions about which Esterhammer writes) or states. Thus the Seven Angels not only declare that they are "not Individuals but States: Combinations of Individuals" (*M*, 32.10), but also claim that they "were combind in Freedom & holy Brotherhood" (*M*, 32.15) while defining themselves against "those combind by Satans Tyranny" (*M*, 32.16), opposing the radicalism associated with the French and American revolutions, as well as the Irish uprising, to the British nationalism that was used against all three.

The conditions under which these "Individuals" were combined also determine the definition of their lineaments: the Seven Angels have "Human Form / Because [they] were combind in Freedom & holy Brotherhood / While those combind by Satans Tyranny . . . are Shapeless

Rocks" (*M,* 32.14–17). In his analysis of Blake's valorization of visual line, Eaves makes an observation that is particularly relevant to this passage in *Milton:* "The distinguishing mark of these mental copies is clear and determinate outline, which the whole force of training, experience, and imagination teaches artists to separate from the blurry cultural ghosts and demons that haunt their minds. Demons (in their New Testament form) are external forces that take up internal residence—a kind of mental parasite that causes the host to be unlike itself."[43] Not only does the latter remark strongly suggest the various mergings of *Milton*—such as "Los had enterd into my soul" (*M,* 22.13), "He hath enterd into the Covering Cherub" (*M,* 23.14), and the infamous "Milton entering my Foot" (*M,* 21.4)—but the former suggests the "Shapeless Rocks" of tyranny that must be superseded by Milton and his "State."[44] Plate 32 of *Milton* defines two States: one, the Angels', is constituted under the ideals of radical politics, has members who therefore have definite form, and gives Milton "vision & dream beatific" (*M,* 32.2); the other, Satan's, is constituted under the tyranny of one who "destroyed the Human Form Divine" (*M,* 32.13), has members who are "Shapeless," and causes both "Sacrifice" and "Chains of imprisonment" (*M,* 32.17). Satan, who is identified at length with the classical, restrictive model, creates a political state of self-sacrifice and bondage—similar to that which the elite promoted by valorizing classical heroism and restraint. This breaks down the human form, just like the diseases that infect Albion in *Jerusalem* and the alienated baggage that is "Cast off" at the end of *Milton* (see chapter 6).

In *A Vision of The Last Judgment,* roughly contemporary with *Milton,* Blake makes a related argument: "Nations Flourish under Wise Rulers & are depressd under foolish Rulers it is the same with Individuals as Nations works of Art can only be produced in Perfection where the Man is either in Affluence or is Above the Care of it. . . . this is A Last Judgment when Men of Real Art Govern & Pretenders Fall. . . . [R]eflect on the State of Nations under Poverty & their incapability of Art" (*VLJ,* 561). While P. B. Shelley argues that the architects of what is good in society are poets—not only artists of all kinds, but "the institutors of laws, and the founders of civil society and the inventors of the arts of life"—and that a decay in social life is coincident with a decay in drama,[45] Blake is more apocalyptic and binary: there is not an evolutionary cycle of rise and fall, but there are "Wise Rulers" creating vital societies and "Real Art," while "foolish Rulers" achieve the converse. Nevertheless, both poets claim that sociopolitical culture and artistic culture are mutually determining. Satan, in this context, is not just the rational selfhood that interferes with vision, as Blake describes it in *A Vision of The Last Judgment:* "I have . . . represented those who are in Eternity by some in a Cloud. . . . [T]hey merely appear as in a Cloud when any thing of Creation Redemption or Judgment are the Subjects of Contemplation, tho their Whole Contemplation is Concerning these things the Reason they so appear is The Humiliation of <the Reasoning & Doubting> Selfhood" (*VLJ*, 563). Satan is also the tyrannical and "foolish Ruler," and his rule has particular features and origins, embedded in culture and the origin of the state. As the "Selfhood" of the national bard, which must be annihilated, the Satanic tyrant is at once the model that infects Albion and the political state that results from that infection.

This perceived conflict between true artistic creation and destructive militarism resonates with contemporary nationalist discourse. In his essay "On the Edge of Europe: Ireland in Search of Oriental Roots, 1650–1850," Joseph Th. Leerssen outlines a pattern that is useful to the present discussion:

> The Canaanites driven from Israel; the Phoenicians, supplanted by the Greek expansion; the Carthaginians, dispossessed by the Romans; and the Gaels, subdued and belittled by the English; in each case, the Phoenicio-Gaelic tradition is "runner-up," unlike victors who have their day and then decline, they are perennial, and form a tradition which links all these phases of Western civilization . . . an orientalist tradition of civility, starting with Solomon's temple . . . a tradition which elevates their cultivation over the military efficiency of their oppressors. An anti-classicist attempt is thus made to impugn the Graeco-Roman tradition as an intolerant, imperialist one, and to link its victims, from Phoenecia to Ireland, into a great tradition in its own right.[46]

In *The Laocoön,* it should be recalled, Blake describes the classical statue as "יה & his two Sons Satan & Adam as they were copied from the Cherubim / of Solomons Temple by three Rhodians & applied to Natural Fact. or. History of Ilium" (*L,* C–D). Blake's anticlassical position is not, of course, fully coincident with the Phoenicianism described by Leerssen; Blake is concerned with the Gothic, not the Gaelic. But as a politicized construct in which the Greco-Roman tradition is aligned with British imperialism and militarism, while an orientalized tradition is aligned with culture and civility, it has useful parallels to the political vision of *Milton.* As discussed in chapter 2, this anticlassicism also had historical support in the rise of gothic nationalism. In his study *National Identity,* Smith notes that neoclassical movements "swept through Europe" in the late eighteenth century, characterizing "classical antiquity as a plateau of civilization that was being realized again in modern Europe but on an even higher plane"—and it is that neoclassical imperialism to which Blake objects so strenuously in *Milton.*[47]

Blake explicitly identifies militarism with imperial classical roots, particularly those of Rome, Greece, and Troy. The Trojans are not only identified with the founding of Rome and, through Virgil's *Aeneid,* aligned with Rome's conflict with Carthage in ways that resonate with Leerssen's observations. The Trojans also played an important role in the nationalist establishment of England's imperial genealogy through Geoffrey of Monmouth's claim that Brutus, the great grandson of Aeneas, was the first king of England.[48] After listing a series of powerful, imperial nations, beginning with "Italy Greece & Egypt" (*M,* 14.6), Blake's Milton complains, "The Nations still / Follow after the detestable Gods of Priam; in pomp / Of warlike selfhood" (*M,* 14.14–16). The Trojan deities are consistently aligned with egotism. Milton concludes his condemnation of the nations with the assertion "I in my Selfhood am that Satan" (*M,* 14.30), while the narrator sees within Milton's "Selfhood deadly" (*M,* 37.10) "the Gods of Ulro dark" (*M,* 37.16), who number twelve (*M,* 37.17, 37.34) and include "Saturn Jove & Rhea" (*M,* 37.33)—and "the Twelve Gods are Satan" (*M,* 37.60). In the poem, selfhood—specifically Milton's selfhood—Satan, and the Trojan gods are linked. Rintrah and Palamabron also condemn the Trojan deities by associating them with self-centeredness: "Asserting the Self-righteousness against the Universal Saviour, / Mocking the Confessors & Martyrs, claiming Self-righteousness . . . With Laws from Plato & his Greeks to renew the Trojan Gods, / In Albion" (*M,* 22.42–43, 22.53–54). Even Greek music is condemned: it is identified with Natural Religion in Rahab and Tirzah's temptation of Milton (*M,* 19.46–47). In Los's vision of oppression and apocalypse, the Trojan gods again appear. In this context, however, their historical alignment is clarified. Los laments,

> Lambeth ruin'd and given
> To the detestable gods of Priam, to Apollo: and at the Asylum
> Given to Hercules, who labour in Tirzahs Looms for bread
> Who set Pleasure against Duty: who Create Olympic crowns

> To make Learning a burden & the Work of the Holy Spirit: Strife.
> T[o] Thor & cruel Odin who first reard the Polar Caves
> Lambeth mourns calling Jerusalem. she weeps & looks abroad
> For the Lords coming, that Jerusalem may overspread all
> Nations. (*M,* 25.48–55)

The Lord is Albion, "our friend and ancient companion" (*M,* 25.62). In this context, the Trojan deities are not identified just with militarism and egotism, but also with cultural formations from capitalism to the valorization of restraint, classical education, and nationalism. The subsequent reference to Odin further ties the classical gods to imperialism. As I have noted elsewhere, contemporary scholarship on northern mythology and antiquities claimed that Odin was not a god but an exile from Asia who participated in a Scythian revolt against the Roman empire and escaped to northern Europe after it failed.[49] Moreover, Odin is vilified in Mallet's *Northern Antiquities* for being a conqueror of northern Europe despite his antiimperialist activities against Rome.[50]

In *Milton,* Blake narrates the self-annihilation of a sacrificial selfhood, ending the sacrificial chain of Protestant martyrdom that Milton began. ("They weave a new Religion from new Jealousy of Theotormon! / Miltons Religion is the cause: there is no end to destruction!" [*M,* 22.38–39].) He also narrates the annihilation of neoclassical, proimperialist, nationalism:

> making War upon the Lambs Redeemed
> To perpetuate War & Glory. to perpetuate the Laws of Sin . . .
> Shewing the Transgresors in Hell, the proud Warriors in Heaven:
> Heaven as a Punisher & Hell as One under Punishment:
> With Laws from Plato & his Greeks to renew the Trojan Gods,
> In Albion. (*M,* 22.44–45, 22.51–54)

This emphasis on the infection of "Albion" by classical thought is a recurring one and it is tied to Blake's critique of sacrifice. Blake is condemning not only classicism and militarism, but also the political iconography prevalent at the time and used to promote sacrifice to the state—particularly, as in West's painting, on the battlefield—propagating a view of the elite as nationalist martyrs, giving their lives to save their country. In *Milton,* Blake repeatedly attacks the influence of classical models on British nationalism and culture and offers in its place his own construction of proper national identity: "We do not want either Greek or Roman Models if we are but just & true to our own Imaginations," and so contest "the detestable Gods of Priam," including Apollo, "Who set Pleasure against Duty" (*M*, 1, 25.49, 25.51). In other words, Milton's self-sacrifice was a terribly classical thing to do—and thus not, for Blake, very English. Satan is constructed as the nexus of these negative features and is the embodiment of the propaganda being distributed during the Romantic period to promote duty among the populace. He is a tyrant who follows the classical gods and selfhood, the destroyer of definite form, an Urizenic dictator from the elite, and a promoter of self-sacrifice. Satan, in other words, figures classically inspired hegemony, marking the interpenetration of culture and politics in the pursuit of glorious empire. Satan is not simply Milton's "Selfhood," but national egotism, the cipher that contains the hegemonic ideologies that were dressed up, through neoclassical heroism, as popular nationalism. To rephrase Milton's declaration by way of illustration, and with apologies to Frye, "I in English nationalism am that frantic jingoism." I am suggesting not that easy equivalences should be drawn between selfhood and nationalism or Satan and jingoism, but that Milton, Satan, and the renovation envisioned in *Milton* are implicated in the national renovation represented in the preface's famous lyric in ways specific to a critique of the prevalent contemporary nationalist ideology and iconography.

"No Part of Me": Nationalist Art(ifice)

At issue here are the implications of the art chosen to represent and propagate national ideals in order to forge a shared nationalist sense of self. In *Milton,* Blake invalidates not only the classical origins of those models, but also the "English" productions on which they are based. In examining the British urge to compete with France on cultural terms, Colley refers to a number of contests held to encourage and uncover native artistic talent, which in turn created a vogue for nationalist collections. English art was placed on a line of genealogical descent from Roman art, just as the English nation was rendered a distant cousin of Rome through claims of a shared Trojan descent, and the classical style formed the basis of artistic education in the period; moreover, when collectors abandoned national works they turned to classical artifacts. It is in this context that Blake declares, in the preface to *Milton,* "Painters! on you I call! Sculptors! Architects! Suffer not the fash[i]onable Fools to depress your powers by the prices they pretend to give for contemptible works or the expensive advertizing boasts that they make of such works. . . . We do not want either Greek or Roman Models" (*M,* 1). Blake counters not just classicism, but also the promotion of classicism as a model for guiding nationalist aspirations. The "fashionable Fools" are "Hirelings in the Camp, the Court, & the University: who would if they could, for ever depress Mental & prolong Corporeal War" (*M,* 1). Such an assertion goes beyond a reference to the elite's support of the Napoleonic Wars, to the promotion of a national identity that was bound up in militarism, self-sacrifice, a sense of national mission, and a broad asceticism in which Milton was specifically implicated—an asceticism that served the interests of those seeking to maintain popular support for the financial and human costs of Britain's excessive military aspirations during the period.

Blake does not limit his critique to the content of the propaganda but also condemns its forms, particularly the epic. As Behrendt shows in "'The Consequence of High Powers': Blake, Shelley, and Prophecy's Public Dimension," biblical prophecy was written from the margins and classical epic from the center, the former seeking to transform society by returning it to lost values and the latter celebrating society's fulfillment of its values and auspicious origins. As discussed earlier, the relationship between the current society and its defining origin—or, rather, the perceived governing paradigm of the current society and the perceived governing paradigm of the origin—is fundamental to this opposition. The historical timeline is reduced to a comparison of the endpoints, and complicated by the different constructions of those endpoints that can be distilled from the "facts." Geoffrey Hill, for instance, suggests that the myth of the "Norman Yoke" places the Magna Carta in a list of concessions that the oppressed Saxons "extorted from their rulers,"[51] so that English history becomes defined by the struggle for liberty. Milton's epic vision was no different, functioning as a construction of national origin that some of Blake's contemporaries found unsettling. In *The Tremulous Private Body,* Francis Barker contends that Milton's essay *Areopagitica,* by arguing that texts should be evaluated and censored after they are published, inaugurates a new model of the relationship between state and subject: "in the Miltonic 'state'—that set of relations marked out in *Areopagitica*—it is already possible to detect the outline of that modern settlement which founds itself on a separation of realms between the public arena of the state apparatus and another domain of civil life. . . . The subject . . . may do as he pleases up to the point of transgression where its activity will be arrested by the agents of the apparatus who patrol the frontier between the two spaces."[52] These are the seeds of the surveillance that Foucault describes in *Discipline and Punish.* Barker argues that transferring the censorship of the text from before to after publication places on the publisher the onus of self-discipline—he should police himself or suffer the consequences, rather than be warned in advance that a work is unacceptable. Barker goes on to suggest that Milton identified self-discipline as an English characteristic, that "all of Milton's descriptions of social life emphasize the stability, maturity and sobriety of the English nation"; thus, by writing laws with certain expectations of the subject, "The state succeeds in . . . pre-constituting that subject as one which is already internally disciplined, censored, and thus an effective support of domination."[53] Blake anticipates this Foucauldian observation in his parenthetical remark, "Temperance, Prudence, Justice, Fortitude, the four pillars of tyranny" (*M,* 29.49). Milton, in other words, arguably helped to construct a national identity that was founded on a dutiful people following, almost inexorably, a religious epic narrative that he himself, with his self-sacrifice and "epic 'true virtue and valour,'" embodied.[54] But Blake associated duty and similar restraints with bondage and slavery. Just as Milton constitutes in his writings a national identity that is innately dutiful, Blake outlines a national identity that has been corrupted by fundamentally foreign writings that promote dutiful behavior—including Milton's.

But it is clear that Blake also posits a national identity that precedes this corruption. Classical "Models" have infected English literature, even the work of its most exemplary poets, and so deflected that tradition from individuals' imaginative visions; but that tradition can be purged: "Shakspeare & Milton were both *curbd* by the general malady & infection from the silly Greek & Latin slaves of the Sword. . . . We do not want either Greek or Roman Models if we are but *just and true to our own Imaginations,* those Worlds of Eternity in which we shall live for ever: in Jesus our Lord" (*M,* 1; my emphasis). This deflection, according to *Milton*'s preface, affects the governing classes of national society, including the military, the aristocracy, and the broader artistic community. Blake's preface argues for England's return to a pastoral ideal purged of classical corruption, specifically rejecting the militaristic and artistic paradigms, and institutions, that he identifies with that alien influence. Hence, in *Milton,* Blake's first published epic, the poet begins with a condemnation of the cultures that produced the models, both poetic and ideological, on which

English literature's notions of epic are founded. "The Stolen and Perverted Writings of Homer & Ovid: of Plato & Cicero. which all Men ought to contemn," declares Blake in the preface, "are set up by artifice against the Sublime of the Bible" (*M,* 1). Milton, along with Shakespeare, is accused of being infected by such artifice. In the opening address of *Jerusalem,* "To the Public," Blake returns to the same poets and again condemns a verse form, this time blank verse:

> When this Verse was first dictated to me I consider'd a Monotonous Cadence like that used by Milton & Shakspeare & all writers of English Blank Verse, derived from the modern bondage of Rhyming, to be a necessary and indispensible part of Verse. But I soon found that in the mouth of a true Orator such monotony was not only awkward, but as much a bondage as rhyme itself. . . . Poetry Fetter'd, Fetters the Human Race! Nations are Destroy'd, or Flourish, in proportion as Their Poetry Painting and Music, are Destroy'd or Flourish![55] (3)

In his address, Blake thus makes an equation between Milton and Shakespeare, a nationally specific form of verse, and bondage, linking free verse form to national vitality. As in *Milton,* artistic forms are linked to destructive and restricting national cultures: "For we have Hirelings in the Camp, the Court, & the University: who would if they could, for ever depress Mental & prolong Corporeal War. . . . [B]elieve Christ & his Apostles that there is a Class of Men whose whole delight is in Destroying" (*M,* 1). In one of the poem's final plates, Blake associates the impoverished versifier with destructive power on a national level:

> To cast aside from Poetry, all that is not Inspiration
> That it no longer shall dare to mock with the aspersion of
> Madness
> Cast on the Inspired, by the tame high finisher of paltry Blots,
> Indefinite, or paltry Rhymes; or paltry Harmonies.
> Who creeps into State Government like a catterpillar to destroy![56]
> (*M,* 41.7–11)

This oppression of the human imagination is tied not only to the promotion of war but also to the creation of neoclassical nationalism.

The poem is traversed by references to nations, especially references to the division of the population and the globe into such political organizations. In the same passage that describes the action of the press on human consciousness, that action is linked to both the existence and production of nations:

> The Wine-press on the Rhine groans loud, but all its central beams
> Act more terrific in the central Cities of the Nations
> Where Human Thought is crushed beneath the iron hand of Power.
> There Los puts all into the Press, the Opressor & the Opressed
> Together, ripe for the Harvest & Vintage & *ready for the Loom*.[57]
> (*M*, 25.3–7; my emphasis)
> you must bind the Sheaves not by Nations or Families
> You shall bind them in Three Classes; according to their Classes
> So shall you bind them. Separating What has been Mixed
> Since Men began to be *Wove into Nations* by Rahab & Tirzah . . .
> When under pretence to benevolence the Elect Subdud All. (*M*, 25.26–31; my emphasis)
> They became Nations in our sight [Los's] beneath the hands of Tirzah. (*M*, 24.16)

This use of weaving to figure the combination of individuals into families and nations is not simply another iteration of the connection between form and state. Inscribed weaving (*textere*) is also used to figure the social structure of the combined state:

> My Garments shall be woven of sighs & heart broken lamentations
> The misery of unhappy Families shall be drawn out into its border. . . .
> I will have Writings written all over it in Human Words
> That every Infant that is born upon the Earth shall read
> And get by rote as a hard task of a life of sixty years
> I will have Kings inwoven upon it, & Councellors & Mighty Men.
> (*M*, 18.6–7,12–15)

There is a complex of related figures here, making up an iconography in which a nation is produced when the populace is oppressed or "Subdud" and then woven into a hierarchical structure governed by kings and "Mighty Men." In broad terms, then, Blake's view of the nation is similar to Gellner's:

> The basic deception and self-deception practised by nationalism is this: nationalism is, essentially, the general imposition of a high culture on society, where previously low cultures had taken up the lives of the majority, and in some cases of the totality, of the population. It means that generalized diffusion of a school-mediated, academy-supervised idiom, codified for the requirements of reasonably precise bureaucratic and technological communication. It is the establishment of an anonymous, impersonal society, with mutually substitutable atomized individuals, held together above all by a shared culture of this kind, in place of a previous complex structure of local groups, sustained by folk cultures reproduced locally and idiosyncratically by the micro-groups themselves.[58]

The garment is a constitution, establishing the national order that contains and restrains the population, and it is such a garment that Milton, in Blake's rewriting of his life, must cast off.[59]

At issue here is not just the relation between form and content, or propaganda and political consensus, but the modeling of the perceptual domain through cultural artifacts. Recognizing the division of societies into technologically or artistically competent cultures only begins to allow us to grasp this. Blake's *Milton* not only condemns classical and commercial paradigms, but also offers new models that redefine the culture of the national state. In the context of a critique of the infection of the national body by Greek and Roman texts and models, Blake's re-visioning of space, time, mythology, the relationship between the individual and the state, and the formation of nations cannot be purely aesthetic in function. As an exercise in modeling, *Milton* ranges from physics to commerce, from geography to history, and from wine making to war. In Blake's later writings, the emphasis on national affiliations in *America* and *Europe* is extended and transformed. Rather than Americans and Daughters of Albion, the engravings *Laocoön* and "On Homers Poetry"/"On Virgil," as well as *Milton* and *Jerusalem,* posit national ideologies that are communicated through cultural artifacts that are historically specific. In *America* and *Europe,* Albion's Guardian oppresses the British and American peoples via the metanational Urizenic book, but in these later texts, "Greek or Roman Models" constrain "our own Imaginations" (*M,* 1) and "Desolate Europe with Wars" ("On Homers Poetry") through a variety of works that are named: in "On Virgil," the culprits are "Homer Virgil & Ovid"; in *Milton,* the list is extended to include "The Stolen and Perverted Writings of

Homer & Ovid: of Plato & Cicero," as well as the classically influenced "Shakspeare & Milton" (*M,* 1). Blake thus historicizes the development of paradigms to which he objects, returning to the model of infection that appears in "Gwin, King of Norway" and locating the responsibility for human actions in cultural forces rather than abstracted or supernatural ones. In *Milton,* Blake describes this process explicitly, or at least with relative explicitness, writing, "This . . . is the Printing-Press / Of Los; and here he lays his words in order above the mortal brain / As cogs are formd in a wheel to turn the cogs of the adverse wheel" (*M,* 27.8–10). In *Milton,* however, Blake does not simply engage the issue of cultural hybridity and the political force of culture. He is specifically concerned with the political iconography that supported a particular brand of British nationalism—militarist, dutiful, self-sacrificing, imperial, and hungry for glory. Through Albion, Blake separates national identity from that brand of nationalism: that nationalism, or "jingoism," does not serve Albion but Satan, and it is not derived from British traditions but from classical ones. The nationalism that government propaganda, and the rehabilitation of Milton, circulated to interpellate the population into a sense of community that valorized a willingness to sacrifice for that community's defining political agenda is thus defamiliarized in the sense of being framed as a nonfamilial strain infecting the proper national familiar and family. In *Milton,* Blake's resistance to interpellation into governing communal paradigms—the linearity of writing in the artistic community; national narratives, in the pseudoantiquarian texts; models of social relations, in *Europe, America,* and *Visions of the Daughters of Albion;* codes of gender and authority, in the preludiums; and prevailing models of political health—is reflected in the putative origin and exemplar of certain nationalist paradigms escaping his own error, and casting off that which is "Not Human."

"ARTFULLY PROPAGATED"

Hybridity, Disease, and the Transformation of the Body Politic

> It is curious to remark, that England, the most fanatical and bigotted country in Europe, has likewise opposed itself, with the greatest obstinacy, to the practice of vaccination.
>
> *Sydney Morgan,* THE O'BRIENS AND THE O'FLAHERTYS (1827)

In the preceding chapters, I have argued that Blake presents the unfamiliar in his texts, contradicting powerful cultural paradigms, from nationalism to bibliographical codes, by rendering the culturally constituted space as a hybrid one. Here, however, I wish to examine more closely the ways in which Blake represents the mechanism through which discursive products affect the cultural-political domain by investigating and characterizing not "how to do things with words," in J. L. Austin's phrase, but how words do things to us.[1] It is this mechanism, or rather the premise that it operates, that not only binds together Blake's radical politics, his innovative approach to genre and media, and the power he ascribes to the bardic voice and the Book of Urizen alike, but also binds Blake to his time. Models of the propagation of ideas in the public domain are legion, but I want to focus here on one figure that is used to great effect in Blake's verse, that of disease and, occasionally, its medical opposite, the restorative. Such "restoratives" are represented propagating virally through the body politic, whether their precise function is to cure a specific "disease" or to invigorate a public body that suffers from a more inchoate or broadly defined problem of sociopolitical health or vulnerability. Restoratives succeed on the basis of their analogous relationship to that which they fight; the distinction between a revitalizing text and a corrupting one is determined ideologically but enforced through the powerful medical connotations of disease, pestilence, cancer, and other unseen, and then largely unmanageable, threats.

What I shall term the "vital/viral" model of textual propagation divides discourse in terms that are at once unimpeachable and extremely vulnerable. Although they appeal viscerally to the will to survive, they are vulnerable to critique and reversal, because the boundary between viral and vital discourse is slippery in a way that its informing medical analogue is not. Words such as "plague" and "cancer" do not conjure up images of ambiguous evil in a medical context, but signal little more than opposition in a political one. Matters became more complicated with the rise of interest in the Eastern practice of vaccination early in the eighteenth century, and public avowals of its efficacy, most famously by Lady Mary Wortley Montagu.[2] With the start of Edward Jenner's experiments in 1796 and the satirical prints that followed, representations of vaccination appeared frequently in the British media during the Romantic period.[3] A folk practice in Britain as well, it was known in eighteenth-century Pembrokeshire as "buying the smallpox."[4] Vaccination involves using one disease to ward off a related one, and so provides a useful paradigm through which to figure the competition to control the sociopolitical domain through circulated discourses rather than legislative ones. "It is," as Tim Fulford and Debbie Lee so cogently put it, "an imaginative means of stemming political change"[5]—or, from the other side of the political fence, stemming the tide of established political might. While legislation offers external restraints through an institutionalized system of punishment and threat, circulated discourses, through the vital/viral model, offer a means by which ideological constructs, from values to laws, can be internalized by each member of the community. In "The Triumph of Life," P.B. Shelley mixes, somewhat uncomfortably, vaccination and the vital/viral paradigm:

"their living melody
Tempers its own contagion to the vein
"Of those who are infected with it—I
Have suffered what I wrote, or viler pain!—
"And so my words were seeds of misery—
Even as the deeds of others."[6]

In Blake's corpus, one can trace a general movement toward a vaccination model, from a sterilization one, within an ongoing concern about ideas that are "artfully propagated" (*PA,* 576). In his earlier texts, Blake emphasizes the eradication of textual disease, often related to external, legislative constraints, through sterilizing fire. But in his later works, *Jerusalem* in particular, Blake turns to a model in which vital and viral texts compete to control the political body. Instead of the "red flames of Orc" (*Am,* 14.11) destroying the "plagues" of the established order (*Am,* 14.20), Blake offers "print" (*J,* 3.9) that will erase the textual errors of various groups and establish his own notion of "harmony" (*J,* 3.10)—a vaccination.

But there is a danger in this. Because Blake frames his own political solution in terms that are similar to those of the systems that he is resisting, many of the gulfs between them are closed. While the renovated Albion that Blake imagines in *Jerusalem* is greatly different from contemporary Britain, there is little difference between the means by which each prevails. In *Jerusalem,* the only distinction between Blake's transformational and harmonizing publication and the Old Testament laws that he condemns in chapter 2, or between the poet's imagined colonization of the globe by Albion and his condemnation of the colonizing spread of rationalism and other systems incommensurable with his own, is the slippery one between viral and vital discourse. While *Jerusalem* has traditionally been read as utopian, and certainly seeks to present itself as such, I thus follow recent critics in tracing the ways in which Blake's utopian vision falls short of its claimed ideals. While Susan Matthews and Anne Janowitz have noted the nationalist dimension of the poem, and Dominic Rainsford attends to Blake's vengeful attacks (for instance, on Schofield) in *Jerusalem* to suggest that the poet's personal concerns sometimes override his ideals,[7] I am interested in the ways in which Blake indulges in imperial discourse and schema in order to fictively generate a New Jerusalem that assimilates, rather than, as in earlier Blake works, celebrates, difference. I shall therefore focus on three issues in the following pages: first, I wish to trace, very briefly, the operation of the vital/viral paradigm of propagation in relation to the circulation of texts, particularly as it appears in the Romantic period; second, I shall examine some exemplary passages in Blake's writings in which this paradigm is at work; third, I shall discuss some of the manifestations of this paradigm in *Jerusalem,* especially those with the often-colonizing Polypus as their locus. This chapter follows from the previous one's examination of the propagation of one political disease in particular—neoclassical nationalism in *Milton*—but here I am most concerned with the application of the general figure of ideological disease as the means by which destructive forms of social hybridity are generated, and ideological vaccination as a means of establishing the proper social order.

Vital/Viral Textual Propagation and Hybridity

The premise that words affect their audience has been fundamental to the ways in which Western societies have regulated published discourse, from education to restrictions on the circulation of certain texts and from propaganda to satire, from classical times to the present. Plato, for instance, has

Socrates suggest in *Phaedrus* that "the true way of writing" is "graven in the soul."[8] Such "inscriptions," however, often had a clear sociopolitical component, having the power to draw the reader or auditor into the ideology of the text, as Socrates discovered when he was accused of distributing a "doctrine which corrupts the youth."[9] In Plato's *Republic,* immediately before the exclusion of poetry and drama from the perfect society on the grounds that, through mimesis, the audience will repeat the errors that they represent, Socrates is drawn into a question about the propagation of his utopia in the domain of the real. Glaucon acknowledges that they have "describe[d]" and "theoretically founded" the perfect society, but expresses "doubt if it will ever exist on earth," to which Socrates replies, "Perhaps . . . it is laid up as a pattern in heaven, where he who wishes can see it and found it in his own heart."[10] Desmond Lee, in a translator's note, indicates that the "literal translation of this well-known phrase is 'and seeing it, establish himself.' The alternative translations commonly given are 'establish himself as its citizen,' or 'establish himself accordingly.'"[11] Socrates and Glaucon produce a utopian ideal in which "he who wishes" can behold the ideal state and will consequently, through the act of beholding, become a citizen of it—or, in Althusserian terms, become interpellated into the ideology and the community that it defines. This idea carries over into Christian theology. Visions, for instance, "present an interpretation of reality and invite the reader or listener to share it," while prophecies, as Behrendt shows, were designed to redirect the audience toward their envisioned ideal.[12] Thus, in William Cowper's "Expostulation," the Jews

> Receiv'd the transcript of th' eternal mind,
> Were trusted with his own graven laws,
> And *constituted guardians of his cause,*
> Theirs were the prophets, theirs the priestly call
> And theirs by birth the Saviour of us all.[13]

Similarly, in Blake's *Jerusalem,* the mere perception of Christ and the Divine Family incorporates the percipient into the familial social structure that Blake valorizes:

> mild the Saviour follow'd him,
> Displaying the Eternal Vision! the Divine Similitude!
> In loves and tears of brothers, sisters, sons, fathers, and friends
> Which if Man ceases to behold, he ceases to exist:

Saying. Albion! Our wars are wars of life, & wounds of love,
With intellectual spears, & long winged arrows of thought:
Mutual in one anothers love and wrath all renewing
We live as One Man; for contracting our infinite senses
We behold multitude; or expanding: we behold as one,
As One Man all the Universal Family; and that One Man
We call Jesus the Christ: and he in us, and we in him,
Live in perfect harmony in Eden the land of life. (*J*, 34.10–21)

Just as the boundary between vital and viral is a slippery one, however, so is the distinction between interpellative and prescriptive inscription: in the latter case, the assimilation of the recipient into the communicated social vision is never as complete as it is in the former case. Prescribed subjects do not, in Althusser's phrase, "work by themselves."[14] While anyone who is healthy fully embodies the definition of health, a patient with a disease never fully embodies the disease—one *is* healthy, and one *has* a disease (or one is diseased, the subject of a passive construction). The characterization of contested discourses as viral or debilitating depends on this unbreachable gap, on positing a natural body, or a political subject, that is necessarily alienated from that which has infected or restrained it. Vital or positively interpellative texts, conversely, offer the elision of such alienation, the promise of a fully integrated subject who has no internal conflicts.

Because of this imputed power to implicate the audience in a particular social organization, the plowshare of discourse can become a sword.[15] This power intersects with paradigms of authority, but is not contained within them. Authorities can contest the status of the circulating discourse as virus or cure, and an authorized text may circulate with the cultural weight of the authority's institution behind it, but the power of discourse to affect the cultural determination of the political subject is not contingent on any *prior* authority—and therein lies its power to transform the body politic, as well as individual subjects. Through the circulation of a text or speech, as those who favor political censorship fear, new authorities can be constituted. From Ovid's expulsion from Rome to the Puritans' closing of the British theaters, ruling classes have sought to secure the political body against the incursions of alternative constructions of society and, as Gellner discusses, to propagate their own. This became particularly difficult, however, in late-eighteenth-century Britain, as the number of readers increased exponentially with the accessibility of the print medium. The considerable growth in the size of the reading public and the commensurate increase in its demographical complexity led to a kind of information revolution that was perceived as threatening to the status quo in Blake's time. Outright fear can be traced in legislation, prosecutions, and espionage throughout much of the so-called long eighteenth century, from the censorship debate out of which Milton's *Areopagitica* arose to the Stage Licensing Act (1737), the Stamp Act (1765), and the expansion of the term "treason" to include speech acts as well as physical ones in the notorious Two Acts (1795). The trend continued in various modulations of press restrictions in the early decades of the nineteenth century. Thomas Muir was charged with "having" merely "lent the works of Thomas Paine,"[16] and his was only one case among many.

While William Godwin, in "Of Choice in Reading," asserts the power of virtue and innocence to defend against corruption by discourse, the premise of censorship is that innocence itself is most vulnerable to such discourses: there is no prophylactic for such a disease and the only preventative measure is the legal equivalent of quarantine, that is, censorship.[17] Thus, in the indictment of William Drennan (1794), a prominent Dublin physician and Irish nationalist, who was later acquitted of all charges, the publication of an address was characterized as an attempt "to excite and diffuse amongst the subjects of this realm of Ireland discontents, jealousies, and suspicions of our sovereign lord the king, and his government, and . . . to incite the subjects of our said lord the king to attempt with force and violence, and with arms, to make alterations in the government, state, and constitution of this kingdom."[18] Propagating outward from the private meeting in which it was written, through various hands as it was published, and finally to the public, the United Irishmen's address threatened to transform not only its readership, but also fundamental institutions of the state. The distinction between words and actions, between reading and being inscribed, between new ideas and new institutional orders, collapses in what the address itself terms "the witchcraft of a proclamation."[19] Such a collapse renders the populace uncontrollable, turning it into an unmappable heterogeneous mix of different reading histories, and so legislators and their agents sought to arrest the hybridization of the populace by preventing the circulation of different, new, or ideologically incommensurable discourses, demonizing them through the rhetoric of disease.[20] Disease is a powerful metaphor for the vehicle by which hybridity is generated: the history of its construction brings together the terror of the uncontrollable transmission of dangerous material, the fear of the invasive entity that not only conquers but transforms that which it invades, anxiety about the unseen and intangible, and, above all, the threat of a conversion of the political body to a different vital agenda.

The term "hybridity" has been applied in recent investigations of colonial and postcolonial politics to characterize the intrusion of the colonizing culture into the colonized cultural space, the reverse of the anxiety that Barrell traces in De Quincey's texts.[21] Discussing Romantic nationalism in Ireland, David Lloyd suggests that

> "hybridization" is necessarily grasped by nationalists as the paradoxically simultaneous process of multiplication or disintegration and homogenization. The flooding of the market with English commodities both disintegrates what is retrospectively constructed as a unified Irish identity and absorbs its residues into the single field of the British industrial and imperial empire. And since the only means to resist this process, in the absence of autonomous national political institutions, appears to be the formation of nationalist subjects through literary institutions, the field of popular literature becomes peculiarly fraught.[22]

Bhabha employs the term differently, using it to refer to an effect of the taxonomical imperial gaze that hoists the empire by its own petard: "If discriminatory effects enable the authorities to keep an eye on them, their proliferating difference evades that eye, escapes that surveillance," and so "[h]ybridity represents that ambivalent 'turn' of the discriminated subject into the terrifying, exorbitant object of paranoid classification."[23] Bhabha and Lloyd are writing about two different nations, India and Ireland, but about the same time and the same empire. Their definitions of "hybridity" differ because of the political position from which "hybridity" is being defined: Lloyd is discussing the hybridity "grasped by nationalists," the splintering of the national identity that they were trying to construct as univocal and coherent; Bhabha, however, is addressing the hybridity generated by imperialists to survey and control, taxonomically, the imperial space—a hybridity that incidentally creates a colonial space so hybridized, so heterogeneous, that it cannot be mapped. In both instances, hybridity marks the loosing of control, the complication of what is knowable and totalizable by that which exceeds such limits. It is at this point that Shklovsky's notion of "defamiliarization" meets Blake's radical politics: the unfamiliar is uncontained by the dominant paradigms that plot the lines of power, and the insertion of the unfamiliar into the realm of public discourse constitutes an intervention in that domain that complicates its configuration and so renders it forever hybrid.

Drawing tropological equations between departures from social codes, the corruption of personal identity, and the physical violation of the body's boundaries was hardly new. The effects that circulate around the drink in Milton's *Comus* constitute only one example among many (although for these purposes it is a particularly apt one, because it reflects moral corruption by turning its imbibers into hybrids of animal and human form).[24] But this trope carried special power during a period of sociopolitical turmoil in which proclamations, propaganda, subversive pamphlets, and speeches fought to control the minds, and arms, of the populace. It is arguably the Enlightenment notion that the mind is a tabula rasa inscribed upon by experience, to use John Locke's formulation in *Enquiry Concerning Human Understanding* (1690), that made the proliferation of readers and readings so dangerous. David Hume, in the early decades of the eighteenth century, makes easy equations between "characters who excite blame" and those who "tend to public detriment and disturbance" while implicitly, but not subtly, drawing a simile between such "characters" and the "malignant humors" of gout as well as the "public" and the body.[25] Because of the anthropocentrism of Western culture, a virus or cancer is not a form of life with which humanity competes, nor even a parasite that can be deconstructively revealed as a host, with the elegance of J. Hillis Miller's rhetoric, but a devouring monster that is the absolute antithesis of the only life that really matters. Arguing that "[t]he case is the same with *moral* as with *physical* ill," as well as explicitly rejecting the notion that disease is proper to the body, Hume can thus posit a "natural" recognition of what is good and evil that is as clear-cut as the distinction between health and the "malignant humors" to which it is implicitly compared.[26] In "The Expostulation" (1782), Cowper uses an extended image of "malignant humors" that are national in scope:

> When nations are to perish in their sins,
> 'Tis in the church the leprosy begins:
> The priest whose office is, with zeal sincere
> To watch the fountain, and preserve it clear,
> Carelessly nods and sleeps upon the brink,
> While others poison what the flock must drink;
> Or waking at the call of lust alone,
> Infuses lies and errors of his own:

His unsuspecting sheep believe it pure,
And tainted by the very means of cure,
Catch from each other a contagious spot,
The foul forerunner of a general rot.[27]

Use of such figures was widespread in the Romantic period, no doubt due in part to the influence of Milton's *Lycidas.* As Barrell has shown, De Quincey "figures the oriental as infection," "terrorised by the fear of an unending and interlinked chain of infections from the East."[28] De Quincey represents cultural contact as an event vulnerable to viral transmission and so invests it with far more sinister overtones than Cowper's more innocuous charge that the British imperialist has thrown out British libertarianism and "[w]ith Asiatic vices stor'd [his] mind."[29] Steven Blakemore finds, "In discussing tradition, [Edmund] Burke uses metaphors of genuine parentage and offspring—authentic blood lines—while the disruption of it is expressed in metaphors of bastard births and venereal disease" that link the subversion of tradition with both disease and corruptions of genealogical lines that hybridize the ruling class, a fear of which was often expressed in similar terms during the Renaissance.[30]

Blake, close to the radical movement suppressed in the 1790s and charged with treasonous utterances himself, was exposed extensively to such tropes. In the 1798 edition of Bacon's *Essays Moral, Economical and Political,* for instance, Blake came across the assertion, "Certainly, the politic and artificial nourishing and entertaining of hopes, and carrying men from hopes to hopes is one of the best antidotes against the poison of discontentments," and wrote, "Subterfuges" (Anno. Bacon, 625). Between 1790 and 1806, arguably Blake's most active years as a writer, four texts were prominently published that employ, and illustrate, the vital/viral model in particularly clear ways. Two of those texts were written by acquaintances of Blake who were, as he was, members of the Johnson circle—that is, Wollstonecraft and Godwin—and a third was written by their political opponent, Burke. The fourth, which almost caused a duel, was written by one of the period's best-known reviewers, Jeffrey, and launches a vitriolic attack on the early work of one of the period's most popular poets, Thomas Moore.

In *A Vindication of the Rights of Woman,* Wollstonecraft compares two kinds of interventions in the sociopolitical domain: "The indolent puppet of a court [i.e., the monarch] first becomes a luxurious monster, or fastidious sensualist, and then makes the contagion which his unnatural state spread, the instrument of tyranny," while "[m]en of abilities scatter seeds that grow up and have a great influence on the forming opinion; and when once the public opinion preponderates, through the exertion of reason, the overthrow of arbitrary power is not very distant."[31] In both instances, the model for the distribution of discourse remains the same: an idea is produced by a singular origin (monarch or author) and then circulates through the political body, transforming it into an entity that is in part determined by that idea. But the metaphors used to figure that model are radically different: "good" ideas are vital ("seeds that grow up") and "bad" ideas are viral ("contagion"). In "Of Choice in Reading" (1797), Godwin is at pains to argue "that the impression we derive from a book, depends less upon its real contents, than upon the temper of mind and preparation with which we read it," but he remains dependent on the same functional model as Wollstonecraft:

> I cannot tell what I should have been, if Shakespear or Milton had not written. The poorest peasant in the remotest corner of England, is probably a different man from what he would have been but for these authors. Every man who is changed from what he was by a perusal of their works, communicates a portion of the inspiration all around him. *It passes from man to man, till it influences the whole mass.* I cannot tell that the wisest mandarin now living in China, is not indebted for part of his energy and sagacity to the writings of Milton and Shakespear, even though it should happen that he never heard of their names.[32]

Despite Godwin's concern with arguing that texts are not inherently moral or immoral, he nevertheless falls into a dependence on the vital/viral paradigm: "Books will perhaps be found, in a less degree than is commonly imagined, the corruptors of the morals of mankind. They form an effective subsidiary to events and the contagion of vicious society; but, taken by themselves, they rarely produce vice and profligacy where virtue existed before. . . . He that would extract poison from them, must for the most part come to them with a mind already debauched."[33] At work here is the premise that corrupting books act on the population in ways that, if not literally corporeal, are best figured through physiological metaphors, while uncorrupting books act on noncorporeal aspects, such as "sagacity," "energy," or what a man "is." Again, we *are* healthy, and we *have* diseases: vital texts, in Godwin's inflection of the paradigm, operate on a profound level of personality, not corporeality. Godwin, moreover, constructs virtue as a prophylactic and vice as a predisposition to the disease of immoral books, while maintaining, on the basis of the innate goodness of humanity, that the influence of books that are not immoral circulates freely through the social body, and even worldwide.[34]

Burke uses a similar model of worldwide propagation but politicizes it as well as renders it more suspect. In *Reflections on the Revolution in France,* Burke notes, "Writers . . . have great influence on the publick mind," and he uses this to suggest that French affairs are not merely domestic in scope but constitute a threat to British sovereignty:

> Formerly your affairs were your own concern only. We felt for them as men; but we kept aloof from them, because we were not citizens of France. But when we see the model held up to ourselves, we must feel as Englishmen, and feeling, we must provide as Englishmen. Your affairs, in spite of us, are made a part of our interest; so far at least as to keep at a distance your panacea, or your plague. If it be a panacea, we do not want it. We know the consequences of unnecessary physic. If it be a plague; it is such a plague, that the precautions of the most severe quarantine ought to be established against it.[35]

Burke, of course, is credited with instigating the suppression of Paine's *Rights of Man* and the legislation that hounded Thomas Muir for loaning books.

Jeffrey provides a useful articulation of the view that Burke supports and Godwin tries to refute, namely that books can corrupt the virtuous. In 1806, anonymously reviewing a volume of Moore's erotic verse, *Epistles, Odes, and other Poems,* Jeffrey charges that Moore wrote the poems "for the purpose of insinuating pollution into the minds of unknown and unsuspecting readers," particularly women, launching "an attack upon their purity" that threatens the entire social order, because "[t]he character and the morality of women exercises already a mighty influence upon the happiness and respectability of the nation."[36] But it is not only the purity of women for which Jeffrey fears. Noting that Moore's verse not only is dedicated to people of "rank and accomplishments," but also expresses a sense of intimacy with them, Jeffrey expresses concern that "[b]y these channels, the book will easily pass into circulation in those classes of society, which it is of most consequence to keep free of contamination; and from which its reputation and its influence will descend with the greatest effect to the great body of the community. . . . [I]f the head be once infected, the corruption will spread irresistibly through the whole body."[37] Unacceptable ideas and attitudes, once published, colonize the political body like a virus, turning that body into a monstrous hybrid of purity and corruption. It is this dangerous hybridity of Moore's poems that lies at the heart of their danger: "the coarse indecencies of Rochester and Dryden . . . can scarcely be regarded as dangerous. There is an antidote to the poison they contain, in the open and undisguised profligacy with which it is presented," while "[i]t seems to be [Moore's] aim to impose corruption upon his readers, by concealing it under the mask of refinement; to reconcile them imperceptibly to the most vile and vulgar sensuality, by *blending* its language with that of exalted feeling and tender emotion."[38] While Godwin's readers must first be receptive to illicit behavior, and virtue is a sure defense—or at least it is a sure defense against anxiety about the uninhibited circulation of such ideas—Moore's poetry, like Comus's drink, seduces all of its imbibers to behave bestially.

Throughout these different models of textual propagation, two points remain the same: the circulation of discourse transforms the social domain through which it moves, or even beyond, to China, in Godwin's argument; ideas or texts consistent with the critic's ideology propagate vitally and ideas or texts inconsistent with that ideology propagate virally. From Plato to Moore, in secular and the sacred traditions, publicly circulated discourse inscribes the ideology of the population, and it can inscribe incommensurable ideologies as well as familiar ones. This is a different matter from constitutional language and the "institutional speech acts" discussed by Esterhammer in the final chapter of *Creating States,* because, to a limited extent, it allows counterhegemonic discourse the same performative power as hegemonic utterances. As the indictment of Drennan and other attempts at censorship reveal, in the so-called age of revolution, the power of non- and counterhegemonic discourse to reconstitute the body politic was all too clear, and the purgation of unacceptable discourse was facilitated by a medical paradigm in which good and evil are clearly delineated.

Blake's transition from the purgative to the vaccination version of the vital/viral paradigm, however, puts him in a more vulnerable position. While he identifies authoritative discourse with disease and revolutionary speech and action with sterilizing fires in his early works, by *Jerusalem* he characterizes his own work as a vaccine that will purge the political body of destructive errors that are often figured as cancerous. But in doing so he makes his own writing susceptible to his own critique of viral discourse as colonizing. *Jerusalem* is rhetorically homologous to the works it condemns; that is, it aims to circulate and so transform the political body into something else.

Battling Infection in the Body Politic

In *The Marriage of Heaven and Hell,* Blake includes the proverb, "Damn. braces: Bless relaxes" (9.57). Blake's resistance to restraints is a commonplace of Blake criticism, but the restraints of which Blake complains are often internalized as ideological dictates through a moral code so that, as Foucault demonstrates so well in *Discipline and Punish,* we do not deal with physical restraints that are separable from the individual. Rather, such restraints produce a hybridized subject, like the females of the preludiums, whose codes of behavior are located in the contested domain between nature and nurture—between what a person is imagined to be in a world without such restraints and what a person is imagined to be if subsumed within the ideology that generates those restraints—in a space in which neither of those defining endpoints exists, except abstractly in attempts to disentangle the mix. Blake not only represents those "braces" as constraints that are produced discursively, as in the houses of *Europe* with "windows wove over with curses of iron: / Over the doors Thou shalt not" (*Eur,* 12.27–28) or the binding texts of *The Laocoön,* but represents their removal as the burning away of a diseased shell. In this trope, the restraining discourse is a stultifying coating that inhibits the growth and health of the (political) body, which remains relatively intact beneath it. In *Vision of The Last Judgment,* Blake offers an unusually personal representation of this restraint:

> <First God Almighty comes with a Thump on the Head Then Jesus Christ comes with a balm to heal it>
> The Last Judgment is an Overwhelming of Bad Art & Science. . . . Some People flatter themselves that there will be No Last Judgment & . . . that Bad Art will be adopted & mixed with Good Art That Error or Experiment will make a Part of Truth . . . I will not Flatter them Error is Created Truth is Eternal Error or Creation will be Burned Up & then & not till then Truth or Eternity will appear It is Burnt up the Moment Men cease to behold it I assert for My self that I do not behold the Outward

> Creation & that to me it is hindrance & not Action it is as the Dirt upon my feet *No part of Me.* (*VLJ,* 565; my emphasis)

America is heavily dependent on the vital/viral model of propagated discourse. In chapter 4, I addressed the vital propagative model employed in *America* and its difference from models that appear in P.B. Shelley's "Ode to the West Wind" and Wollstonecraft's *Vindication.* To reiterate, Orc proposes a model that closely recalls the vital half of Wollstonecraft's model; in it, the scattered pages of the text are like seeds that "make the desarts blossom" (*Am,* 8.8). Orc's model departs from Wollstonecraft's, however, in severing the connection between the author and the fertilization of the public domain. Instead of envisioning a poet spreading his word, as in P.B. Shelley's ode, Orc envisions the torn text as the means of liberating the individual from the conformity enforced through mass-produced books. The torn text is thus a subversion of the propagated tyrannical books whose production is described, in the preludium to *Europe,* through a metaphor that recalls the other half of Wollstonecraft's model, while tying the propagation of tyranny more explicitly to the publication of texts. But the torn text is also a catalyst for another level of propagation. It "renew[s] the fiery joy" (*Am,* 8.9) "that Urizen perverted to ten commands" (*Am,* 8.3) and it is fire that destroys the pestilence produced by the tyrants in the final conflict. Throughout the poem, "pestilence is shot from heaven" (*Am,* 1.6) or, more literally, from tyrants in the cause of maintaining tyranny:

> a heavy iron chain
> Descends link by link from Albions cliffs across the sea to bind
> Brothers & sons of America, till our faces pale and yellow. (*Am,* 3.7–9)
> Arm'd with diseases of the earth to cast upon the Abyss,
> Their [Albion's Angels'] numbers forty millions, must'ring in the eastern sky. (*Am,* 13.15–16)
> Albions Angel [gave] the thunderous command:
> His plagues obedient to his voice flew forth out of their clouds
> Falling upon America, as a storm to cut them off
> As a blight cuts the tender corn when it begins to appear . . .
> And as a plague wind fill'd with insects cuts off man & beast. (*Am,* 14.3–8)
> their ensigns sick'ning in the sky
> The plagues creep on the burning winds. (*Am,* 15.10–11)

Disease is the weapon of the tyrant, controlling the population by limiting its health and vitality. Blake would later write, "A Tyrant is the Worst disease & the Cause of all others" (Anno. Bacon, 625).

But, in *America,* it is the tyrants who are most noticeably infected by the pestilence. In the early plates of the poem, the narrator declares that "Albion is sick" (*Am,* 4.4) and Boston's Angel asks, "Must the generous tremble & leave his joy, to the idle: to the pestilence! / That mock him?" (*Am,* 11.6–7). Moreover, during the great conflict, the tyrants are "smitten with their own plagues" (*Am,* 16.18). The plagues are implicitly identified with syphilis through the disease's contemporary association with a remarkable susceptibility to the cold and the belief that leprosy was a late stage of syphilitic infection: "Pestilence began in streaks of red / Across the limbs of Albions Guardian, the spotted plague smote Bristols / And the Leprosy Londons Spirit, sickening all their bands" (*Am,* 15.1–3); "Albions Guardian writhed in torment . . . teeth chattering / Howling & shuddering his legs quivering; convuls'd each muscle & sinew / Sick'ning lay Londons Guardian, and the ancient miter'd York" (*Am,* 15.6–9); "the Guardians of Ireland and Scotland and Wales . . . [are] spotted with plagues" (*Am,* 15.13–14); "the Bard of Albion felt the enormous plagues" (*Am,* 15.16); Urizen has both a "leprous head" and "Leprous . . . limbs" (*Am,* 16.3, 16.11). Just as the Great Fire of 1666 rid London of the Black Plague, the purifying fires of Orc turn back the tyrants' syphilitic pestilence and liberate the populace. The "fiery joy" destroys the leprous elite but leaves undamaged the healthy political body: "Fires inwrap the earthly globe, yet man is not consumd" (*Am,* 8.15). Just as the soldiers' disrobing marks their refusal to be complicit in the British government's attempt to suppress liberty (see chapter 3), the cleansing fires mark the purging from society of a hegemony that only inhibited the vitality of those that it ruled.

The "fiery joy" reappears at the apocalyptic resolution of *Milton,* and again it destroys only that which corrupts the body politic. After Ololon descends "Into the Fires of Intellect that rejoic'd in Felphams Vale" (*M,* 42.9), Christ is draped in her clouds, "folded as a Garment dipped in blood / Written within & without in woven letters: & the Writing / Is the Divine Revelation in the Litteral expression: / A Garment of War" (*M,* 42.12–15). The passage that follows, closing the poem, echoes the final lines of *Europe.* But I am more interested here in the lines that precede the arrival of the apocalypse:

> To bathe in the Waters of Life; to wash off the Not Human

> I come in Self-annihilation & the grandeur of Inspiration
> To cast off Rational Demonstration by Faith in the Saviour
> To cast off the rotten rags of Memory by Inspiration
> To cast off Bacon, Locke & Newton from Albions covering
> To take off his filthy garments, & clothe him with Imagination
> To cast aside from Poetry, all that is not Inspiration. (*M,* 41.1–7)

The innumerable, convoluted mergings of the preceding plates end here in a series of divisions that "cast off," "cast aside" and "take off" all that is not proper to the identity that Blake imagines, all that is "Not Human." Just as the American soldiers cast off their uniforms before the apocalyptic purging, Milton casts off his "false Body: an Incrustation over [his] Immortal / Spirit" (*M,* 40.35–36), anticipating the moment when Jesus "shall wholly purge away with Fire" (*M,* 41.27) such alien graftings. In defining that "false Body," Blake emphasizes pretence, just as he does in the nationalist passage from his *Public Address* I discussed in chapter 1 (*PA,* 576). In *Milton,* however, the pretence is specifically associated with discursive inadequacies. It is the false, and pretentious, writers who infect the government of Albion:

> the tame high finisher of paltry Blots,
> Indefinite, or paltry Rhymes; or paltry Harmonies.
> Who creeps into State Government like a catterpillar to destroy
> To cast off the idiot Questioner who is always questioning,
> But never capable of answering; who sits with a sly grin
> Silent plotting when to question, like a thief in a cave;
> Who publishes doubt & calls it knowledge . . .
> These are the destroyers of Jerusalem, these are the murderers
> Of Jesus . . .
> These are the Sexual Garments, the Abomination of Desolation
> Hiding the Human Lineaments as with an Ark & Curtains
> Which Jesus rent: & now shall wholly purge away with Fire.
> (*M,* 41.9–15, 41.21–22, 41.25–27)

Just as the valorization of copying generates a false Englishness (*PA,* 576), the discursive failures of poets, legislators, and scientists produce a "false Body," the "Not Human." In the apocalyptic resolution to *Milton,* there is no separation of the saved and not saved, but rather the purgation of identity from that which is alien to it, leaving only what Blake considered proper, whether to the body, religion, politics, poetics, or, as discussed in the previous chapter, the nation.

Earlier in *Milton,* Blake suggests that this infectious error is circulated textually. Arguably, this is established in the very title: by aligning the reformation of a poet and essayist with the renovation of British society, Blake establishes a fundamental synergy between the writer and the state. Blake raises the issue at length in the preface to *Milton,* linking ideological sickness to fatality by again identifying tyrannical pestilence with war, suggesting that the classical "slaves of the Sword" propagate "the general malady & infection" (*M,* 1). But "when the New Age is at leisure to Pronounce; all will be set right" and the "ancient" artistic order will be reestablished, replacing the militarist classical one (*M,* 1). Satan, the representative of the neoclassical imperialist hegemony, is depicted propagating his view textually:

> He created Seven deadly Sins drawing out his infernal scroll,
> Of Moral laws and cruel punishments upon the clouds of
> Jehovah
> To pervert the Divine voice in its entrance to the earth
> With thunder of war & trumpets sound, with armies of disease.
> (*M,* 9.21–24)

Like the divinity that "purge[s] away" the "Not Human" at the end of the second book (*M,* 41.27, 41.1), Satan's texts cast off that which is incommensurable with the ideology that he seeks to propagate. Satan declares,

> I am God alone
> There is no other! let all obey my principles of moral individuality
> I have brought them from the uppermost innermost recesses
> Of my Eternal Mind, transgressors I will rend off for ever,
> As now I rend this accursed Family from my covering.
> (*M,* 9.25–29)

Satan anticipates the model that is expounded in the final plates of *Milton* but reverses its placement of the contending ideologies, locating divinity in the exterior and his own "principles" in a privileged interiority. But the formulation of the relationship between what is proper and what is alien, and the means by which the alien can be "cast off," remains the same. While Blake is still using the image of fire to mark the eradication of ideological disease, he here approaches a vaccination model in which two similar diseases compete to control the body politic.

The transposition of an image from *Milton* to *Jerusalem* marks a further step away from the sterilizing model to the vaccination one. In *Milton,* the complicity of texts in the propagation of infectious militarism is made explicit: "This Wine-press is call'd War on Earth, it is the Printing-Press / Of Los; and here he lays his words in order above the mortal brain / As cogs are formd in a wheel to turn the cogs of the adverse wheel" (*M,* 27.8–10). The passage thus does not simply refer to the influence of texts on the subject, but harks back to the preface: "We do not want either Greek or Roman Models if we are just and true to our own Imaginations." The Printing-Press "prolong[s] Corporeal War" because it, like the classical models, deflects subjects from their "own Imaginations," controlling the brain as an "*adverse* wheel," at once opposed and unwilling—like a virus. Thus "The Wine-press on the Rhine groans loud . . . Where Human Thought is crushd beneath the iron hand of Power" (*M,* 25.3, 25.5). Blake reiterates this passage in *Jerusalem,* referring to "ornaments" that mimic "the Wheels of Albions sons" "as cogs / Are formd in a wheel, to fit the cogs of the adverse wheel" (*J,* 13.12–14). In *Jerusalem,* however, the wheels are not identified with the printing press, and thus with the mass production of texts, but with the distribution of systems that are fundamentally compulsive, as if the complicity of Blake's own text in such a project has become too uncomfortable to suggest when its "wondrous writing" might resolve all.

The Wheels of *Jerusalem* are implicated in often unspecified machines that enforce rigidity of thought and political division, such as "the Wheels of Albions Sons: / Fixing their Systems, permanent: by mathematic power / Giving a body to Falshood" (*J,* 12.11–13) and "intricate wheels invented, wheel without wheel: / To perplex youth in their outgoings, & to bind to labours in Albion" (*J,* 65.21–22).[39] These wheels are also poisonous:

> They saw their Wheels rising up poisonous against Albion
> Urizen, cold & scientific: Luvah, pitying and weeping
> Tharmas, indolent & sullen: Urthona, doubting and despairing
> Victims to one another & dreadfully plotting against each other
> (*J,* 38.1–4)

"In opposition deadly, and their Wheels in poisonous / And deadly stupor" (*J*, 74.5–6). The power of the wheels to affect, or "perplex," thought is thus characterized as sickening as well as mechanistically violent. In Eden, however, there is no sickness:

> I turn my eyes to the Schools & Universities of Europe
> And there behold the Loom of Locke whose Woof rages dire
> Washd by the Water-wheels of Newton. black the cloth
> In heavy wreathes folds over every Nation; cruel Works
> Of many Wheels I view, wheel without wheel, with cogs tyrannic
> Moving by compulsion each other: not as those in Eden: which
> Wheel within Wheel in freedom revolve in harmony & peace.
> (*J*, 15.14–20)

Only the wheels of the fallen world are identified with both the textual and the tyrannical, while the Edenic resolution of difference promised by the first preface to *Jerusalem* produces cogless wheels in which all struggle has ended and difference has been resolved. Other images of the influence of compulsive systems repeat these figures of interlocutory interlocking, the infectious disease, surreptitious poison, and cancer. In chapter 1 of *Jerusalem*, for example, Blake appropriates Sir Philip Sidney's conceit of the sugared pill, in which the medicinal properties of the didactic text are surrounded by seductive aesthetic qualities:

> his cold
> Poisons rose up: & his sweet deceits coverd them all over
> With a tender cloud. . . . Listen!
> Be attentive! be obedient! (*J*, 8.4–6, 8.8–9)

Throughout these references to compulsion by pestilence-like texts and disease-infested rulers, Blake's central anxiety is located at the interpenetration of the diseased and the healthy—the meshed cogs of the opposing wheels of text against as-yet-uncompelled brain, the epidermal boils and encrustations of the corrupted, the caterpillar-like destroyer of government, the military that invades the state like a disease attacks a body, and the circulation of false texts in the public domain. Or, rather, Blake marks his difference from certain views by aligning his utopian ideal with health and the target of his satiric pen with disease. Blake thus alienates from the political body that to which he objects, making it strange, and so facilitates the conversion of the reader to a view in which such restraints must be excised through the powerful resonances of the medical discourse that he has appropriated. The power of this trope goes beyond the simplicity of "disease is bad and health is good." Medical discourse is framed to deal with symptoms in a very particular way: it tells the patient what in his or her body does not belong or has ceased to work properly, separating the subject from a part of his or her own body through reference to the ideal body of the medical imagination. Acculturated into the prevailing ideologies, Blake's readers must also be alienated from a part of themselves; Blake must imagine the ideal political body through which they can divide their culture's paradigms into healthy and diseased before they can purge the latter. But, by appropriating the vital/viral paradigm to affect his readers, Blake also infects his own discourse with that of the hegemony. To communicate effectively with those who have been interpellated into the ideologies to which he objects, he must graft the rhetoric of those ideologies onto his own, or risk being completely obscure and failing to achieve his polemic ends.

Excising the Cancer: Hybridity and Jerusalem

The vital/viral paradigm is implicit in Leonard W. Deen's description of the power of *Jerusalem*'s text: "the poem *Jerusalem* is itself a system in part, and what is a systematizing of error in it is designed to fall away, to move back so that it no longer looms in the foreground and overwhelms the mind, and can thus be seen in the perspective that reveals error. What remains when Satan is annihilated is simply the risen Albion, the great body of universal humanity, the family of men living in universal brotherhood."[40] The circulated text marks and cures the disease and, like any good medical treatment, leaves the body pure of any taint, restored to its ideal condition. But, as I have already discussed, such pathologies are sensitive to the very critique and reversal that Blake proposes: classifications that delineate what is "error" and what is "universal humanity" become much more vulnerable to question. While Blake criticism has usually focused on the narrative of *Jerusalem,* the quest for the reunion of Albion and his Emanation, a mystical version of the conventional marriage plot, I wish to focus on the work's construction as an assemblage of four polemics that are directed at specific audiences: the Jews, the Deists, the public, and the Christians.[41] By representing these audiences in particular ways, Blake makes his concern with "error," like his solution to it, culturally specific. Blake's "family of men" is fundamentally British and Christian, and can be achieved only if cultural and ideological difference—termed "error"—is excised from the "great body of universal humanity."

Jerusalem, perhaps precisely because it is Blake's most "consolidated" work (*J,* 3), is also his most tyrannical, plotting the assimilation of the globe into his own political and religious vision. Despite Blake's early opposition to imperialism, *Jerusalem* envisions a kind of imaginative colonization, and religious proselytization, in which Albion's and Jerusalem's prior universality is reinstated over the national and cultural divisions of the present: "Awake! Awake Jerusalem! O lovely Emanation of Albion / Awake and overspread all Nations as in Ancient Time" (*J,* 97.1–2), when "London coverd the whole Earth. England encompassd the Nations: / And all the Nations of the Earth were seen in the Cities of Albion" (*J,* 79.22–23). Matthews suggests that, "in *Jerusalem,* the language hesitates between the national and the universal," but it is an imperial hesitation, as the valorized nation is identified with the proper human type.[42] While Los complains of those who "murder by analyzing, that [they] / May take the aggregate" (*J,* 91.26–27), this is, on one level, precisely the strategy that Blake's final epic enacts in its vision of resolving differences into "harmony."[43] The return to the lost Jerusalem is repeatedly figured as the purging of the political body of invasive difference, and it is achieved through "the wond'rous art of writing" (*J,* 3.4): "Therefore I print; nor vain my types shall be: / Heaven, Earth & Hell, henceforth shall live in harmony" (*J,* 3.9–10). While Dominic Rainsford provocatively suggests that Blake's "aggressive and egotistic presence within the text [*The Marriage of Heaven and Hell*] can easily be read as being itself a product of deliberate excess, so that what we are offered is less a self-portrait than a self-caricature; and this encourages the reader to be rebellious or eccentric in his or her turn,"[44] there is no such boisterous author figure in *Jerusalem.* Instead we have the presentation of *Jerusalem* playing "cowpox," so to speak, to the prevailing "smallpox." The text itself is offered as a restorative that will not only eradicate invading viruses, but also establish a political body that is invulnerable to further incursions. But sustaining this model of his epic's social power requires that Blake negotiate some difficult waters between the Charybdis, which threatens to subsume *Jerusalem* in the colonizing discourse that it condemns, and the Scylla, which might destroy its effectiveness as a means of harmonizing a cacophony of cultural voices.

Throughout *Jerusalem,* corrupting influences "writhe their arms into the nether deep" (*Am,* 2.11). Schofield, for example, "is like a mandrake in the earth before Reubens gate: / He shoots beneath Jerusalems walls to undermine her foundations!" (*J,* 11.22–23). The most interesting of the poem's many invasive, and subversive, root systems is the Polypus. According to the *OED,* not only is "polypus" a species of tentacled marine life, but it has also been a common term for tumors, particularly the rhinal variety, since the fourteenth century. By the eighteenth century, it was also being applied to tumors of the heart and of the uterus. It is the latter meaning of "polypus" that resonates in *Jerusalem.* The Polypus is represented not simply as a monster, but as an invasive monster that is, at one point, explicitly identified with uterine cancer. It is also implicitly associated with tumors through its identification with the growing roots of trees and other images of creeping invasion. The Polypus thus not only refers to a member of a species that can be described as "'colonial' organisms of individuals" and so can operate as a figure for social collectives,[45] it is also a persistent trope for representing the propagation of ideologies to which Blake objects as destructively colonizing. The Polypus of each chapter is explicitly identified with the quality that Blake's corresponding preface establishes as the error of the group under scrutiny—an error that forestalls the establishment of Blake's own "harmony." The Polypus marks the invading paradigm that corrupts the group from the ideal that Blake's text imagines in the postapocalyptic moment of his own ideology's successful colonization—or, from another perspective, entangles the group in an otherness, an unassimilable hybridity, that halts the colonizing momentum of that ideal.

In chapter 3 of *Jerusalem,* for instance, Blake addresses "the Deists," contending, "Those who Martyr others or who cause War are Deists, but never can be Forgivers of Sin. The Glory of Christianity is, To Conquer by Forgiveness. All the Destruction therefore, in Christian Europe has arisen from Deism, which is Natural Religion" (*J,* 52). It is the Deists who "Arose with War," "forgd the Law into a Sword," and turned "Grecian Mocks & Roman Sword / Against this image of his Lord" (*J,* 52.8, 52.19, 52.23–24). As we have seen, Blake persistently identifies Rome and Greece with military imperialism in contemporary works, from *Milton* to *The Laocoön* and "On Virgil." Blake thus associates the Deists with violent conquest, imperialism, and rationalism—and, in chapter 3, the Polypus is represented in similar terms:

the Great Polypus of Generation covered the Earth
In Verulam the Polypus's Head, winding around his bulk

Thro Rochester, and Chichester, & Exeter & Salisbury,
To Bristol: & his Heart beat strong on Salisbury Plain
Shooting out Fibres round the Earth, thro Gaul & Italy
And Greece, & along the Sea of Rephaim into Judea
To Sodom & Gomorrah: thence to India, China & Japan.
(*J,* 67.34–40)

O Double God of Generation
The Heavens are cut like a mantle around from the Cliffs of
Albion
Across Europe; across Africa; in howlings & deadly War
A sheet & veil & curtain of blood is let down from Heaven
Across the hills of Ephraim . . .
He sees the Twelve Daughters naked upon the Twelve Stones
Themselves condensing to rocks & into the Ribs of a Man
Lo they shoot forth in tender Nerves across Europe & Asia.
(*J,* 68.18–22, 68.24–26)

Colonizing root systems spread outward from England to Africa and Asia, through the Polypus's tentacles, the Daughters' nerves, or the woven threads of a mantle. While the nonconsensual pregnancies of the female of *Europe*'s preludium produce tyrannical books, the "infernal bondage" (*J,* 69.9) of the warriors' culture produces a colonizing cancer that propagates the philosophies of the Deists:

Then all the Males combind into One Male & every one
Became a ravening eating Cancer growing in the Female
A Polypus of Roots of Reasoning Doubt Despair & Death.
Going forth & returning from Albions Rocks to Canaan:
Devouring Jerusalem from every Nation of the Earth.
Envying stood the enormous Form at variance with Itself
In all its Members. (*J,* 69.1–7)[46]

The Polypus is a compelling figure for hybridity. "[A]t variance with Itself" (*J,* 69.6), it is devouring, parasitical, and invasive, as well as colonizing. It is that which corrupts the political body but will leave it in its prior state of health once excised.

In chapter 1, "To the Public"—or, perhaps, "To the [British] Public"—the Polypus is identified with nationalism and appears in a series of plates that return over and over again to issues of nationalism and exile.

After an extensive geographical and architectural description of the City of Golgonooza (*J,* 12.45–14.34), Blake turns from that "museum in which Blake shores eternal forms against the ruins of time"[47] to "Hampstead Highgate Finchley Hendon Muswell hill" (*J,* 16.1), moving from the Platonist ideal to a lapsarian particular of that ideal. The intervening passage plots fibrous strangulations by the Polypus and polypus-like entities that are structurally similar but ethically the opposite of the "Fibres of love from man to man thro Albions pleasant land" (*J,* 4.8) that will spread after the renovation. The Polypus is the basis for the topography of the fallen, divided world mapped in the lines that follow its appearance, marking the transformation of the abstract landscape from Golgonooza to its fallen British iteration. The first reference to the Polypus envisions another colonization of the globe, again imaged in terms of rooting and the mandrake-like soldier "Skofeld":

> And Hand & Hyle rooted into Jerusalem by a fibre
> Of strong revenge & Skofeld Vegetated by Reubens Gate
> In every Nation of the Earth till the Twelve Sons of Albion
> Enrooted into every Nation: a mighty Polypus growing
> From Albion over the whole earth. (*J,* 15.1–5)

A few lines later, such serpentine entanglements are identified with other texts available "To the Public":

> Bacon & Newton sheathd in dismal steel, their terrors hang
> Like iron scourges over Albion, Reasonings like vast Serpents
> Infold around my limbs, bruising my minute articulations
> I turn my eyes to the Schools & Universities of Europe
> And there behold the Loom of Locke whose Woof rages dire
> Washd by the Water-wheels of Newton. black the cloth
> In heavy wreathes folds over every Nation; cruel Works
> Of many Wheels I view, wheel without wheel, with cogs tyrannic
> Moving by compulsion each other. (*J,* 15.11–19)

Beginning with what could be a description of *The Laocoön,* surrounded as the encircled figures are with Blake's own "minute articulations," the passage ends with the iteration of an image from *Milton,* "cogs are formd in a wheel to turn the cogs of the adverse wheel" (*M,* 27.10), in the Printing-

Press of Los. To drive home the point, Blake ends the passage with an anticipation of the time when Los will begin "cutting the Fibres from Albions hills / That Albions Sons may roll apart over the Nations" (*J*, 15.23–24).

In chapter 1, the Polypus is thus implicated in limitations that are complicit in the production of national divisions. These divisions are enthusiastically erased in the opening and closing lines of the poem, as Jerusalem "overspread[s] all Nations" (*J*, 97.2), so that "the Reader will be with [the author], wholly One in Jesus" (*J*, 3) and "Heaven, Earth & Hell, henceforth shall live in harmony" (*J*, 3.10). Interconnections and harmonies are valorized in the first preface, "To the Public": from Blake's praise of "those with whom to be connected, is to be [*blessed*]," the "consolidated" poem, and the religious Ancients who were "absorb'd in their Gods," to his condemnation of "the modern bondage of Rhyming," the poet represents the erasure of constraints as a union with a larger collective—rather than as simple liberty or engagement with the imagination, as he had so often before. The Polypus intervenes in this uninterrupted collectivity, marking the nations through its fibrous, invasive roots, guided by "strong revenge" (*J*, 15.2) and anticipating the entwining texts of the rationalists and the imposed cartography of the following lines in which the gates, counties, and points of Britain and Ireland are "fixd down" (*J*, 16.28), "fixing" (*J*, 16.31), and "divided" (*J*, 16.43, 16.51, 16.52).

Later in chapter 1, the Polypus reappears, again in connection with violence, devouring imperialism, boundaries, and the nation: "Building Castles in desolated places, and strong Fortifications. / Soon Hand mightily devour'd & absorb'd Albions Twelve Sons. / Out from his bosom a mighty Polypus, vegetating in darkness" (*J*, 18.38–40). In the fractured syntax of the passage, moving "forth from [a] bosom" (*J*, 18.42) or absorbing into the bosom through eating ("devour'd & absorb'd") becomes part of a chain of repetitions, "Like Wheels from a great Wheel reflected in the Deep" (*J*, 18.43), that mark the violation of the closed boundary of personal territory (the body)—the first stage of invasion. The Polypus is revealed as a figure for the agents of a war who intend to conquer rather than defend territory: "Hyle & Coban were his two chosen ones, for Emissaries / In War: forth from his bosom they went & return'd" (*J*, 18.41–42); "His Children exil'd from his breast pass to and fro" (*J*, 19.1). The conquerors are, of necessity, in exile from the place proper to them. In the ensuing lines, the Polypus-invaded landscape takes on the features of the Polypus, especially poison, hate, devouring, disease, and any "Form at variance with Itself" (*J*, 69.6). All of it is traced to the same source as the Polypus, the bosom of Hand:

> from within his witherd breast grown narrow with his woes:
> The corn is turn'd to thistles & the apples into poison:
> The birds of song to murderous crows . . .
> And self-exiled from the face of light . . . he wanders up and down. (*J*, 19.9–11, 19.13–14)
> All his Affections now appear withoutside: all his Sons . . . each Double-form'd . . .
> Raging against their Human natures, ravning to gormandize
> The Human majesty and beauty of the Twentyfour.
> Condensing them into solid rocks with cruelty and abhorrence
> Suspition & revenge, & the seven diseases of the Soul.
> (*J*, 19.17, 19.20, 19.23–26)

When Albion finally "br[eaks] silence" (*J*, 20.42) to speak to Jerusalem, he locates himself in the Polypus-like web of poison, divided against himself and diseased:

> The disease of Shame covers me from head to feet: I have no hope
> Every boil upon my body is a separate & deadly Sin.
> Doubt first assaild me, then Shame took possession of me
> Shame divides Families. Shame hath divided Albion in sunder!
> First fled my Sons, & then my Daughters, then my Wild Animations
> My Cattle next, last ev'n the Dog of my Gate . . . drivn forth by my disease. (*J*, 21.3–8, 21.10)

In the following lines, Albion blames words for this destruction, lamenting, "What have I said? What have I done? O all-powerful Human Words! / You recoil back upon me in the blood of the Lamb" (*J*, 24.1–2). He also condemns the education that he has offered: "I have taught my children sacrifices of cruelty" (*J*, 23.17); "I have educated you in the crucifying cruelties of Demonstration" (*J*, 24.55).

In the closing lines of chapter 1, the features of the Polypus reappear in the lament for the loss of Jerusalem, for a past in which "In the Exchanges of London every Nation walkd / And London walkd in every Nation mutual in love & harmony / Albion coverd the whole Earth, England encompassd the Nations" (*J*, 24.42–44). The imposition of national boundaries is again figured as a wounding that is associated with revenge (*J*, 15.2, 19.26), planting or rooting, and the serpentine:

> Why did you take Vengeance O ye Sons of the mighty Albion?
> Planting these Oaken Groves: Erecting these Dragon Temples
> Injury the Lord heals but Vengeance cannot be healed . . .
> Vengeance is the destroyer of Grace & Repentance in the bosom
> Of the Injurer: in which the Divine Lamb is cruelly slain.
> (*J*, 25.3–5, 25.10–11)[48]

This figuring of war, regional boundaries, nationalism, and colonization as a kind of invasive Polypus protects the possibility of the survival of an uncorrupted identity. The vision of a past Jerusalem can be resurrected in the present only if that Polypus can be excised, and the wounds it created healed through an apocalyptic transformation like that which appears at the end of *Milton:* "Descend O Lamb of God & take away the imputation of Sin" (*J*, 25.12). Yet again, renewal is represented as the "casting off" of that which is not proper to the (healthy) body.

In chapter 3, addressed "To the Jews," the correspondence between preface, Polypus, and text is more overt; it is one of Blake's most extended elaborations of the vital/viral paradigm, and it is the chapter most explicitly concerned with the written word. Texts are emphasized throughout, even to the narrator asserting, "Record the terrible wonder . . . Shudder not, but Write, & the hand of God will assist you! / Therefore I write Albions last words" (*J*, 47.14, 47.17–18). In such remarks, Blake emphasizes the textuality of the narrative in a way that he does not in other chapters, as the religion of the book, writing, and disease intersect in his condemnation of Old Testament "Law." In the Polypus's only explicit appearance in chapter 3, Blake writes, "O Polypus of Death O Spectre over Europe and Asia / Withering the Human Form by Laws of Sacrifice for Sin" (*J*, 49.24–25). This apostrophe precisely echoes the prefatory verse:

> [Satan] witherd up sweet Zions Hill,

From every Nation of the Earth:
He witherd up Jerusalems Gates,
And in a dark Land gave her birth.
He witherd up the Human Form,
By laws of sacrifice for sin. (*J*, 27.49–54)

But the Polypus is also implicit in the "deadly Tree" of the chapter's opening lines, repeating the images of enrooting, poison, and limitation found in other chapters' representations of the Polypus:

A deadly Tree, he nam'd it Moral Virtue, and the Law
Of God who dwells in Chaos hidden from the human sight.
The Tree spread over him its cold shadows, (Albion groand)
They bent down, they felt the earth and again enrooting
Shot into many a Tree! an endless labyrinth of woe! (*J*, 28.15–19)

Such labyrinthine twinings are then identified with writing:

I am your Rational Power O Albion & that Human Form
You call Divine, is but a Worm seventy inches long
That creeps forth in a night & is dried in the morning sun
In fortuitous concourse of memorys accumulated & lost
It plows the Earth in its own conceit, it overwhelms the Hills
Beneath its winding labyrinths . . .
And shall Albions Cities remain when I pass over them
With my deluge of forgotten remembrances over the tablet.
(*J*, 29.5–10, 29.15–16)

While the inscription of memories by the "Human Form" is figured as plowing and so recalls the traditional conceit of writing as plowing, so closely connected to the vital paradigm in Hugh Latimer's *Sermon on the Ploughers* (1549),[49] it appears here in a pejorative, violent variation of that metaphor. It recalls as well the plowing of the globe into divided nations that recurs throughout *Milton* and *Jerusalem* and echoes the inscriptions of the "Spectrous Chaos," carved in cold tablets of stone.

The conceit of plowed land as an inscription of mental contents is later extended to explicitly include "error," as the same "Hills" lament Albion's disease: "Albion is sick! said every Valley, every mournful Hill / And every River: our brother Albion is sick to death," for "They have perswaded him of horrible falshoods! / They have sown errors over all his fruitful fields" (*J*, 36.11–12, 36.19–20). This is the plate that, as Stephen Leo Carr has noted, visually develops a contrast that is made more explicit as Blake's revisions progress and is related to the vital/viral imagery I am tracing:

> In the last complete version of *Jerusalem* (copy F), Blake carefully revised the left margin of plate 36 [40], transforming it into a clearly delineated tree. . . . This monochrome plate offers a more definite representation of a tree than does the sole illuminated version (E). Yet both late revisions establish a similar thematic contrast with the scene in the right margin: its exuberant human activity and ripe grapes are now counterbalanced by a stark, almost leafless (lifeless?) tree. The newly formed tree also plays off numerous other marginal designs, especially in *Jerusalem* 34 [38], whose chainlike vegetation is echoed at the top of plate 36, and in *Jerusalem* 49, which depicts a similar desolate tree.[50]

The Spectre is also physically identified with the Polypus, or "many footed,"

> Having a white Dot calld a Center from which branches out
> A Circle in continual gyrations. this became a Heart
> From which sprang numerous branches varying their motions
> Producing many Heads three or seven or ten, & hands & feet
> Innumerable at the will of the unfortunate contemplator
> Who becomes his food[:] such is the way of the Devouring
> Power. (*J*, 29.19–24)

I cite this description of the Spectre at length not only because it echoes the anatomy of the Polypus, as well as its medical association with tumors of the heart (repeated in chapter 1, in which the Polypus is repeatedly rooted in the bosom), but also because of this reference to "the unfortunate contemplator." It is in this chapter that "becoming what he beheld" becomes a chorus, and receives its only elaboration. In Blake's attempted rhetorical conversion of the Jews, the Polypus-like entity propagates the legislative constraints of the Old Testament and, as those who read it "become what they behold," consumes those exposed to it.

In chapter 2, after condemning the "Laws" against "Sin," Blake writes, "they looked on one-another & became what they beheld," and then,

> all terrified fled: they became what they beheld.
> If Perceptive Organs vary: Objects of Perception seem to vary:
> If the Perceptive Organs close: their Objects seem to close also:
> Consider this O mortal Man! O worm of sixty winters said Los
> Consider Sexual Organization & hide thee in the dust.
> (*J*, 30.50, 30.54–58)

Such "beholding" is repeatedly identified with disease:

> does Mercy endure Atonement?
> No! It is Moral Severity, & destroys Mercy in its Victim.
> So speaking, not yet infected with the Error & Illusion,
> Los shudder'd at beholding Albion, for his disease
> Arose upon him pale and ghastly. (*J*, 35.25–36.2)
> Have you also caught the infection of Sin & stern Repentance?
> I see Disease arise upon you! (*J*, 38.75–76)

"Strucken with Albions disease they become what they behold" (*J*, 39.32): "these Laws" "are death / To every energy of man" (*J*, 31.11–12), and they spread virally from their inscription to the population.

While the commandments of the Old Testament propagate virally, Christianity offers the vital half of the model—a vaccine that is structurally similar but medically antithetical to the disease that it destroys. Instead of a "deadly Tree" named "Moral Virtue" (*J*, 28.15) and an Albion "perswaded" of "horrible falshoods" (*J*, 36.19), a Bard "speak[s] the words of God / In mild perswasion: bringing leaves of the Tree of Life" (*J*, 41.8–9). The Saviour addresses Albion,

> Displaying the Eternal Vision! the Divine Similitude!
> In loves and tears of brothers, sisters, sons, fathers, and friends
> Which if Man ceases to behold, he ceases to exist:
> Saying. Albion! . . .
> We live as One Man; for contracting our infinite senses
> We behold multitude; or expanding: we behold as one,
> As One Man all the Universal Family; and that One Man
> We call Jesus the Christ: and he in us, and we in him,
> Live in perfect harmony. (*J*, 34.11–21)

Again, that word "harmony" erases difference, but in this case it is produced by beholding the "Eternal Vision," as the population again "becomes what it beholds," by regarding the Christian ideal as propounded by Blake—within the text as well as through it.

In the final chapter, hybridity is condemned to be erased by that vision. Just before the final crisis,

> Los terrified cries: trembling & weeping & howling! Beholding
> What do I see? The Briton Saxon Roman Norman amalgamating
> In my Furnaces into One Nation the English: & taking refuge
> In the Loins of Albion. The Canaanite united with the fugitive
> Hebrew, whom she divided into Twelve, & sold into Egypt
> Then scatterd the Egyptian & Hebrew to the four Winds!
> This sinful Nation Created in our Furnaces & Looms is Albion.
> (*J*, 91.58–92.6)

Albion's death, "closed apart from all Nations" (*J*, 94.14), and then his resurrection into "Friendship & Brotherhood" (*J*, 96.16), facilitates the transcendence of these divisions:

> Albion stood before Jesus in the Clouds
> Of Heaven Fourfold among the Visions of God in Eternity
> Awake! Awake Jerusalem! O lovely Emanation of Albion
> Awake and overspread all Nations. (*J*, 96.42–97.2)

The production of this unity is represented in a passage that transmutes the features of the Polypus and its brethren into a divine version:

> in regenerations terrific or complacent varying
> According to the subject of discourse & every Word & Every Character
> Was Human according to the Expansion or Contraction, the Translucence or
> Opakeness of Nervous fibres such was the variation of Time & Space
> Which vary according as the Organs of Perception vary & they walked
> To & fro in Eternity as One Man reflecting each in each & clearly seen

> And seeing: according to fitness & order. And I heard Jehovah speak
> Terrific from his Holy Place & saw the Words of the Mutual Covenant Divine. (*J*, 98.34–41)

At the same time, the Polypus-like trees disappear: "Where is the Covenant of Priam, the Moral Virtues of the Heathen / Where is the Tree of Good & Evil that rooted beneath the cruel heel / Of Albions Spectre" (*J*, 98.46–48).

Like Bhabha's colonial agents, Blake divides the population with which he is concerned into different kinds that can then be controlled through means specific to their differences; and, like Lloyd's anxious nationalists, he condemns hybridity wherever he finds (and does not obviously produce) it—as he writes at the outset, "Every Thing has its Vermin" (*J*, 1). In *Jerusalem*, Blake goes beyond the apocalyptic moment to imagine what the postapocalyptic future will hold, and, because that future knows no religious or national divisions, the fall that precedes apocalyptic renewal is framed in precisely those terms. For Blake's Christian, nationally specific utopia to prevail, the Jews and Deists must convert, and the Public and the Christians must acknowledge that Britishness is a product of national interminglings that can contain the global erasure of national differences as well as submit to Blake's definitions of a true public and a legitimate Christianity.

As Barrell has shown, Blake's representations of "the Public" are, to a large extent, defined as Blake's ideal audience: as Barrell succinctly puts it, "[W]hen the judgment of the audience is correct, it is a public; it remains a mere audience when its judgment is mistaken."[51] In colonizing these cultural spaces, subsuming them in his artistic, religious, and national rubric, Blake falls back on the mechanisms and rhetoric of the more usual imperialists, from the transformative power of texts and the administrative command of taxonomies to the propagandist force of an identification of the unacceptable with disease. By dividing *Jerusalem* into four prefaces and four chapters, with each section addressed to a different division of the population—the Public, the Jews, the Deists, and the Christians—and providing a prosaic and then more oblique poetic critique directed at persuading that group to accede to his general vision, Blake submits his readership to an administrative taxonomy. This taxonomy facilitates his management of the differences that he would erase in plotting the return of a metanational Jerusalem and the homogeneity that Blake's new acceptance of the term "harmony" implies.[52] At the same time, he characterizes the continuance of such differences as disease, infection, pestilence, cancerous growths, roots invading the earth, poison, intoxicating liquids, and pollution while locating his own text as the revitalizing doppelgänger of those destructive propagative mechanisms, different in its social effects but not in its mode of operation. In imagining a universal renovation, Blake "buys the smallpox" and becomes what he has so long beheld—the producer of "print" that "murder[s] by analyzing, that [he] / May take the aggregate."

We see here the forerunners of the twentieth-century cliché that the first step in a revolution is to seize the radio station. In each of these works, published discourse bears with it, as a term of its publication, the possibility of sociopolitical change. Regardless of its truth value or prophetic authority, the circulated text affects the way in which its readers perceive the world around them. During the eighteenth century and Romantic period, the battlefield of political discourse shifted from Runnymede to any publicly accessible domain. By "the witchcraft of a proclamation," popular opinion could be formed and transformed outside of the bounds of authority. Hegemony could no longer depend on treaties, deeds, legislation, and wealth to sustain its control, but needed to maintain its claim to authority by controlling public representations of itself and its areas of responsibility. And, with an increasingly literate, wealthy, and politicized populace, popular opinion was becoming very difficult to determine, or even manage, while the ability of conventional authority to sell ideology became compromised through its widely disseminated association with the taint of Cowper's fountain and "the iron hand of Power" (*M,* 25.5). Thus, while the government seized control over the publication of discourse—by censoring print, banning large meetings, expanding the definition of treason to include utterances, and establishing a network of spies to monitor private speech—its supporters infiltrated counterhegemonic discourse by producing ballads of their own, distributing narratives in the voice of the disenfranchised, and printing cheap engravings of paintings that characterized those in power as heroic and self-sacrificing.[53] Blake's verse is part of this battle over representational control, and it employs the same weapons, including the vital/viral paradigm and the medical discourse that invests it with such power, as well as "the form of a national epic,"[54] as each side tries to purge the political body of matter that it characterizes as foreign or unhealthy in order to justify and sanctify its purgation.

Conclusion

In these final pages, I would like to return to some of the ways in which Blake has already been represented by contemporary scholarship as strange—or as more normal than we might realize—by way of a prelude to considering the sociopolitical implications of his formal, defamiliarizing strategies. In *The Political Theory of Painting,* Barrell argues that in both U.S. and British streams of Blake criticism, "Blake becomes a founding father of the liberal individualism which has been the prevailing ideology of 'Blake Studies,' and which can understand the public only as an invasion of private space—as 'standardization,' as 'big government.'"[1] Barrell proceeds to suggest that Blake had the same agenda as Sir Joshua Reynolds, namely the constitution of a civic public, and disagreed only on some of the precise terms of its constitution.[2] Blake conceived of individuality not as "unique," but as, according to Barrell, "what constitutes the ground of his unity with eternity . . . with Christ, and so with other men insofar as they acknowledge their generic character"; individuality is thus the basis of a community that transcends the divisions of the mundane, fallen world.[3] As Damrosch writes, "Imaginative experience is valid because it is guaranteed by the Divine Imagination, but its expressive symbols are contaminated by the fallen world from which they are drawn. The languages in which symbols are represented—visual as well as verbal—are 'stubborn structures,' barriers to vision as well as aids to it."[4] And herein lies the problem of recuperating the individual character described by Barrell: it can be described only generically, in fallen language, and relative to the mundane world to which it is antagonistic. The absolute unity of the alternative community that Blake posits in his later works arguably reflects not its character, but the limits of mundane access to it. In *Jerusalem,* Blake locates social unity just beyond the horizon of the limitations of the mundane:

> We live as One Man; for contracting our infinite senses
> We behold multitude; or expanding: we behold as one,

> As One Man all the Universal Family; and that One Man
> We call Jesus the Christ. (*J*, 34.17–20)

At the point of ultimate contraction and expansion, the center and the circumference (to use P. B. Shelley's phrase) of possibility, "We live as One Man" and "we behold as one." But even as Blake holds out the possibility of this transcendental unity, he withdraws it from the world of the social present: "that One Man / We call Jesus the Christ." We "call" it "Jesus the Christ" and so even the utopian community is grafted onto the world of linguistic production and mediated by finite senses.

Barrell's model of the differentiation of communities, "this/that/the other," is useful here. In *The Infection of Thomas De Quincey,* Barrell posits a dynamic in which the working classes operate as a medial figure between the hegemonic definition of Englishness and its Oriental Other. "That" is at once an ally of Englishness against the latter and the site of an internal orient that threatens "this" by its very proximity; "that" is also the hybrid space that is at once strange but assimilable because its strangeness is only partial and so can be purged once it is identified. The strategy rests on defamiliarizing the opposition while allowing the possibility that it may yet be assimilated to "this," and instituting one's own familiarity as the communal one—a strategy used far beyond the construction of a non-Oriental Englishness.[5] As Eaves shows in *The Counter-Arts Conspiracy,* art and nation were discursively entangled during Blake's lifetime, and the compromise of one was grasped as a threat to the other. Eaves suggests that Blake's different inflection of "English-school art history" arises from his dependence on the Bible as the basis of artistic value, a dependence for which every step away from the original is dogged by error; "where intellectual change is necessarily a scandal that can be accounted for only as theft and self-betrayal, significant historical difference is assigned entirely to the intellectual crime rate."[6] Conspirators, strongly identified with foreign influences, pervert the growth of British art,[7] and this misdirected development appears in *Jerusalem* as cancer and disease, a perilous cultural invasion. But Eaves's emphasis on conspiracy leaves open the other side of the question, namely the terms on which Blake's work sought to circulate as a purgative medicine or as revitalizing nourishment against the pressure of legislation that would characterize much of it (including his utterances to Schofield) as viral. The world of "that" contains both "this" and "other," and it moves between those poles. Thus, Blake does not identify the Bible as a "foreign" influence but assimilates it into his definition of Englishness via Milton's nationalist identification of England with the New Jerusalem, while the Old Testament is rejected as an Urizenic text. The Bible makes possible Blake's critique of contemporary culture as alien but not irrecuperable because of its very hybridity relative to that culture: it enacts, through the typological relations between the Old and New Testaments, the purgation of error that leaves valued elements of the culture intact. The defamiliarizing strategies of Jesus noted by James L. Resseguie are appropriated by Blake, to similar ends—to purge the best culture that currently exists, the Gothic-Hebraic, of that which prevents it from fulfilling its utopian potential as a Christian Albion.[8] In Blake's deployment of the model, the prevailing cultural codes constitute "that": Blake's subject is rendered hybrid by its engagement with a corrupting and false exteriority, and the cultural space is itself rendered hybrid by its infection by false and alien paradigms, but neither is so corrupt that it cannot be purged and corrected through the circulation of truths by visionaries such as Blake. Blake's texts map the sites of hybridity in British culture, the mergings of alien and familiar in which the flawed familiar can be renovated through the alien and the flawed alien can be purged from the familiar, but in doing so reflect the circulation of that same model of hybridity and familiarity in the public domain.

In *The Laocoön,* Blake offers a condensed but complex articulation of such entanglements: the snakes sent by the gods to punish the priest for speaking are visually and verbally echoed by the texts with which the struggling figures are encircled. The bibliographical and historiographical dependence on linearity, the formation of disciplinary codes (art, science, religion) that limit and divide the possible, and the identification of cultural with national identity—all appear in *The Laocoön* as the form of the engraving challenges their key premises. Blake's critique of these restraints, as I have tried to show in preceding chapters, typically proceeds in this way, that is, simultaneously on the level of content and form. Blake defamiliarizes the forms that encode content, calling attention to that which is skimmed rather than challenged because it looks familiar, and forcing a level of engagement from all of his readers rather than simply expecting it from a minority of them. Blake's illuminations and manipulations of literary genre, from the ballad and the lyric to the aphorism and the epic, as well as his resistance to the regularity of typeface or even post-Johnson orthography, do not simply mark the uniqueness of Blake but enact a critique of what marks the normality of most of his contemporary authors and artists. His eccentricities are not always comprehensible, nor are the variants in his texts always explainable, but a pattern of resistance informed by contemporary theories of art, history, politics, gender, and hermeneutics nevertheless emerges from his corpus. The search for Blake in these texts raises the same problematic as the characters in Blake's works, that is, we see Blake caught in and struggling with a maelstrom of cultural forces rather than gaining special access to his interiority.

In "Dangerous Blake," W. J. T. Mitchell proposes the "defamiliarization and the rediscovery of Blake's exotic, archaic, alien, and eccentric character," suggesting that Blake's "madness, obscenity, and incoherence" are incompatible with conventional parameters of critical discourse: thus, for Frye, he suggests, "to speak of madness in Blake or any other artist is to renounce the claim to speak critically."[9] Mitchell argues, "The greatest challenge and the most threatening scandal for the formalist appropriation of Blake is the threat of incoherence, nonsense, failure to communicate; the presence of accident, random sloppiness, lack of technical facility,"[10] marking as threatening the gulf between practice and theory, between the actuality of Blake's art and the imagined essence of art. Quietly at work in Mitchell's representation of formalism, and of what is acceptably visible to its critical discourse, are a series of academic hierarchies that we rarely examine and are anything but "disinterested," hierarchies that exoticize, alienate, or otherwise dismiss that which does not fit into a complex of paradigms in which a state of mind that impedes an individual's productivity is "madness," earthiness is "obscenity," and an untotalized text is "incoherent." These paradigms—roughly capitalist, puritan, and rationalist, in that order—are fundamentally aligned with the British hegemony of Blake's time, a period in which Britain developed an identity that was insistently commercial, as well as intrinsically "civilized" and Protestant, and everything, from the raced, classed, and gendered political subject to the work of art to a subspecies in a botanical taxonomy, had to be "in its fit place," a phrase that Mitchell repeats as the hallmark of a formalist aesthetic.[11] We must ask ourselves where Coleridge's notion of organic poetic form slides into a natural political order in which there is, as Jeffrey insists, a head in control of a body. Or, to put it another way, how far do the structures of power that informed Romantic-era formulations of social order inform Romantic theories of poetic form, and vice versa?

For Blake, as for many of his contemporaries, the division between the aesthetic and the substantial, form and content, and the ideology of genre and the genre of ideology was effectively a fuzzy one. Late-eighteenth-century England cried out for a contemporary school of art that would adequately reflect its national, and imperial, importance; propagandist engravings and tracts were circulated to sway public opinion; and treason was redefined to reflect the power of the word to effect political change. The Two Acts of 1795 extended the provenance of the term "treason" to include speeches and publications, marking the recognition, or at least the fear, that the publication of words, vocally or textually, constitutes an "overt action," and, moreover, an action that can alter the political order as surely as the sword. The network of spies that crisscrossed Britain and Ireland during the period, as well as legislation that prohibited meetings beyond a particular size and required that texts be "stamped" by an official institution before publication, testify to the government's intense, and wide-ranging, concern with what people were saying to each other. As Paul Keen's recent study, *The Crisis of Literature in the 1790s,* reveals, moreover, the anxiety over the circulation of print—and who gets to write that print, and how—can be traced throughout British media at the turn of the century.[12]

The effects of legislation and the wider cultural debate in which it intervened permeate Blake's texts, and inform the terms of their production. Each of his engravings for *The Book of Job* includes the crucial phrase "Published as the Act directs," but many other privately printed works do not, highlighting the context in which Blake's publishing had to operate. The period saw a stunning transformation of the configuration of the political domain and the way in which it was policed—to secure the continuation of the status quo by securing the circulation of discourse—as the sphere of political activity was extended from the body to the book. In this transformation, the range of genres and media increased exponentially with the segments of society included in the debate, as formal elements were used to target particular groups (as in, for instance, the circulation of political ballads metrically amenable to oral delivery among the newly literate and still illiterate, and of turgid epics among the middle and upper classes).

Blake's contention that art is a reflection of the national condition, his figuring of national bards, his many statements on the power of art to alter perception, his nationalist defense of the English language, and his libertarian condemnation of rhyme in the proclamation "Poetry Fetter'd, Fetters the Human Race!" (*J,* 3)—all of these assertions are implicated in the extension of textual political power from parliamentary and coffeehouse debate to the fundamentally transformed and extended domain of popular allegiances and opinions. Because of this transformation, Blake, and many like him, were not only perceived to be "dangerous," but legally defined as a danger to social order. They were the virus against which the state demanded inoculation and cure through, for instance, the sedition laws that allowed Blake's prosecution in the Schofield affair. In taking formal as well as verbal risks, Blake does not endanger a formalist aesthetic, but—from *Poetical Sketches* to *Jerusalem, The Laocoön* and the curses he hurled at Schofield—poses a threat to the concealment of its investments.

Notes

INTRODUCTION

1. Benedict Anderson, *Imagined Communities: Reflections on the Origin and Spread of Nationalism,* rev. ed. (New York: Verso, 1991).

2. Ernest Gellner, *Nations and Nationalism* (Oxford: Blackwell, 1983), 7.

3. "Of a National Character in Literature," *Blackwood's Edinburgh Magazine* 3 (September 1818): 707.

4. Gellner—suggestively given this remark, in *Blackwood's,* that the author is lost in the nation—argues repeatedly that writers on nationalism historically "did not really make much difference": "In the case of nationalism (though the same is not always true of other movements), the actual formulation of the idea or ideas, the question concerning who said or wrote precisely what, doesn't matter much. The key idea is in any case so very simple and easy that anyone can make it up almost at any time, which is partly why nationalism can claim that nationalism is always natural" (*Nations and Nationalism,* 124, 126).

5. Ibid., 133.

6. Nicholas M. Williams, *Ideology and Utopia in the Poetry of William Blake* (Cambridge: Cambridge University Press, 1998), 26.

7. Leopold Damrosch Jr., *Symbol and Truth in Blake's Myth* (Princeton: Princeton University Press, 1980), 3.

8. See, for example, David Hume, "Of National Characters," in *David Hume: The Philosophical Works,* 4 vols., ed. Thomas Hill Green and Thomas Hodge Grose (Aalen, Germany: Scientia Verlag, 1964), 3:244–58.

9. Ibid., 31.

10. M. H. Abrams, *Natural Supernaturalism: Tradition and Revolution in Romantic Literature* (New York: Norton, 1971), 13.

11. Linda Colley, *Britons: Forging the Nation, 1707–1837* (New Haven: Yale University Press, 1992).

12. Gellner, *Nations and Nationalism,* 125.

13. David V. Erdman, *Blake: Prophet against Empire: A Poet's Interpretation of the History of His Own Times,* rev. ed. (Garden City, N.Y.: Doubleday, 1969), xii; W. J. T. Mitchell, "Dangerous Blake," *Studies in Romanticism* 21 (1982): 410–16.

14. Susan Fox, *Poetic Form in Blake's* Milton (Princeton: Princeton University Press, 1976), 4; Damrosch, *Symbol and Truth,* 350. Further examples abound: Tilottama Rajan suggests that a passage from *Milton* has "the effect of defamiliarizing Milton's perversity" (*The Supplement of*

Reading: Figures of Understanding in Romantic Theory and Practice [Ithaca: Cornell University Press, 1990], 206); Donald Ault describes his study of *The Four Zoas* as an "attempt to defamiliarize the reader with Blake's poetics" (*Narrative Unbound: Re-Visioning Blake's* The Four Zoas [Barrytown, N.Y.: Station Hill, 1987], xi); Jon Mee offers "a less familiar context for understanding Blake" (*Dangerous Enthusiasm: William Blake and the Culture of Radicalism in the 1790s* [Oxford: Clarendon, 1992], 226); Williams refers to "the exhilarating newness of his conceptions" (*Ideology and Utopia,* 2); and Angela Esterhammer, taking Fox's point further, suggests that, "in Blake's case, his use of historical names is unavoidably influenced by his admixture of names like 'Los' and 'Enitharmon,' which flaunt the fact that they do not refer, at least not to any referent the reader has experience of. Blake's use of unfamiliar names defamiliarizes the whole concept of naming, exposing the fact that names in imaginative literature do not function the way they are supposed to in real-world discourse" (*Creating States: Studies in the Performative Language of John Milton and William Blake* [Toronto: University of Toronto Press, 1994], 182).

15. Victor Shklovsky, "Art as Technique" (1917), in *Russian Formalist Criticism: Four Essays,* trans. Lee T. Lemon and Marion J. Reis (Lincoln: University of Nebraska Press, 1965), 5–24. The *OED* does not list any earlier occurrences of the word "defamiliarization" and defines it first as a translation of Shklovsky's term that is specific to literary theory, "esp. Russian Formalist." The supplementary definition describes its more casual usage in post-1971 discourse, while still connecting it to its Russian Formalist roots.

16. Regarding the difficulties of translating Shklovsky's phrase *priem ostranenija* ("the device of making strange"), see R. H. Stacy, *Defamiliarization in Language and Literature* (Syracuse: Syracuse University Press, 1977), 2–3. Stacy includes "estrangement" as a possible translation of *ostranenija,* suggesting the social implications of removing the percipient from a socially constructed frame of reference.

17. Charles Robert Maturin, *Melmoth the Wanderer: A Tale* (1820), ed. Alethea Hayter (Markham, Ontario: Penguin, 1984), 298–99 (latter emphasis mine).

18. Pierre Bourdieu, "Censorship and the Imposition of Form," in *Language and Symbolic Power,* ed. John B. Thompson, trans. Gino Raymond and Matthew Adamson (Cambridge: Harvard University Press, 1991), 138, 139.

19. I use the term "codes" in a sense similar to that used in the English translation of Michel Foucault's *The Order of Things:* "The fundamental codes of a culture—those governing its language, its schemas of perception, its exchanges, its techniques, its values, the hierarchy of its practices—establish for every man, from the very first, the empirical orders with which he will be dealing and within which he will be at home" (*The Order of Things: An Archaeology of the Human Sciences* [1966; New York: Random House, 1970], xx).

20. Bourdieu, "Censorship," 158. Shklovsky's theory of the effects and value of defamiliarization sometimes overlaps with Romantic aesthetics. Shklovsky argues, "The technique of art is to make objects 'unfamiliar,' to make forms difficult, to increase the difficulty and length of perception because the process of perception is an aesthetic end in itself and must be prolonged" ("Art as Technique," 12). He also extends the aesthetic into the epistemological, maintaining that *ostranenija* facilitates art's attempt "to make the stone stony. The purpose of art is to impart

the sensation of things as they are perceived and not as they are known" (12). Readers of Romantic literature will find these statements somewhat familiar: "Poetry lifts the veil from the hidden beauty of the world, and makes familiar objects be as if they were not familiar" (Percy Bysshe Shelley, "A Defence of Poetry," in *Shelley's Poetry and Prose,* ed. Donald H. Reiman and Sharon B. Powers [New York: Norton, 1977], 487); "to combine the child's sense of wonder and novelty with the appearances, which every day for perhaps forty years had rendered familiar . . . this is the character and privilege of genius" (Samuel Taylor Coleridge, *Biographia Literaria or Biographical Sketches of My Literary Life and Opinions,* 2 vols., ed. James Engell and W. Jackson Bate, 1:80–81. Vol. 7 of *The Collected Works of Samuel Taylor Coleridge* [Princeton: Princeton University Press, 1983]).

Behind P. B. Shelley's and Coleridge's assertions is the premise that the reader has turned from a suprafamiliarity that all share towards the false familiar generated by experience and paradigms, and it is this general epistemological taxonomy that contains, but is not limited to, the aesthetic. William Wordsworth claims for his verse this suprafamiliarity and distinguishes it from the unnatural excess of other literature but, in doing so, isolates literature along national lines. By extensively characterizing his literature as familiar and briefly decrying other literature as "frantic," "extravagant," "sickly," and "outrageous," Wordsworth defamiliarizes the properly unfamiliar and familiarizes what he classifies as properly familiar, valorizing it by claiming that the familiar is the resource of good poetry: "The remotest discoveries of the Chemist, the Botanist, or Mineralogist, will be as proper objects of the Poet's art as any upon which it can be employed, if the time should ever come when these things shall be familiar to us" (preface to the *Lyrical Ballads* in *William Wordsworth,* ed. Stephen Gill [New York: Oxford University Press, 1989], 599, 607). Stacy notes this double agenda of defamiliarization: "the artist familiarizes by defamiliarizing, in the sense that, if successful, he brings to our recognition a new or different or more striking vision; he renews our familiarity, or even refamiliarizes us, with some more or less ordinary facet of reality, image, literary tradition, or resource of the language" (*Defamiliarization in Language and Literature,* 49).

21. Edmund Burke, "Speech on Opening of Impeachment" (15 February 1788), in *India: The Launching of the Hastings Impeachment, 1786–1788,* ed. P. J. Marshall, vol. 6 of *The Writings and Speeches of Edmund Burke,* ed. Paul Langford (Oxford: Clarendon, 1991), 271.

22. Ibid., 275.

23. Ibid., 278.

24. Steven Goldsmith, *Unbuilding Jerusalem: Apocalypse and Romantic Representation* (Ithaca: Cornell University Press, 1993), 153, 160.

25. Ibid., 164.

26. Mee, *Dangerous Enthusiasm,* 1–2.

27. Northrop Frye, *Fearful Symmetry: A Study of William Blake* (1947; reprint, Princeton: Princeton University Press, 1969), 70; Erdman, *Prophet against Empire,* 202.

28. S. Foster Damon, *A Blake Dictionary: The Ideas and Symbols of William Blake,* rev. ed. (London: Brown University Press, 1988), xxv.

29. Benedict Anderson, *Imagined Communities,* 4; Anthony D. Smith, "Neo-Classicist and Romantic Elements in the Emergence of Nationalist Conceptions," in *Nationalist Movements,*

ed. Anthony D. Smith (London: Macmillan, 1976), 75. Gellner, rather than characterizing nationalism as a consequence of revolutionary fear, Napoleonic aggression, or the post-Enlightenment strain against neoclassicism, argues that the industrial age created the social conditions through which nationalism could emerge, by, for instance, requiring education and mass communication to produce competent workers for the new economy (*Nations and Nationalism*).

30. *A Full Report of the Trial at Bar in the Court of King's Bench, of William Drennan, MD Upon an Indictment Charging Him with Having Written and Published a Seditious Libel with the Speeches of Counsel, and the Opinions of the Court at Large* (Dublin: Rea and Johnson, 1794), in *The Trial of William Drennan,* ed. John Francis Larkin (Dublin: Irish Academic Press, 1991), qtd. 39.

31. John Barrell, *The Political Theory of Painting from Reynolds to Hazlitt: 'The Body of the Public'* (New Haven: Yale University Press, 1986), 237.

32. William Richey, "The French Revolution: Blake's Epic Dialogue with Edmund Burke," *ELH* 59 (1992): 824.

33. Barrell, *Political Theory of Painting,* 254.

34. Homi K. Bhabha, "Introduction: Narrating the Nation," in *Nation and Narration,* ed. Homi K. Bhabha (New York: Routledge, 1990), 3.

35. Charles Bernstein, preface to *The Politics of Poetic Form: Poetry and Public Policy,* ed. Charles Bernstein (New York: ROOF, 1990), vii. I take the term "crisis of literature" from Paul Keen's excellent study *The Crisis of Literature in the 1790s* (Cambridge: Cambridge University Press, 1999).

36. Stuart Peterfreund, "The Problem of Originality and Blake's Poetical Sketches," *ELH* 52 (1985): 699. This essay is reprinted in the important collection *Speak Silence: Rhetoric and Culture in Blake's Poetical Sketches,* ed. Mark L. Greenberg (Detroit: Wayne State University Press, 1996), 71–103, but all quotations are taken from the *ELH* version.

37. Paul Youngquist, "Reading the Apocalypse: The Narrativity of Blake's *Jerusalem,*" *Studies in Romanticism* 32 (1993): 601–2.

38. Molly Anne Rothenberg, "Parasiting America: The Radical Function of Heterogeneity in Thomas Paine's Early Writings," *Eighteenth-Century Studies* 25 (1992): 331–51.

39. John Lucas, *England and Englishness: Ideas of Nationhood in English Poetry, 1688-1900* (London: Hogarth, 1990), 76. In recent years, a number of investigations of nationalism in English Romantic literature have appeared, including numerous articles—among them such notables as Marlon B. Ross's "Romancing the Nation State: The Poetics of Romantic Nationalism," in *Macropolitics of Nineteenth-Century Literature: Nationalism, Exoticism, Imperialism,* ed. Jonathan Arac and Harriet Ritvo (Philadelphia: University of Pennsylvania Press, 1991), 56–85—and such volume-length studies as David Aram Kaiser, *Romanticism, Aesthetics, and Nationalism* (Cambridge: Cambridge University Press, 1999); Cannon Schmitt, *Alien Nation: Nineteenth-Century Gothic Fictions and English Nationality* (Philadelphia: University of Pennsylvania Press, 1997); and Katie Trumpener, *Bardic Nationalism: The Romantic Novel and the British Empire* (Princeton: Princeton University Press, 1997). The emphasis as yet is on Scottish and Irish nationalisms, but competing notions of English nationhood, as Lucas demonstrates, were important to English literature.

CHAPTER 1

1. "Vagaries," as Keats seems to be fully aware, is derived from the Latin *vagari,* "to wander": this playful wandering links the images of this passage in the letter, from his attempt to "run away from what was in [his] head" to the leaping checkers and the leapfrogging poets (letter to John Hamilton Reynolds [3 May 1818], in *Letters of John Keats,* ed. Robert Gittings [Oxford: Oxford University Press, 1986], 94).

2. Ibid.

3. Jonathan Goldberg, *Writing Matter: From the Hands of the English Renaissance* (Stanford: Stanford University Press, 1990).

4. See Roland Barthes, *S/Z,* trans. Richard Miller, preface by Richard Howard (1970; New York: Hill and Wang, 1974).

5. David Punter, "Blake: Social Relations of Poetic Form," *Literature and History* 8 (1982): 185.

6. Marshall McLuhan, *Understanding Media: The Extensions of Man* (Toronto: McGraw-Hill, 1964), 174, 175. On the ways in which Blake's own printing practices disrupted such repetition, see Edward Larrissy, "Spectral Imposition and Visionary Imposition: Printing and Repetition in Blake," in *Blake in the Nineties,* ed. Steve Clark and David Worrall (New York: St. Martin's, 1999), 61–77.

7. Jacques Derrida, *Of Grammatology,* trans. Gayatri Chakravorty Spivak (Baltimore: Johns Hopkins University Press, 1976), 59.

8. In much of the secondary literature and criticism, the name of the statue and the Homeric character is variously spelled "Laocoön" or "Laocoon," while references to Lessing's text often use the German form, *Laokoon.* When quoting, I have retained the author's or translator's spelling, but I consistently use "Laocoön" otherwise, since that is the spelling that appears in the editions of Blake that I consulted. To add to the confusion, there are four Laocoöns circulating in this chapter: Lessing's text, Blake's work, the Rhodians' statue, and the priest in Homer's *Iliad.* I have tried to make the distinctions clear.

9. Essick and Viscomi use the recent discovery of an 1826 watermark on one of the two extant impressions of the plate and other features of the paper used for those prints to suggest that both "were most likely the quarters of the same Whatman 1826 sheet" (Robert N. Essick and Joseph Viscomi, eds., *Milton, A Poem and the Final Illuminated Works,* vol. 5 of *The Illuminated Books of William Blake,* ed. David Bindman [Princeton: Princeton University Press, 1998], 241). They convincingly support that dating further through reference to changes in Blake's printing and engraving practices as well as the content of his writings (see 241–43).

10. See Essick and Viscomi, *Milton, A Poem,* 241.

11. For a discussion of the influence of emblem books on Blake, see Jean H. Hagstrum, *William Blake, Poet and Painter: An Introduction to the Illuminated Verse* (Chicago: University of Chicago Press, 1964), esp. 48–57.

12. David Bindman, introduction and notes to *The Complete Graphic Works of William Blake,* ed. David Bindman (London: Thames and Hudson, 1986), 487 n.

13. Mark Poster, *The Mode of Information: Poststructuralism and Social Context* (Chicago: University of Chicago Press, 1990), 11.

14. Morris Eaves, *William Blake's Theory of Art* (Princeton: Princeton University Press, 1982); Morris Eaves, *The Counter-Arts Conspiracy: Art and Industry in the Age of Blake* (Ithaca: Cornell University Press, 1992).

15. I refer throughout to the McCormick translation: Gotthold Ephraim Lessing, *Laocoön: An Essay on the Limits of Painting and Poetry* (1766), trans. Edward Allen McCormick (Baltimore: Johns Hopkins University Press, 1984), and cite page references parenthetically.

16. Simon Richter, *Laocoon's Body and the Aesthetics of Pain: Winckelmann, Lessing, Herder, Moritz, Goethe* (Detroit: Wayne State University Press, 1992), 19.

17. Regarding the pervasiveness of the Laocoön in eighteenth-century German art criticism, see Richter, *Laocoon's Body*, esp. 16–23.

18. Lessing is cited in passing with reference to *ut pictura poesis* by Hagstrum, *William Blake, Poet and Painter,* 8; and David Wagenknecht, afterword to *Critical Paths: Blake and the Argument of Method,* ed. Dan Miller, Mark Bracher, and Donald Ault (Durham, N.C.: Duke University Press, 1987), 316. Robert N. Essick mentions Lessing twice on the subject of natural signs, citing Lessing's *Laocoön* once, but not with reference to Blake's engraving of that name (*William Blake and the Language of Adam* [Toronto: Oxford University Press, 1989], 71–72, 77). Winckelmann is much better represented in Blake criticism, particularly in Morris Eaves's work.

19. Yvonne M. Carothers, "Space and Time in *Milton:* The 'Bard's Song,'" in *Blake in His Time,* ed. Robert N. Essick and Donald Pearce (Bloomington: Indiana University Press, 1978), 120, 121.

20. Morton D. Paley, "'Wonderful Originals'—Blake and Ancient Sculpture," in *Blake in His Time,* 196 n.

21. For a discussion of this, see Martin Bidney, *Blake and Goethe: Psychology, Ontology, Imagination* (Columbia: University of Missouri Press, 1988), xi–xii.

22. Blake possessed a copy of the translation and, according to Paley, it "was obviously of considerable importance to him" ("'Wonderful Originals,'" 196 n).

23. Describing a conversation with Fuseli about his aphorisms on painting, Mrs. Federica Lock wrote to Fanny Burney on 20 June 1789, "These were the subjects of his discussion—he considers the finest antique Statues—the Apollo, Laocoon, and Hercules and then describes what produces their particular beauty" (*The Collected English Letters of Henry Fuseli,* ed. David H. Weinglass [London: Kraus, 1982], 44). Fuseli refers to the statue often in his *Lectures on Painting* ([1801], in *The Life and Writings of Henry Fuseli,* 3 vols., ed. John Knowles [London: Kraus, 1982]).

24. Eudo C. Mason suggests, "The opening sentences of Fuseli's third Lecture are an almost literal translation of [an early] passage in Lessing" (*The Mind of Henry Fuseli* [London: Routledge, 1951], 206). The passages in question are the eighth and following paragraphs of Lessing's preface (4) and the first paragraph of part 1 of Fuseli's third lecture, "Invention"; see Henry Fuseli, *Lectures on Painting,* 2:133–34. For a comprehensive examination of connections between Blake's and Fuseli's thought, see Carol Louise Hall, *Blake and Fuseli: A Study in the Transmission of Ideas* (New York: Garland, 1985).

25. Some of the works that included engravings by Blake were reviewed in the *Analytical Review,* such as G. A. Burger's *Leonora,* J. G. Stedman's *Narrative to Surinam,* and C. G. Salzmann's *Elements of Morality;* see G. E. Bentley Jr., *Blake Records* (Toronto: Clarendon, 1969), 38–39, 55, 613

n. (Blake's contribution to *Elements of Morality* is not definitively established [see Bentley, *Blake Records,* 39 n]).

26. Mason, *Mind of Henry Fuseli,* 207.

27. R. R., review of *An Essay on the Picturesque, as compared with the sublime and the beautiful; and, on the Use of Studying Pictures, for the Purpose of improving real Landscape,* by Uvedale Price, *Analytical Review* 20 (1794): 259.

28. Ibid., 259 n.

29. Johann Joachim Winckelmann, *The History of Ancient Art,* 4 vols., trans. G. Henry Lodge (1764; 4 vols. in 2, Boston: James R. Osgood, 1880), 3–4:232–34.

30. Ibid., 3–4:228, 453 n.

31. Mason, *Mind of Henry Fuseli,* 48.

32. Essick and Viscomi, *Milton, A Poem,* 231.

33. Fuseli, *Lectures,* 2:134, 135.

34. Ibid., 2:137–38.

35. Ibid., 2:136–37.

36. Eaves, *The Counter-Arts Conspiracy,* 23.

37. Many of Blake's differences with Reynolds are derived from Reynolds's advocacy of the sequential view of art history: "*It is not in Terms that Reynolds & I disagree* Two Contrary Opinions can never by any Language be made alike. I say Taste & Genius are Not Teachable or Acquirable but are born with us Reynolds says the Contrary" (Anno. Reynolds, 659; my emphasis). This position is reiterated throughout the annotations (see, for instance, Anno. Reynolds, 639, 646, 656).

38. For a useful narrative of the Laocoön's alterations and duplications, see Richter, *Laocoon's Body,* esp. 23–24. Winckelmann not only addresses questions about the statue's authenticity, noting that the statue "is composed of two pieces, and not formed of a single block, which Pliny asserts of the group in the Baths of Titus" (*History of Ancient Art,* 3–4:231), but also refers explicitly to the modifications to the recovered statue: "Michael Angelo thought of restoring the right arm of Laocoön, which is wanting, and has been replaced by one in terra cotta. . . . This arm, around which the serpents are twined, was to have been held in a bent position across the head of the statue. It may have been the intention of Michael Angelo, in this approximation of the arm to the head, to render the idea of suffering in Laocoön. . . . But it seems as if the arm, bent over and across the head, would divide the principal attention. . . . For this reason Bernini extended the arm when he restored it in terra cotta," *History of Ancient Art,* 3–4:229–30. In other words, the Laocoön was reinterpreted and modified, under the guise of restoration, according to different aesthetic criteria.

39. Essick and Viscomi, *Milton, A Poem,* 230.

40. Janet A. Warner, *Blake and the Language of Art* (Kingston: McGill-Queen's University Press, 1984), 20; Winckelmann, *History of Ancient Art,* 3–4:229.

41. See 1 Kings 6–8, Ezekiel 42, and 2 Chronicles 2–4. In this context, it is also worth noting that Blake often used the Latin term for "carved," *sculptilis,* when identifying himself as the engraver. For example, in a number of engravings after designs by Thomas Stothard, Blake identified their different roles in Latin abbreviations: a circular design for *The Fall of Rosamond*

(1783) is signed "Blake Sculpt" on the right undercurve and "Stothard Delin." along the left undercurve; the frontispiece for the first volume of *The Wit's Magazine; or, Library of Momus* (1784), edited by Thomas Holcroft, is signed "Blake sculp" on the right and "Stothard Del." on the left. The distinction between sculpting and engraving collapses in the common Latin nomenclature, as in *The Laocoön.*

42. See Paley's essay "'Wonderful Originals'" for an examination of the sources in which Blake could have found arguments that coincided with his in claiming that the plastic arts began in the culture of the Old Testament. Paley takes his title and his primary subject from a passage with a similar argument in Blake's *Descriptive Catalogue of Pictures:*

> The two Pictures of Nelson and Pitt are compositions of a mythological cast, similar to those Apotheoses of Persian, Hindoo, and Egyptian antiquity . . . being preserved from some stupendous originals now lost or perhaps buried. . . . The Artist having been taken in vision into the ancient republics, monarchies, and patriarchates of Asia, has seen those wonderful originals called in the Sacred Scriptures the Cherubim, which were sculptured and painted on walls . . . and erected in the highly cultivated states of Egypt, Moab, Edom, Aram, among the Rivers of Paradise, being originals from which the the Greeks and Hetrurians copied . . . all the grand works of ancient art. (530–31)

43. Victor Anthony Rudowski, "Lessing *contra* Winckelmann," *Journal of Aesthetics and Art Criticism* 44 (1986): 241; Carol Jacobs, "The Critical Performance of Lessing's *Laokoon,*" *Modern Language Notes* 102 (1987): 487–88.

44. Jacobs, "Critical Performance of Lessing's *Laokoon,*" 488.

45. Qtd. Jacobs, "Critical Performance of Lessing's *Laokoon,*" 495 n; McCormick does not include the epigraph in his translation of Lessing's text.

46. Winckelmann, *History of Ancient Art,* 3–4:230.

47. Lessing's expression of distaste for systematic books anticipates his combative analysis of Winckelmann's works. Winckelmann, especially in the *History of Ancient Art,* systematically divided his subject into topics, subtopics, and sub-subtopics: "Art Among the Greeks," for instance, has a section on "Beauty of Individual Parts of the Body," which has subsections entitled "The Eyelids," "Objections to Joined Eyebrows," "The Ears Generally," and "Ears of Athletes or Pancratiasts" (*History of Ancient Art,* 1–2:xv). As Winckelmann puts it, "In considering beauty I have proceeded analytically, that is, from the whole to the parts. . . . [A]s a knowledge of general principles must, in every regular system, be presumed before any particular observations are made . . . I have given a preference to the analytical mode of proceeding" (*History of Ancient Art,* 1–2:380).

48. I allude here to Hagstrum's useful formulation of Blake's relationship to his artistic sources as "generic as well as genetic" (*William Blake, Poet and Painter,* 48).

49. Fuseli, *Lectures,* 2:133–34. Goethe also addresses this issue, concluding his discussion of the statue as a work of art by comparing it to Virgil's account of the incident in terms that recall Lessing's distinction between visual and verbal media: "We are doing a great injustice to Virgil and poetry in general if we compare, even for a moment, the most self-contained of all

sculptural masterpieces with the episodic treatment the subject receives in the *Aeneid*" (Johann Wolfgang von Goethe, "On the *Laocoon* Group" [1798], in *Essays on Art and Literature,* ed. John Gearey, trans. Ellen von Nardroff and Ernest H. von Nardroff [New York: Suhrkamp, 1986], 23).

50. Stephen C. Behrendt suggests that "*Milton* is in fact an interdisciplinary analogue to grand style eighteenth-century painting, an exercise in 'Sublime Allegory' that directly engages artist, subject and audience in a community activity of consciousness-raising" (*Reading William Blake* [New York: St. Martin's, 1992], 155). But it also brings writing closer to painting, as Lessing defined it, through what Behrendt terms "the Blakean principle of simultaneity that governs the entire work" (157); see also Fox, *Poetic Form.*

51. Lawrence Lipking, *The Ordering of the Arts in Eighteenth-Century England* (Princeton: Princeton University Press, 1970), 164–65.

52. See David E. James, "Blake's *Laocoön:* A Degree Zero of Literary Production," *PMLA* 98 (1983): 228.

53. Essick and Viscomi, *Milton, A Poem,* 220. For similar characterizations of the texts as axiomatic or aphoristic, see, for example, Eaves, *Counter-Arts,* 134; Max Plowman, ed., *William Blake: Poems and Prophecies* (1927; reprint with an introduction by Kathleen Raine, London: Dent, 1984), 288; and Hazard Adams, ed., *William Blake:* Jerusalem, *Selected Poems, and Prose* (New York: Holt, Rinehart and Winston, 1970), 585.

54. Walter Scott, *Waverley; or, 'Tis Sixty Years Since* (1814), ed. Andrew Hook (Markham, Ont.: Penguin, 1985), 60.

55. The two passages to which I refer are "The whole Business of Man Is / The Arts & All Things Common" (*L,* B) and

> What can be Created
> Can be Destroyed
> Adam is only
> The Natural Man
> & not the Soul
> or Imagination. (*L,* B)

Note that these two passages bracket the seventeen-line passage on the design, though their line of writing is perpendicular to it. I exclude examples in which capitalization is consistent with Blake's practice in prose, as when the next line is a new sentence or begins with a noun.

56. Essick and Viscomi, *Milton, A Poem,* 229 (my emphasis).

57. For instance: "See Luke Ch 2 v I" (*L,* D), "See Virgils Eneid. Lib. VI. v 848" (*L,* B), and "Read Matthew CX. 9 & 10 v" (*L,* B).

58. See, for instance, the "Greek for 'Ophiucus,' the serpent holder" and the Hebrew for "Lilith" (Essick and Viscomi, *Milton, A Poem,* 272 n, 273 n).

59. Gavin Edwards, "Repeating the Same Dull Round," in *Unnam'd Forms: Blake and Textuality,* ed. Nelson Hilton and Thomas A. Vogler (Berkeley: University of California Press, 1986), 46, 47. For a related argument about the *Marriage,* see Dan Miller, "Contrary Revelation: *The Marriage of Heaven and Hell,*" *Studies in Romanticism* 24 (1985): 491–509.

60. Blake's investment in the so-called aphorisms has only rarely been called into question.

For characterizations of the aphorisms as assertions of Blake's beliefs, see, for instance, Irene Tayler, "Blake's *Laocoön,*" *Blake Newsletter: An Illustrated Quarterly* 10 (1976–77): 72; James, "Blake's *Laocoön,*" 230; Geoffrey Keynes, ed., *Blake: Complete Writings* (1957; reprint, Oxford: Oxford University Press, 1972), 923 n. Passing invocations of one of the aphorisms to support a reading of another Blake text are too numerous to mention. Damrosch, however, suggests that the statements' "status as aphorisms allows them to make gnomic claims that are not easily sustained in the myth as a whole" (*Symbol and Truth,* 246).

61. Jerome J. McGann, *The Textual Condition* (Princeton: Princeton University Press, 1991), 53, 56.

62. Ibid., 53.

63. Essick and Viscomi, *Milton, A Poem,* 268.

64. Plowman, *William Blake,* 287–88; Keynes, *Blake: Complete Writings,* 775; Adams, *William Blake,* 585–87; Mary Lynn Johnson and John E. Grant, eds., *Blake's Poetry and Designs* (New York: Norton, 1979), 425; David V. Erdman, ed., *The Complete Poetry and Prose of William Blake,* rev. ed. (New York: Doubleday, 1988), 273–75.

65. Essick and Viscomi not only keep the four lines under the statue together, but, for instance, the words "around the right arm of the central figure," separated by a number of lines in other editions, and the passages around the central figure generally (*Milton, A Poem,* 268).

66. Ibid., 268–71.

67. Erdman, *Complete Poetry,* 273.

68. Compare the second letter of the second word, an aleph, under "The Angel of the Divine Presence" (*L,* A–B) to Erdman's transcription (*Complete Poetry,* 273). Erdman uses the modern form while, as Martin Kreiswirth noted in a private conversation, Blake uses a now unusual form.

69. Erdman, "Textual Notes," in *The Complete Poetry and Prose of William Blake,* 814.

70. I am indebted to Robert Essick for his explanation of the presence of the reverse image in Erdman's latest edition of Blake's writings.

71. Nicole Brossard, "Poetic Politics," in *The Politics of Poetic Form: Poetry and Public Policy,* ed. Charles Bernstein (New York: ROOF, 1990), 78, 79.

72. Michael Joyce, "Notes Toward an Unwritten Non-linear Electronic Text, 'The Ends of Print Culture,'" *Postmodern Culture* 2.1 (September 1991): 14.

73. V. A. De Luca, "A Wall of Words: The Sublime as Text," in *Unnam'd Forms,* 218–41.

74. Brossard, "Poetic Politics," 76; Mary Ann Caws, *The Art of Interference: Stressed Readings in Verbal and Visual Texts* (Princeton: Princeton University Press, 1989), 16.

75. Poster, *The Mode of Information,* 15.

76. We are familiar with the ways in which Blake's script mutates into designs, as *ys,* for instance, trail off into ivies, in what Nelson Hilton poetically terms "words strain[ing] to become pure graphic form" (*Literal Imagination: Blake's Vision of Words* [Berkeley: University of California Press, 1983], 3). But *The Laocoön* offers a rare instance of Blake's use of different print-like scripts, invoking the different fonts (gothic) and letter forms (English, Hebrew) in use in European print culture rather than challenging the distinction between graphic and verbal lines.

77. Essick and Viscomi, *Milton, A Poem,* 272 n.

78. Caws suggests that this deformation of verbal assemblages into linear sequences is

engrained at a perceptual level even when it is avoided at a textual level: "all too often the linear structure from which contemporary readers have learned, more or less easily, to tear themselves away in the reading of texts seems to retain its traditional hypnotic effect on our perception" (*The Art of Interference,* 16).

79. Damrosch uses the same figure in addressing a similar point regarding the form of Blake's poetry, suggesting that Blake's practice of producing plates that could be reorganized and supplemented "leads to a kind of poetry almost entirely recalcitrant to theories of organic form. The poetic whole is made up of interpenetrating symbolic facets that can be juxtaposed with each other in an almost infinite variety of ways; the poems are kaleidoscopes" (*Symbol and Truth,* 350).

CHAPTER 2

1. Eaves, *Counter-Arts,* 158. The *Public Address* also belongs to a body of Blake's work in which he engages the emergent discourse of the instructional framing of exhibitions as described by C. S. Matheson in "The Royal Academy and the Annual Exhibition of the Viewing Public," in *Lessons of Romanticism: A Critical Companion,* ed. Thomas Pfau and Robert F. Gleckner (Durham, N.C.: Duke University Press, 1998), 280–303.

2. Edmund Burke, *Reflections on the Revolution in France* (1790), ed. Conor Cruise O'Brien (Markham, Ont.: Penguin, 1986), 120.

3. Erdman deduces the date from topical allusions in the work (see "Textual Notes," 849).

4. Frye, *Fearful Symmetry,* 167.

5. Marilyn Butler, "The Bristol Model: Romanticism as Provincial Nationalism" (paper presented at the biannual conference of the British Association for Romantic Studies, Glasgow, Scotland, 10 July 1993).

6. On the subject of correspondences between Gray's *Descent of Odin* and Blake's poetry, see, for instance, Erdman, *Prophet against Empire,* 262 n; and Mark Schorer, *William Blake: The Politics of Vision* (New York: Holt, 1946), 405–6 n. Regarding the influence of Gray, Collins, and Thomson's interest in antique material on Blake, see, for example, Peterfreund, "Problem," 698–99; and Lucas, *England and Englishness,* 5. Blake's debt to Stukeley, Mallet, and other antiquarians is also well established; references to antiquarianism are almost plentiful in two of the seminal works of Blake criticism, Frye's *Fearful Symmetry* and Harold Bloom, *Blake's Apocalypse: A Study in Poetic Argument* (Garden City, N.Y.: Doubleday, 1963). Most recently, Mee has addressed Blake's use of primitivism; see his chapter "Northern Antiquities" in *Dangerous Enthusiasm.* Moreover, as Hagstrum has shown, Blake was also influenced by medieval illuminated manuscripts (*William Blake, Poet and Painter,* 30–33).

7. Peterfreund, "Problem," 699.

8. Thomas Percy, translator's preface to *Northern Antiquities,* by Paul Henri Mallet (1770), 2 vols. (New York: Garland, 1979), xii–xiii.

9. Lucas, *England and Englishness,* 43, 44.

10. Ibid., 47.

11. Anthony D. Smith, *National Identity* (1991; reprint, Reno: University of Nevada Press, 1991).

12. Besides the antiquarianism with which this chapter is primarily concerned, there were, of course, other radical theories that characterized contemporary culture as corrupt but were less amenable to nationalism; see, for example, Thomas Paine's notion of inherent and equal rights in *Rights of Man* (1791–1792), ed. Henry Collins (Markham, Ontario: Penguin, 1983).

13. Burke, *Reflections on the Revolution,* 119 (my emphasis).

14. As the Ossian controversy shows, the line between a forgery and good scholarship is a rather fuzzy one, particularly during a period in which the terms of good scholarship were still being established. The authenticity of Macpherson's Ossian poems is still being contested, because Macpherson did base his work on authentic material: his alterations to the material can be understood as a revision of the kind that takes place without note in popular culture rather than as Macpherson's creation of a text distinct from the Scottish material. On this subject, see Howard Gaskill, "'Ossian' Macpherson: Towards a Rehabilitation," *Comparative Criticism* 8 (1986): 113–46; and Clare O'Halloran, "Irish Re-Creations of the Gaelic Past: The Challenge of Macpherson's Ossian," *Past and Present* 124 (1989): 69–95, esp. 69–70.

15. Walter Scott parodies such rewritings of the nation in his Waverley novel, *The Antiquary* (1816). The title character encourages a young poet to write an epic in which Scotland repels a historical Roman invasion: after acknowledging that "the invasion of Agricola was *not* repelled," the antiquary yet offers to "write the critical and historical notes on each canto, and draw out the plan of the story" (*The Antiquary* [1816], vol. 3 of *The Waverley Novels* [Edinburgh: Black, 1873], 119).

16. For a wide-ranging discussion of antiquarian nationalism in novels of the period, see Trumpener, *Bardic Nationalism.*

17. Stephen C. Behrendt, "'The Consequence of High Powers': Blake, Shelley, and Prophecy's Public Dimension," *Papers on Language and Literature* 22 (1986): 256–57.

18. Ibid., 255.

19. Lucas, *England and Englishness,* 44–45. This is the "poet-as-bard, whose epic voice cannot authentically be raised in praise of a society where freedoms are being stifled" and who ought to be "a poet of the people" (47–48). I am simplifying Lucas's discussion of Thomson, Gray, and Collins considerably to tease out the general precepts that they found in the northern tradition. Lucas shows that the poets were uncomfortable, at best, with the radical implications of the tradition that they found so seductive.

20. I use "iteration" in the sense that Jacques Derrida outlines in "Signature Event Context," trans. Alan Bass, in *Limited Inc.,* ed. Gerald Graff (Evanston, Ill.: Northwestern University Press, 1988), 1–23.

21. Homi K. Bhabha, "DissemiNation: Time, Narrative, and the Margins of the Modern Nation," in *Nation and Narration,* 297.

22. Ibid.

23. Molly Anne Rothenberg, *Rethinking Blake's Textuality* (Columbia: University of Missouri Press, 1993), 112; for a more structural analysis of the narrative conundrums posed by *Jerusalem,* see Morton D. Paley, *The Continuing City: William Blake's* Jerusalem (Oxford: Clarendon, 1983), esp. chap. 6.

24. Rothenberg, *Rethinking Blake's Textuality,* 111.

25. Goldsmith, *Unbuilding Jerusalem,* 160–61.

26. Peterfreund, "Problem," 673–74.

27. Frye, *Fearful Symmetry,* 177.

28. Margaret Ruth Lowery, *Windows of the Morning: A Critical Study of Blake's* Poetical Sketches, *1783* (New Haven: Yale University Press, 1940), 201.

29. William Richey suggests that the seasonal poems' "allusions to various ancient cultures reflect both [Blake's] eclectic brand of primitivism and his characteristically neoclassical desire to return art to its once purer and more vigorous form" (*Blake's Altering Aesthetic* [Columbia: University of Missouri Press, 1996], 37). But this desire is fundamental to nationalism and the Hebraic tradition of prophecy, both of which are relevant to the *Poetical Sketches,* and the classical is less associated with the classical-world-as-primitive than the Renaissance pastoral, a nationalist pastoral that prioritizes the northern over the southern European, most obviously in "To Summer."

30. Peterfreund, "Problem," 698–99; Lucas, *England and Englishness,* 73. The songs also set their audience "at ease." Lucas argues that the song is part of a tradition of "shared, collective utterance," a genre whose "anapaestic metres, stanza forms, rhyme schemes [are] knowable, familiar, 'owned' by those who are excluded from the society of the great cage" "of the Augustan couplet" (79, 71). The conventional themes of Blake's songs—love, a "black ey'd maid," rural life, communion with nature—further their recognizability.

31. Harold Bloom, "Commentary," in *The Complete Poetry and Prose of William Blake,* rev. ed., ed. David V. Erdman (Toronto: Doubleday, 1988), 969.

32. Susan Wolfson, "Sketching Verbal Form: Blake's *Poetical Sketches,*" in *Speak Silence: Rhetoric and Culture in Blake's Poetical Sketches,* ed. Mark L. Greenberg (Detroit: Wayne State University Press, 1996), 33, 51. Wolfson offers a suggestive reading of the tropes and musical devices of this poem, 51–54.

33. Robert F. Gleckner, *Blake's Prelude:* Poetical Sketches (Baltimore: Johns Hopkins University Press, 1982), 117.

34. Gleckner, *Blake's Prelude,* 164 n.

35. Seamus Deane, "Civilians and Barbarians," in *Ireland's Field Day,* Field Day Theatre Company (Notre Dame: University of Notre Dame Press, 1986), 33.

36. Lucas, *England and Englishness,* 41.

37. See not only the antiquarian texts already mentioned and Mallet's *Northern Antiquities,* but also John Lemprière's *Classical Dictionary of Proper Names Mentioned in Ancient Authors Writ Large,* 3rd ed., (1788; reprint, New York: Routledge, 1984) and John Bell's *New Pantheon* (1790), both of which include nonclassical references, and William Jones's orientalist researches.

38. Frye, *Fearful Symmetry,* 187.

39. David V. Erdman, "The Symmetries of *The Song of Los,*" *Studies in Romanticism* 16 (1977): 179.

40. Mee, *Dangerous Enthusiasm,* 121.

41. Jerome J. McGann, "The Idea of an Indeterminate Text: Blake's Bible of Hell and Dr. Alexander Geddes," *Studies in Romanticism* 25 (1986): 324; Mee, *Dangerous Enthusiasm,* 17.

42. Williams, *Ideology and Utopia,* 129.

43. See, for instance, Essick's important *William Blake and the Language of Adam.*

44. Mee, *Dangerous Enthusiasm,* 126; Rajan, *Supplement of Reading,* 201.

45. Rajan, *Supplement of Reading,* 201.

46. The phrase "action at a distance" refers to events in which one object affects another with which it is not in observable contact, either directly or through intermediary objects. Magnetic and gravitational effects are thus instances of the phenomena, but not a chain of falling dominoes. These, and many other instances of "action at a distance," including the propagation of viruses and other diseases, were still unexplained in Blake's day.

47. Williams, *Ideology and Utopia,* 129.

48. John Lemprière, *Classical Dictionary,* 496. Lemprière also notes the legend that Pythagoras "appeared on the same day and at the same instant in the cities of Crotona and Metapontum" (538), recalling Urizen's feat (*SL,* 3.6–8).

49. The timeline is fundamentally Judeo-Christian, but Blake does not mix the Old and New Testaments. He marks the divide between them by locating nonbiblical mythic figures and pre-Christian thinkers before the interlude, "Times rolled on o'er . . . time after time" (*SL,* 3.20), and only biblical mythic figures and Christian thinkers after it; only his own, pseudomythic figures occupy both sides of that poetic divide.

50. This collapsing of histories and geographical spaces, I would argue, complicates readings of Blake's Africa as the site of the "perversion of human energy," as James McCord puts it in "Historical Dissonance and William Blake's *The Song of Los,*" *Colby Library Quarterly* 20 (1984): 26.

51. Michel Foucault, "Nietzsche, Genealogy, History," in *The Foucault Reader,* ed. Paul Rabinow (New York: Pantheon, 1984), 76–100. For a suggestive analysis of the ways in which the verbal and visual dimensions of the work cooperate to challenge other kinds of containment, see Kathleen Lundeen, "Urizen's Quaking Word," *Colby Library Quarterly* 25 (1989): 12–27.

52. Bloom, "Commentary," 907.

53. Patricia Parker, for instance, identifies the blazon with a rhetoric of property in which the woman's body is "inventoried" (*Literary Fat Ladies: Rhetoric, Gender, Property* [New York: Methuen, 1987], 126).

54. Betsy Bolton, "'A Garment Dipped in Blood': Ololon and Problems of Gender in Blake's *Milton,*" *Studies in Romanticism* 36 (1997): 61.

55. Fox, *Poetic Form,* 24. Fox, for example, argues that the definitions of the "Three Classes" "accrue," so that "our fullest understanding of them does not come until nearly the end of the poem" (22).

56. Andrew M. Cooper, "Blake's Escape from Mythology: Self-Mastery in *Milton,*" *Studies in Romanticism* 20 (1981): 90–91.

57. Albert J. Rivero, "Typology, History, and Blake's *Milton,*" *Journal of English and Germanic Philology* 81 (1982): 31.

58. Derrida, "Signature Event Context," 12.

59. Carothers, "Space and Time in *Milton,*" 116–27.

60. Similarly, the opening and closing plates of the poem, marking the start of Enitharmon's song and the second historical interruption of it, are linked through repetition: first, the "secret child" "Descended thro' the orient gates" (*Eur,* 3.2, 3.3) and "all the troops like shadows fled to their abodes" (*Eur,* 3.4), and later "morning ope'd the eastern gate" (*Eur,* 14.35) and "every one fled to his station" (*Eur,* 14.36). Thus, the crossings from history into myth and from myth into history share images associated with time (the "eastern" or "orient" gates of sunrise) and space (the proper places of the different troops).

61. Will McConnell, "Blake, Bataille, and the Accidental Processes of Material History in *Milton,*" *CLIO* 26 (1997): 467.

CHAPTER 3

1. For a psychological, rather than a political, view of alienation in Blake's works, see Steven Shaviro, "'Striving With Systems': Blake and the Politics of Difference," *boundary 2* 10 (1982): 229–50.

2. Friedrich Nietzsche, "On Truth and Lying in an Extra-Moral Sense" (1873), in *Friedrich Nietzsche on Rhetoric and Language,* trans. Sander L. Gilman, Carole Blair, and David J. Parent (New York: Oxford University Press, 1989), 247.

3. Roland Barthes, "Myth Today," in *Mythologies* (1957), trans. Annette Lavers (Toronto: Paladin Grafton Books, 1973), 155.

4. Georges Bataille, "The Psychological Structure of Fascism," *Visions of Excess: Selected Writings, 1927–1939,* ed. Allan Stoekl, trans. Allan Stoekl with Carl R. Lovett and Donald M. Leslie Jr., vol. 14 of *Theory and History of Literature* (Minneapolis: University of Minnesota Press, 1991), 137–38.

5. Foucault, *Order of Things,* xx.

6. Barthes, for example, suggests in "Myth Today," "Statistically, myth is on the right. There, it is essential; well-fed, sleek, expansive, garrulous, it invents itself ceaselessly. It takes hold of everything, all aspects of the law, of morality, of aesthetics, of diplomacy, of household equipment, of Literature, of entertainment" (162).

7. Ault, *Narrative Unbound,* 3.

8. Rothenberg, "Parasiting America," 347, 348. The ideological and social links between Paine and Blake are well established. Erdman traces some of the tenuous evidence linking Blake to Paine via the Johnson circle, which also included Godwin, Wollstonecraft and Fuseli (*Prophet against Empire,* 154–56). Blake also wrote, but did not publish, a defense of Paine, and Erdman suggests that Tharmas is modeled, in part, on Paine (299–302). Moreover, as Essick shows, Blake and Paine

not only are linked ideologically and socially, but also share "common . . . rhetorical strategies" ("William Blake, Thomas Paine, and Biblical Revolution," *Studies in Romanticism* 30 [1991]: 194).

9. See Bertholt Brecht, *Brecht on Theatre: The Development of an Aesthetic,* ed. and trans. John Willett (New York: Hill and Wang, 1964).

10. David L. Clark, "'The Innocence of Becoming Restored': Blake, Nietzsche, and the Disclosure of Difference," *Studies in Romanticism* 29 (1990): 93.

11. Jacques Derrida, "La Parole Soufflée," in *Writing and Difference,* trans. Alan Bass (Chicago: University of Chicago Press, 1978), 194.

12. David Gross, "'Mind Forg'd Manacles': Hegemony and Counter-Hegemony in Blake," *The Eighteenth Century: Theory and Interpretation* 23 (1986): 6–7.

13. Frye, *Fearful Symmetry,* 238.

14. Susan Fox, "The Female as Metaphor in William Blake's Poetry," *Critical Inquiry* 3 (1977): 513; Rajan, *Supplement of Reading,* 248.

15. I here depart from the recuperative position, articulated, for instance, by Fox, that Oothoon "passes from Innocence through Experience to a confident new vision of reality that subsumes both. . . . The whole poem may be seen as a dialectic between her comprehensive perspective and their fragmented perspectives" (*Poetic Form,* 8). Oothoon's perspective may be outside of certain "fragmented perspectives" and comprehend them, but it is nevertheless still limited, as indicated by her interrogatory declamations and, more importantly, her far-from-confident "wailing" and lamentatory closing lines.

16. As Rajan notes, "Since it is Oothoon who plucks the marigold, it is not entirely clear that she is raped according to then-prevailing legal definitions of the term" (*Supplement of Reading,* 248).

17. Nelson Hilton, "An Original Story," in *Unnam'd Forms,* 78; Nancy Moore Goslee, "Slavery and Sexual Character: Questioning the Master Trope in Blake's *Visions of the Daughters of Albion,*" *ELH* 57 (1990): 101–28.

18. Damrosch, *Symbol and Truth,* 199.

19. In the late eighteenth century, definitions of rape were changing as notions of female sexuality and reproduction altered. Thomas Laqueur notes that, until the 1820s, many medical texts claimed that rape could not result in pregnancy, citing, among others, Samuel Farr's assertion, "in the first legal-medicine text to be written in English (1785)," that "without an excitation of lust, or enjoyment in the venereal act, no conception can possibly take place," although such a defense probably did not succeed in court (*Making Sex: Body and Gender from the Greeks to Freud* [Cambridge: Harvard University Press, 1990], 161, 162). Bromion's assertion that Oothoon has conceived is therefore additionally insidious because it could be interpreted as his attempt to preemptively deny charges of rape by tacitly claiming her consent.

20. Goslee suggests that, while "Bromion and Theotormon attempt to work out new ways of looking at their worlds, [Oothoon] works out a new way of looking at such defilement" ("Slavery and Sexual Character," 111); but Bromion and Theotormon are also dealing with the rape, albeit in egocentric terms. Bromion rewrites the rape by calling Oothoon an object of conquest as well as a "harlot," "believ[ing] that his victim was asking for it" (Alicia Ostriker, "Desire Gratified and Ungratified: William Blake and Sexuality," *Blake: An Illustrated Quarterly* 16 [1982–83]: 157). Theotormon projects his emotional response to the rape onto the natural world

(*VDA,* 3.22–4.11), an approach that Bromion takes up by turning his attention to the world "unvisited by the voyager" (*VDA,* 4.17), arguably a euphemistic way of saying "unconquered" (given the close linkage between discovery and conquest as the British Empire began its rapid expansion), as well as a gesture toward what Frye terms "an unthinkably mysterious and remote world beyond his reach" (*Fearful Symmetry,* 239).

21. See Goslee on the text's ambiguous hints that Oothoon and Theotormon are married ("Slavery and Sexual Character," 108).

22. I invoke here Williams's point that the poem is the site of "the battle between the 'is' and the 'will be,' the ideological and the utopian" (*Ideology and Utopia,* 86).

23. James A. W. Heffernan, for instance, writes that "Oothoon remains a fascinating outsider because her attitude will not fit the structures of power and submission with which societies customarily organize themselves"; yet he laments that "she neither converts the men who oppress her nor liberates herself from them" ("Blake's Oothoon: The Dilemmas of Marginality," *Studies in Romanticism* 30 [1991]: 18). Thomas A. Vogler, on the other hand, suggests that "nothing will change in this story until Oothoon pays more attention to why her proselytizing (whether for free love, prophecy, or imagination) is not working" ("'in vain the Eloquent tongue': An Un-Reading of *VISIONS of the Daughters of Albion,*" in *Critical Paths: Blake and the Argument of Method,* ed. Dan Miller, Mark Bracher, and Donald Ault [Durham, N.C.: Duke University Press, 1987], 305).

24. See also, for example, Goslee, "Slavery and Sexual Character," 115; Hilton, "An Original Story," 102; David Wagenknecht, *Blake's Night: William Blake and the Idea of Pastoral* (Cambridge, Mass.: Belknap, 1973), 206; Michael Ferber, "Blake's Idea of Brotherhood," *PMLA* 93 (1978): 444.

25. See Rachel Blau DuPlessis, *Writing beyond the Ending: Narrative Strategies of Twentieth-Century Women Writers* (Bloomington: Indiana University Press, 1985), 1.

26. Erdman, *Prophet against Empire,* 236.

27. Mark Bracher, "The Metaphysical Grounds of Oppression in Blake's *Visions of the Daughters of Albion,*" *Colby Library Quarterly* 20 (1984): 165, 166.

28. Rothenberg, "Parasiting America," 347. Paine here runs into the same dilemma as Blake. In his discussion of *Visions,* Ferber notes, "His passionate hatred of oppression and tyranny sometimes leads Blake into accounts of human differences that seem to threaten the very possibility of human fraternity" ("Blake's Idea of Brotherhood," 444).

29. This suggests a possible reading of the poem's motto, "The Eye sees more than the Heart knows" (*VDA,* title page). Oothoon has arguably turned from the perspective of her eye to that of her heart, from observing Theotormon to sympathizing with him (in the specific sense outlined by Enlightenment notions of sensibility; see, for instance, Adam Smith, *Theory of Moral Sentiments* [1759; reprint, New York: Kelley, 1966]). This is reflected in the direction of Oothoon's gaze. When she is distinguishing herself from the system that she ascribes to Theotormon, she declares that she is "Open to joy and to delight where ever beauty appears . . . there my eyes are fix'd" (*VDA,* 6.22, 6.23); but when she turns to "my Theotormon," she declares instead, "I'll lie beside thee on a bank & view their wanton play / In lovely copulation bliss on bliss with Theotormon" (*VDA,* 7.25–26). Quite apart from the problems critics have found in Oothoon's later declaration, it reveals a considerable narrowing of her perspective. Instead of fixing her eyes "where ever beauty appears," she directs them to follow only Theotormon.

30. The final portion of Oothoon's speech undermines the optimistic view of Oothoon's

transcendence, articulated by Ostriker ("Desire Gratified and Ungratified," 158). As Damrosch writes, "Oothoon's voyeurist fantasy—she will *watch* their play—does not sound like something Blake would recommend" (*Symbol and Truth,* 198).

31. Behrendt, *Reading William Blake,* 86, 133.

32. David Blake and Elliott Gruner, "Redeeming Captivity: The Negative Revolution of Blake's *Visions of the Daughters of Albion,*" *Symbiosis: A Journal of Anglo-American Literary Relations* 1 (1997): 28.

33. Throughout, I use "prophecy" to indicate the portion within *America* and *Europe* that is designated as such rather than the entire work.

34. For a discussion of linear and circular time in the poem, see James E. Swearingen, "Time and History in Blake's *Europe,*" *CLIO* 20 (1991): 109–21. For a set of related oppositions in other works by Blake, see W. J. T. Mitchell, "Visible Language: Blake's Wondrous Art of Writing," in *Romanticism and Contemporary Criticism,* ed. Morris Eaves and Michael Fischer (Ithaca: Cornell University Press, 1986), 68.

35. Georges Bataille, *Theory of Religion* (1973), trans. Robert Hurley (New York: Zone Books, 1992), 37.

36. Foucault, *Order of Things,* 25.

37. Ostriker, "Desire Gratified and Ungratified," 161.

38. Suzanne Araas Vesely, "The Daughters of Eighteenth-Century Science: A Rationalist and Materialist Context for William Blake's Female Figures," *Colby Quarterly* 34 (1998): 19.

39. There are (at least) three possible divisions of lines 3.9–4.14 among the speakers: Erdman has Los speak lines 3.9–14, the sons of Urizen speak lines 4.3–9, and Enitharmon begin on line 4.10 (*Prophet against Empire,* 266 n); Bloom contends that Los quotes the sons of Urizen, and that they do not speak for themselves, so that Los speaks lines 3.9–4.9, and then Enitharmon begins ("Commentary," 904); Johnson and Grant suggest that all of the disputed lines could be spoken by either Enitharmon or Los (*Blake's Poetry and Designs,* 126 n).

40. Mark Anderson notes, for instance, that, in the context of Enitharmon's previous speech, Enitharmon's "feelings . . . seem to be contradictory" ("Why Is That Fairy in Europe?" *Colby Library Quarterly* 21 [1985]: 131); while Johnson and Grant remark that the first summoning of Rintrah and Palamabron, on plate 5, contradicts Enitharmon's previous call for Orc to arise (*Blake's Poetry and Designs,* 127 n).

41. My reading of the prescriptive lines as the heavens' speech, rather than Enitharmon's, arguably adds further weight to Mee's association of these lines with Blake's critique of "the theology of future rewards and punishments" (*Dangerous Enthusiasm,* 96): a theological, rather than a misogynistic, spin to these lines makes the heavens a more appropriate source than Enitharmon within a Protestant context.

42. Enitharmon's laughter has often been identified as her response to the oppression of the Europeans rather than their liberation, the cause of Orc's laughter three lines earlier. For my argument against this identification, see chapter 4.

43. Peterfreund, "Problem," 680.

44. Stephen Greenblatt, *Shakespearean Negotiations: The Circulation of Social Energy in Renaissance England* (Berkeley: University of California Press, 1988), 64; Michel Foucault,

Discipline and Punish: The Birth of the Prison (1977), trans. Alan Sheridan (New York: Random House, 1979).

45. Terry Castle, *Masquerade and Civilization: The Carnivalesque in Eighteenth-Century English Culture and Fiction* (Stanford: Stanford University Press, 1986), 5.

46. Ibid., 79, 78, 79.

47. Castle notes that cross-dressing was not uncommon at masquerades (Ibid., 46–47, 63–64).

48. Mary Brunton, *Discipline* (1814; reprint, London: Pandora, 1986), 48.

49. William Keach, *Shelley's Style* (New York: Methuen, 1984), 24–27.

50. Essick, *William Blake,* 64; Rothenberg, "Parasiting America," 346.

51. Thomas Paine, *Common Sense* (1776), ed. Isaac Kramnick (Markham, Ontario: Penguin, 1982), 71; Paine, *Rights of Man,* 104.

52. Paine, for instance, discredits the aristocracy by characterizing the law of primogeniture as "a law against every law of nature, and Nature herself calls for its destruction," *Rights of Man,* 104. See Essick regarding Blake's response to Paine's assumption of a natural ground ("William Blake, Thomas Paine," 200–202).

53. Paine, *Rights of Man,* 92.

54. Ibid., 146.

55. Bloom, *Blake's Apocalypse,* 154.

56. James E. Swearingen makes a similar point about *Jerusalem:* "Blake's 'giant forms' are not clearly defined entities with predictable functions. Each functions differently in different textual environments ("William Blake's Figural Politics," *ELH* 59 [1992]: 127).

57. Mallet, *Northern Antiquities,* 87. As I have argued elsewhere, Mallet's description of Odin's participation in battles, as translated by Percy, is remarkably similar to that of Orc's contribution to the conflicts in *Europe* and *America.* But the Thirteen Angels are also types of Odin here, following the same pattern, in which a flaming mythic figure joins a real battle; see Julia M. Wright, "'Empire is No More': Odin and Orc in *America,*" *Blake: An Illustrated Quarterly* 26 (1992): 27.

58. Colley, *Britons,* 185–87.

59. See Judith Butler, "Imitation and Gender Subordination," in *Inside/Out,* ed. Diana Fuss (New York: Routledge, 1991), 13–31.

60. Rodney M. Baine, *The Scattered Portions: William Blake's Biological Symbolism* (Athens Ga.: privately printed, 1986), 130.

61. Erdman, *Prophet against Empire,* 236.

62. Fox, "Female as Metaphor," 512–13; Ostriker, "Desire Gratified and Ungratified," 158.

63. There is a further implication that is beyond the purview of this chapter but needs to be mentioned. In a time of increasingly gendered reading, in which the boundaries of proper reading for each gender, as well as the classification of writing (especially novels) by women as reading for women, were being more rigorously policed, Blake offers an interesting gendering of readers and writers: Oothoon speaks, even though she does not recognize it, to a female audience (the Daughters) as well as a male one (Theotormon), but the text is written by a man and for a generally male readership (insofar as Blake controlled the circulation of his texts at this

time through personal sales of hand-produced illuminated prints). In other words, *Visions* offers a scene of women writing and reading, but in a text that circulates outside of the boundaries of "women's writing," not only in the material conditions of its production and circulation, but also in its non-novelistic form.

64. Ferber, "Blake's Idea of Brotherhood," 438.

CHAPTER 4

1. Patrick Power translates this passage as follows:

Yet blind as I was, I wouldn't yield
To the substanceless voice of those who made speech,
A purposeless foolish mocking or baiting,
Till the truth of the tale by her womb was related.
'Twasn't frivolous gossip or lying chatter,
Or woman-tells-woman-it type of yarn,
But the deed spoke out with truth and maturity

(*Cúirt an Mhean-Oíche / The Midnight Court* [1780], by Brian Merriman, trans. Patrick C. Power [Dublin: Mercier Press, 1971], 523–29).

2. See, for example, Terry Castle, "Lab'ring Bards: Birth *Topoi* and English Poetics, 1660–1820," *Journal of English and Germanic Philology* 78 (1979): 193–208; Susan Stanford Friedman, "Creativity and the Childbirth Metaphor: Gender Difference in Literary Discourse," *Speaking of Gender*, ed. Elaine Showalter (New York: Routledge, 1989), 73–100; Sandra M. Gilbert and Susan Gubar, *The Madwoman in the Attic: The Woman Writer and the Nineteenth-Century Literary Imagination* (New Haven: Yale University Press, 1979); Laqueur, *Making Sex;* and Parker, *Literary Fat Ladies*.

3. Castle, "Lab'ring Bards," 202, 203.

4. Friedman, "Creativity and the Childbirth Metaphor," 75.

5. Mary Whateley, "On the Author's Husband Desiring Her to Write Some Verses" (1780/1794), in *Eighteenth-Century Women Poets: An Oxford Anthology,* ed. Roger Lonsdale (Oxford: Oxford University Press, 1989), lines 30–31.

6. Mary Barber, "To a Lady, who commanded me to send her an Account in Verse, how I succeeded in my Subscription" (1734), in *Eighteenth-Century Women Poets,* lines 34–35.

7. I use "dissemination" throughout this chapter in an etymologically aware sense, as a "sowing of seed" that suggests the impregnations and plantings of texts, by male figures, in *America* and *Europe.* It also links this chapter to the next, in which images of published texts' ability to revitalize the political domain, including representations of published words as scattered seeds, are discussed.

8. In recent years, greater attention has been paid to this aspect of Blake's work. Mee, for

example, suggests that the female's "rending pains" "reflect[ ] the unsatisfactory nature of Orc's male and still patriarchal revolt in relation to the daughter" (*Dangerous Enthusiasm,* 104). See also, for example, Steven Bidlake, "Blake, the Sacred, and the French Revolution: Eighteenth-Century Ideology and the Problem of Violence," *European Romantic Review* 3 (1992): 1–20.

9. In such arguments, which Blake critics are now questioning, the female is associated with the earth, but Orc retains his maleness and personhood (see Bloom's "best hint for reading William Blake: every female personage finally relates to, or is, a form of nature; every male at last represents humankind, both male and female" [*Blake's Apocalypse,* 119]). Erdman, for example, interprets the female's response to her seizure in *America* as a response to "patriots . . . making love to good earth" (*Prophet against Empire,* 261); Bloom argues, "The silence of the shadowy female identifies her with nature, barren when not possessed by man" ("Commentary," 902); and John Howard writes that the female "partly personifies the physical earth of the American continent," as well as being, "[t]o the sexuality of Orc . . . the matrix to be inseminated" (*Infernal Poetics: Poetic Structures in Blake's Lambeth Prophecies* [Toronto: Associated University Presses, 1984], 116). The female of *Europe* is similarly described. Michael J. Tolley, for instance, calls her "a kind of personified womb" ("*Europe,*" 121); Leonard W. Deen identifies her as "the Eternal Female who seems all womb" (*Conversing in Paradise: Poetic Genius and the Identity-as-Community in Blake's Los* [Columbia: University of Missouri Press, 1983], 61), and Bloom identifies her as "the mother of all that is mortal in man" (*Blake's Apocalypse,* 147).

10. Tolley, "*Europe,*" 121; John Howard, *Infernal Poetics,* 116.

11. Mary Wollstonecraft, *A Vindication of the Rights of Woman* (1792), ed. Miriam Brody (Markham, Ontario: Penguin, 1985), 79.

12. For discussions of Wollstonecraft and the victimization of women in Blake's texts, see, for example, Fox, "Female as Metaphor"; Heffernan, "Blake's Oothoon"; Anne K. Mellor, "Blake's Portrayal of Women," *Blake: An Illustrated Quarterly* 16 (1982–83): 148–55; and Ostriker, "Desire Gratified and Ungratified."

13. As Paul A. Tipler describes it, under the heading "Wave-Particle Duality," "light, which we ordinarily think of as a wave motion, exhibits particle properties when it interacts with matter. . . . It might be tempting to say that [it] is both a wave and a particle, but the meaning of such a statement is not clear. In classical physics the concepts of waves and particles are mutually exclusive" (*Physics,* 2nd ed. [New York: Worth, 1982], 984). Light itself—ironically, given its association with enlightenment—thus disrupts scientific closure. Similar problems arise when the relationship between the noncorporeal and the corporeal aspects of a human being is addressed, and the problems are complicated by the ideological bias of the terms that can be applied to each aspect, or to their sum—even the division along corporeal lines is itself ideologically implicated. I will use "self" to refer to the sum, as a term with less baggage than most, and "subject" to refer to the noncorporeal aspect, unless a term is offered by the passage under discussion, because the usage of "subject" is the most consistent with the position that I perceive the females to represent, namely being caught within a discursive framework that they try to engage, and loosen, through language. In this regard, I am particularly indebted to Emile Benveniste, *Problems in General Linguistics,* trans. Mary Elizabeth Meek (Coral Gables: University of Miami Press, 1971); and Kaja Silverman, *The Subject of Semiotics* (New York: Oxford University Press, 1983).

14. For the argument that the females are one character, see especially the influential work of S. Foster Damon, *A Blake Dictionary,* 369. Damon's work is followed with apparent unanimity on this point. Taking up Damon's equation of the females, however, leads to an awkward genealogy in which the female is the daughter of Urthona in *America* (1793) and of Los in *Europe* (1794). Although Los is the name given to a "manifestation" of Urthona in *The Four Zoas* (1797) and *Jerusalem* (1804) (see Damon, 246, 426–27), Los refers to Urthona in the third person in *Europe* (3.10), so that it is necessary to use the late poems—despite the lack of supportive evidence, as well as evidence to the contrary, in *Europe* and *America*—to construct a genealogy in which the two females can be equated. Moreover, the descriptor "shadowy female" is not capitalized in *America* and *Europe,* as it is in the later works, *Milton* and *The Four Zoas.*

15. Swearingen, "Time and History," 112.

16. Michael Ferber, "Blake's *America* and the Birth of Revolution," in *History and Myth: Essays on English Romantic Literature,* ed. Stephen C. Behrendt (Detroit: Wayne State University Press, 1990), 82.

17. Fox, "Female as Metaphor," 513; Bloom, *Blake's Apocalypse,* 147.

18. Minna Doskow, "William Blake's *America:* The Story of a Revolution Betrayed," *Blake Studies* 8 (1979): 176. The rape has been associated with various events of mystical significance. Stephen C. Behrendt, for example, asserts that "the 'rape' is a necessary rite of passage that frees both figures into a more enlightened perspective" ("'This Accursed Family': Blake's *America* and the American Revolution," *The Eighteenth Century: Theory and Interpretation* 27 [1986]: 41); Erdman suggests a religious allegory in which "[t]his ritual copulation reunites man and earth, and she recognizes the Christ-like seed planted for resurrection" (*Prophet against Empire,* 261); and Leslie Tannenbaum similarly associates it with the Incarnation, as "a rape and a birth, signifying . . . the Word again made flesh" (*Biblical Tradition in Blake's Early Prophecies: The Great Code of Art* [Princeton: Princeton University Press, 1982], 142).

19. The female's complaint, "thy fire & my frost / Mingle in howling pains" (*Am,* 2.15–16), presents a provocative variation on "[a] common Petrarchan antithesis," in which fire is associated with "love" and ice with "egotism and pride," as James M. Saslow puts it in his notes on Michelangelo's poetry in *The Poetry of Michelangelo: An Annotated Translation* (New Haven: Yale University Press, 1991), 208 n. Blake, an admirer of Michelangelo, who often uses such images, radically modifies the conventional antithesis by presenting the beloved's perspective and addressing the torment that she feels because of his fiery expressions of desire.

20. Doskow, "William Blake's *America,*" 176.

21. Bloom suggests that, through the rape, Orc "seeks to give his voice, and his passion, to silent nature" (*Blake's Apocalypse,* 120).

22. Regarding the pervasiveness of the alignment of male/female with these and similar oppositions in Western thought since classical Greece, see Ian Maclean, *The Renaissance Notion of Woman: A Study in the Fortunes of Scholasticism and Medical Science in European Intellectual Life* (New York: Cambridge University Press, 1983), esp. 2–3, 8, 54, 62.

23. This synergy recalls Ault's discussion of "self-differing" in Blake's *Four Zoas,* in which "the text announces . . . a radical, unresolvable disjunction between its totality and its divisions"

(*Narrative Unbound,* xiii). See also Rajan, who argues that "The 'whole,' instead of being what the parts fit into, is a perpetually shifting effect of the (part)iculars through which we view it" (*Supplement of Reading,* 203).

24. David Blake and Elliott Gruner, "Redeeming Captivity," 29.

25. Victor Brombert, "The Happy Prison: A Recurring Romantic Metaphor," *Romanticism: Vistas, Instances, Continuities,* ed. David Thorburn and Geoffrey Hartman (Ithaca: Cornell University Press, 1973), 62–79.

26. Mitchell, "Visible Language," 68.

27. For discussions of Blake's position(s) regarding the mechanical reproduction of texts, see, for example, Eaves, *Theory of Art;* Morris Eaves, "Blake and the Artistic Machine: An Essay in Decorum and Technology," *PMLA* 22 (1977): 903–27; John H. Jones, "Printed Performance and Reading *The Book[s] of Urizen:* Blake's Bookmaking Process and the Transformation of Late Eighteenth-Century Print Culture," *Colby Quarterly* 35 (1999): 73–89; Paul Mann, "*The Book of Urizen* and the Horizon of the Book," in *Unnam'd Forms,* 49–68; and Mitchell, "Visible Language," 63–80.

28. Erdman, *Prophet against Empire,* 267 n.

29. John P. Feather, "From Censorship to Copyright: Aspects of the Government's Role in the English Book Trade, 1695–1775," in *Books and Society in History,* ed. Kenneth E. Carpenter (New York: Bowker, 1983), 184. In 1794, the year that *Europe* is dated, a "register of pamphlets in the Stamp-office," Francis Lestrange, was called as a witness in the trial of William Drennan (*Full Report,* 79); he was asked to identify those involved in the publication of an address deemed seditious. Under the law and in some notorious trials of the 1790s, publishing and stamping were explicitly linked.

30. This is not to suggest that Blake is describing his own method of producing plates, which remains a mystery to scholars but clearly underwent many refinements (see Bindman, introduction and notes to *Complete Graphic Works of William Blake,*13–15).

31. This representation of tyrannical publication resonates suggestively with Gellner's argument about the medium being the message of nationalism: "The media do not transmit an idea which happens to have been fed into them. It matters precious little what has been fed into them: it is the media themselves, the pervasiveness and importance of abstract, centralized, standardized, one to many communication, which itself automatically engenders the core idea of nationalism, quite irrespective of what in particular is being put into the specific messages transmitted" (*Nations and Nationalism,* 127).

32. Edward Larrissy, "A Description of Blake: Ideology, Form, Influence," in *1789: Reading Writing Revolution,* ed. Francis Barker et al. (Colchester, U.K.: University of Essex, 1982), 102, 103.

33. John Milton, *Areopagitica,* in *Milton's Prose Writings* (New York: Dutton, 1958), 175 (my emphases).

34. Percy Bysshe Shelley, "Ode to the West Wind," in *Shelley's Poetry and Prose,* lines 66–69; Bloom, *Blake's Apocalypse,* 123.

35. Wollstonecraft, *Vindication,* 99 n.

36. Rothenberg, "Parasiting America," 351.

37. Mitchell, "Visible Language," 62; Gross, "'Mind Forg'd Manacles,'" 20.

38. Rajan, *Supplement of Reading,* 203.

39. Ibid., 258.

40. See, for example, Erdman, *Prophet against Empire,* 269; and John Howard, *Infernal Poetics,* 144.

CHAPTER 5

1. Frye goes as far as to suggest that "[f]or Blake, . . . to imitate Milton is to imitate Jesus, just as, for Virgil, to imitate Homer was to imitate 'nature'" (*Fearful Symmetry,* 322). The power of this reading of *Milton* is such that the poem is central to Bloom's formulation of the dynamics of poetic influence. As early as 1970, Bloom wrote that it is the "anxiety of influence" that Blake "had labored heroically to overcome in *Milton*" ("Blake's *Jerusalem:* The Bard of Sensibility and the Form of Prophecy" [1970], reprinted in *The Ringers in the Tower* [Chicago: University of Chicago Press, 1971], 75). In *Anxiety of Influence,* Bloom depends on Blake's poem for a language to discuss that anxiety, from applying the States to the stages of "Poetic Influence" to identifying the Covering Cherub with "creative anxiety" (*The Anxiety of Influence: A Theory of Poetry* [New York: Oxford University Press, 1973], 30, 36). William Dennis Horn argues, "For Bloom this story [*Milton*] stands as a type for the dynamics of influence in which the newcomer can overcome his belatedness only by assimilating and then correcting his precursor" ("Blake's Revisionism: Gnostic Interpretation and Criticial Methodology," in *Critical Paths,* 73). This issue is too fundamental to Blake criticism to enumerate fully the more interesting examinations of it, but Joseph Wittreich's study warrants special mention: Joseph Anthony Wittreich Jr., *Angel of Apocalypse: Blake's Idea of Milton* (Madison: University of Wisconsin Press, 1975). Jackie DiSalvo pays scant attention to *Milton,* but generatively traces Milton's influence through the rest of Blake's corpus in *War of Titans: Blake's Critique of Milton and the Politics of Religion* (Pittsburgh: University of Pittsburgh Press, 1983).

2. Critics vary in their assessments of the degree of secularity of this individual renovation. Frye, for instance, suggests, "*Milton* is an individual prologue to the omen of something universal coming on. The Last Judgment lies on the distant horizon, and is prophesied in the final line of the poem" (*Fearful Symmetry,* 323); and calls it "the great poem of individual awakening" (*A Study of English Romanticism* [Chicago: University of Chicago Press, 1968], 38). Bloom maintains that "Milton . . . is shown casting off his own selfhood and moving toward a visionary emancipation that Blake desires as his own," but, "What belonged to religious convention or 'moral virtue' in the historical Milton is of no help to Blake, nor was it to Milton himself, in Blake's view" ("Commentary," 909). Erdman argues for a more secular version of apocalyptic renovation, a "*mental* liberation" after which "Blake" is "mentally ready for the Great Harvest," which has apocalyptic overtones (*Prophet against Empire,* 423). See also Florence Sandler, "The Iconoclastic Enterprise: Blake's Critique of 'Milton's Religon,'" *Blake Studies* 5 (1972): 13–57);

Thomas R. Frosch argues, "In *Milton,* Blake expands his analysis of the obstructions within the imagination" (*The Awakening of Albion: The Renovation of the Body in the Poetry of William Blake* [Ithaca: Cornell University Press, 1974], 41).

3. Damon argues, "The act of the poem is one, but the causes are so complex that Blake had to invent an original structure, to suggest the simultaneousness of all the material. He introduced material without any preparation, abruptly changing the subject over and over" (*A Blake Dictionary,* 280). More recently, critics have noted that this narrative fragmentation is also a fragmentation of narrative perspective, whether "anti-perspectivism" (Frosch, *Awakening of Albion,* 116) or "the shifting of visionary perspectives" (Bloom, *Blake's Apocalypse,* 310). See also, for instance, Fox, *Poetic Form,* 6; Wittreich, *Angel of Apocalypse*; and Mark Bracher, *Being Form'd: Thinking Through Blake's* Milton (Barrytown, N.Y.: Station Hill, 1985).

4. Bloom, for instance, writes, "Blake goes with Los to the gate of the city of Golgonooza. . . . One point of this incident is to show us that Blake is now distinct from Palamabron" (*Blake's Apocalypse,* 334). While contesting the theoretical premises behind the "readiness of even sympathetic readers to confuse a poet's life and his imagination," Frye maintains that "[t]here are . . . border-line cases where it is impossible wholly to separate art and biography, and Blake's *Milton* is one of them" (*Fearful Symmetry,* 326, 327). It is my position that the "I" of the poem is always distinct from Blake; while the poem contains some references that suggest a correspondence between a figure in the poem and the historical Blake, their signification is transformed by their poetic context.

5. It is worth noting that Blake did not include the preface in two of the copies of *Milton,* C and D, though Essick and Viscomi suggest that it was provisionally included in copy C (*Milton, A Poem,* 39 n). There are various theories regarding why the preface was excluded in the later copies of the poem, but no textual or extratextual evidence has yet emerged to give us clear direction on the subject.

6. Wittreich, *Angel of Apocalypse,* 239.

7. Bloom, *Blake's Apocalypse,* 308.

8. Wordsworth, "London, 1802," in *William Wordsworth,* 286. Paul Keen uses Wordsworth's sonnet to begin his discussion of the poet's ideological transition from radicalism to a more Burkean position, indicating the utility of Milton in a more conservative nationalism than one might expect, given his earlier status as a regicide apologist; see Paul Keen, "Critical Leapfrog: Wordsworth's Canonical Ambivalence," *Critical Mass* 3 (1992): 21–29.

9. Lucas, *England and Englishness,* 12.

10. Wittreich, *Angel of Apocalypse,* 271 n. Regarding the reception of Milton's support of regicide during the eighteenth century, see, for example, James King, "Cowper, Hayley, and Samuel Johnson's 'Republican' Milton," in *Studies in Eighteenth-Century Culture,* vol. 17, ed. John Yolton and Leslie Ellen Brown (East Lansing, Mich.: Colleagues Press, 1987), 229–38; Lucas, *England and Englishness,* 45–46; and Wittreich, *Angel of Apocalypse,* 272 n. Pre-Romantic discomfort with Milton's politics extended to his works. John Dennis thus stressed its "formal achievement," and, in an illustrated edition of *Paradise Lost,* "the radical intention of Milton's work is . . . deliberately subverted, or undercut" (Lucas, *England and Englishness,* 17, 16).

11. William Hazlitt, *Lectures on the English Poets* (1818; reprint, Toronto: Oxford University Press, 1952), 100.

12. Francis Jeffrey, "Review of *Specimens of the British Poets; with Biographical and Critical*

Notices, and an Essay on English Poetry," by Thomas Campbell, *Edinburgh Review* 31 (March 1819): 478.

13. Frye, *Fearful Symmetry,* 340.

14. Boyd C. Shafer, *Faces of Nationalism: New Realities and Old Myths* (New York: Harcourt Brace Jovanovich, 1972), 35.

15. Colley, *Britons,* 28.

16. Besides Colley, see, for example, Shafer, *Faces of Nationalism,* esp. 121–22. The Schofield incident is relevant in this context, not because Blake's swift dismissal of the soldier from his Felpham garden and his anxiety over the ensuing trial for sedition gives us a deeper sense of Blake's antimilitarist feeling during the years that he wrote *Milton,* but because of the larger dynamic at work. As G. E. Bentley Jr. points out, "the journal of John Marsh, among other documents, indicates that popular support for the military in Sussex in 1803 and 1804 was very muted" ("*Rex v. Blake:* Sussex Attitudes toward the Military and Blake's Trial for Sedition in 1804," *Huntington Library Quarterly* 56 [1993]: 88). Such evidence lends further support to Colley's argument, in *Britons,* that many regions of Britain were less than enthusiastic when it came to supporting the national military. The Schofield incident was arguably, as Bentley proposes in "*Rex v. Blake,*" "not so much *Rex v. Blake* as *Rex v. Vox Populi* or *The Military v. the People*" (88), complicating attempts to arouse nationalist support for military efforts.

17. Behrendt, *Reading William Blake,* 154.

18. Ibid., 154, 155.

19. See Colley, *Britons,* 178–82.

20. Ibid., 179.

21. To quote a passage from Gellner already cited in the introduction, "Far from revelling in the defiant individual will, nationalists delight in feelings of submission or incorporation in a continuous entity greater, more persistent and more legitimate than the isolated self" (*Nations and Nationalism,* 133).

22. Colley, *Britons,* 167–68.

23. Ibid., 179.

24. I take the term "cult of self-sacrifice" from Daniel J. O'Neil, "The Cult of Self-Sacrifice: The Irish Experience," *Éire-Ireland* 24 (1989): 89–105. O'Neil's comments on Italian nationalism during World War I are also applicable here: "the nation-building effort seems intimately intertwined with the cult of sacrifice. Even a peaceful, revolutionary transition to nationhood often must be elevated to heroic status with its pantheon of martyrs. The nation cannot be born without blood and suffering" (93).

25. Thomas Hughes, *Tom Brown's Schooldays* (1857) (Markham, Ontario: Puffin, 1971), 243.

26. Cindy McCreery, "Satiric Images of Fox, Pitt, and George III: The East India Bill Crisis, 1783–1784," *Word & Image* 9 (1993): 177–78.

27. John Keats, "Ode on a Grecian Urn," in *The Poems of John Keats,* ed. Jack Stillinger (Cambridge: Harvard University Press, 1978), lines 31, 45, 17–18, 2–3.

28. Michael Ferber tentatively points to such a reading, suggesting that Blake's critique of self-sacrifice or atonement contends that the "elect" "create themselves (their Selves) by their belief in the atonement" (*The Social Vision of William Blake* [Princeton: Princeton University

Press, 1985], 77). My aim here is to historicize that contention, and suggest that Blake was identifying an influential cultural construct rather than simply engaging a theological point.

29. Ernest Renan, "What Is a Nation?" trans. Martin Thom, in *Nation and Narration*, 19.

30. John Milton, *Paradise Regain'd,* in *The Complete Poetry of John Milton,* ed. John T. Shawcross, rev. ed. (Garden City, N.Y.: Doubleday, 1971), 3.71–72, 3.74–84.

31. My concern here is with nationalism and anticlassicism in *Milton,* particularly in connection to the rhetoric of sacrifice invoked by neoclassical nationalist ideology. I have dealt with other issues related to this line of enquiry—Blake's representation of Cromwell's Latin secretary, Milton, apocalyptic critiques of imperialism, and imperial genealogies (Greece, Rome, Egypt, Britain)—elsewhere, in my essay "'Greek & Latin Slaves of the Sword': Rejecting the Imperial Nation in Blake's *Milton,*" in *Milton and the Imperial Vision,* ed. Elizabeth Sauer and Balachandra Rajan (Pittsburgh: Duquesne University Press, 1999), 255–72.

32. Moore's satire was published in 1809 and therefore appeared in the first part of the period in which Blake's *Milton* may have been composed.

33. See, for example, the identification of Satan's false exterior with "the Wicker Man of Scandinavia" (*M,* 37.11) and the reference to "Satans Druid sons" who "Offer the Human Victims throughout all the Earth" (*M,* 11.7, 11.8).

34. This distinction has certain continuities with the formal distinction discussed in chapter 2: self-sacrifice operates, in a sense, like a linear narrative, combining individuals into a coherent aggregate through bonds of causation; self-annihilation, however, is closed off from the whole, and so its iterations are not contained within a governing narrative or causal relationship.

35. Colley, *Britons,* 180.

36. O'Neil, "The Cult of Self-Sacrifice," 91–92. O'Neil suggests that Burke, the Romantic period's great defender of the status quo, exemplified this type of thinking.

37. Ibid., 92.

38. Colley, *Britons,* 69–70.

39. Eaves, *Counter-Arts,* 68. Eaves here refers to engraver and print seller John Boydell (for a short biographical sketch of Boydell, see Eaves, *Counter-Arts,* xxiv).

40. Damon, for example, defines "States" as "stages of error" (*A Blake Dictionary,* 386); Fox argues, "Each of these units [states] shelters a collection of fallen individuals, who pass successively from unit to unit, 'state' to 'state,' until they may pass beyond states altogether" (*Poetic Form,* 141); Frosch suggests that it is "Blake's literal contention that worlds, total fabrics of internal and external being, are as fluid and changeable as psychic states. The state of mind is instead the new way in which we are to see ourselves in relation to our condition," *Awakening of Albion,* 94; and Bloom contends, "The State of Milton . . . is a state of self-annihilation" (*Blake's Apocalypse,* 348–49). For one of the more nuanced and comprehensive examinations of Blakean states and individual conditions, see Jeanne Moskal, *Blake, Ethics, and Forgiveness* (Tuscaloosa: University of Alabama Press, 1994), chap. 3. See also, for example, Edward J. Rose, "Blake's Metaphorical States," *Blake Studies* 4 (1971): 9–31.

41. Esterhammer, *Creating States,* 203–4. As Esterhammer added in a conference version of some of this material, "In a historical period when Blake heard of political states being created and abolished all around him, in revolutionary France, in all parts of Europe, and throughout

the British Empire, political connotations are close at hand" ("Blake's *Jerusalem* and the Language of Constitutions" [paper presented at the inaugural conference of the North American Society for the Study of Romanticism, London, Canada, 29 August 1993]). For some examples of Blake's clear use of the term "state" in its political sense, see the Annotations to Bacon's *Essays Moral, Economical and Political,* in which, for instance, Blake writes, "Is Nobility a portion of a State i.e Republic" (624).

42. Damrosch, *Symbol and Truth,* 154.

43. Eaves, *Theory of Art,* 29.

44. See also Eaves's remark, "The picture of emotion as shapeless is embedded in a number of familiar ideas about art: in the usual eighteenth-century definition of sublimity, for instance, where strong, impetuous emotion is associated with vagueness" (*Theory of Art,* 59).

45. Percy Bysshe Shelley, "A Defence of Poetry," 482, 492.

46. Joseph Th. Leerssen, "On the Edge of Europe: Ireland in Search of Oriental Roots, 1650–1850," *Comparative Criticism* 8 (1986): 100, 101.

47. Smith, *National Identity,* 87, 88.

48. The story of Brutus appears in Geoffrey of Monmouth's twelfth-century text *Historia Regum Britanniae,* and was regularly cited by English writers over the next five hundred years, from Layamon, who penned a poem titled *Brut* (c. 1200), to William Warner's *Albion's England or Historical Map of the Same Island* (1586) and Milton's *History of Britain.* Brutus is represented as the conqueror of the indigenous population, but the founder of the writer's people, so that the English are not the descendants of brutes, so to speak, but the imperial Brutus.

49. Thomas Warton, "Of the Origin of Romantic Fiction in Europe" (1774), *The History of English Poetry,* 3 vols., additional notes by Ritson, Ashby, et al. (London: Tegg, 1840), 1:xx; John Bell, *Bell's New Pantheon,* 2 vols. (1790; reprint, New York: Garland, 1979), 2:233; Mallet, *Northern Antiquities,* 1:59–62.

50. See Wright, "'Empire Is No More,'" 28.

51. Geoffrey Hill, "The Norman Yoke," *Puritanism and Revolution: Studies in Interpretation of the English Revolution of the Seventeenth Century* (London: Secker and Warburg, 1958), 57.

52. Francis Barker, *The Tremulous Private Body: Essays in Subjection* (New York: Methuen, 1984), 46.

53. Ibid., 46, 47.

54. Lucas, *England and Englishness,* 45. Arguably, this elision of Milton with his "strong words" informs what S. H. Clark identifies as a "contest" in *Milton* "between prophetic voice and the play of writing" ("Blake's *Milton* as Empiricist Epic: 'Weaving the Woof of Locke,'" *Studies in Romanticism* 36 [1997]: 463).

55. Erdman suggests that the composition of *Milton* and *Jerusalem* overlapped and that the preface to *Milton* in particular might be of later date ("Textual Notes," 809), so linking that preface to an early plate in *Jerusalem* is not necessarily anachronistic. However, I would suggest that similarities between the genre and concerns of the two plates are sufficient grounds for placing them in conjunction; if they are not contemporary, the later plate is arguably an allusion to the earlier, though we may never know which was which.

56. It is tempting to suggest that Blake's description of the uninspired was influenced by Robert Southey's appointment to the position of poet laureate in 1813. Our inability to fix a date

for the poem makes this suggestion at once possible to speculate and difficult to assert: the first three copies of the poem are printed on 1808 paper, and Erdman suggests that the plates were engraved in 1809–1810, but the fourth copy was printed on 1815 paper; plate 41 is common to all four versions, and Erdman's dating of the plates is contingent on the assumption that *Milton* was nearly complete when Blake wrote *Public Address* (see "Textual Notes," 806).

57. By linking the printing press to the "Wine-press on the Rhine," Blake may be alluding to the story that Johann Gutenberg's first press was a modified wine press.

58. Gellner, *Nations and Nationalism,* 57.

59. Compare Paine's discussion of the language of the English and French constitutions and of the significance of other writings when discussing the French state (esp. 111–16). Paine asserts, for instance, "As Mr Burke has not written on constitutions, so neither has he written on the French revolution" (*Rights of Man,* 115).

CHAPTER 6

1. I allude here to J. L. Austin's *How to Do Things with Words* (1962; reprint, Oxford: Clarendon, 1975).

2. According to Peter Razzell, the "first medical account of inoculation to appear in England was that written by Dr Emanuel Timoni, an abstract of which was published in the *Philosophical Transactions* in 1714" (*The Conquest of Smallpox: The Impact of Inoculation on Smallpox Mortality in Eighteenth Century Britain* [Newhaven, U.K.: Caliban, 1977], 2). Timoni, a doctor in Constantinople, was quickly followed into print by Peter Kennedy (*An Essay on External Remedies* [1715]) and Jacob Pylarni ("*Nova et tuta excitandi per transplatationem methodus; nuper inventa et in usum tracta,*" in *Philosophical Transactions* [1716]), and by Lady Mary Wortley Montagu in a letter (1717) (see Razzell, *Conquest of Smallpox,* 2–3, 162 n). In 1721, Montagu had her daughter inoculated in London.

3. Razzell notes, "Jenner's first experiment in vaccination took place on the 14th May, 1796, when he inoculated James Phipps with cowpox taken from the hand of the milkmaid Sarah Nelmes" (*Edward Jenner's Cowpox Vaccine: The History of a Medical Myth* [Newhaven, U.K.: Caliban, 1977], 8). Jenner published his findings in works such as *An Inquiry into the Causes and Effects of the Varioliae Vaccinae* (1798), *Further Observations on the Variolae Vaccinae or Cow-Pox* (1799), and *A Continuation of Facts and Observations Relative to the Variolae Vaccinae or Cowpox* (1800). Jenner's decision to add the colloquial term for the disease to the medical one after 1798 suggests the expectation of a wider, nonmedical audience for his studies. For a wide-ranging discussion of the cultural representations of Jenner's work at the turn of the century, see Tim Fulford and Debbie Lee, "The Jenneration of Disease: Vaccination, Romanticism, and Revolution," *Studies in Romanticism* 39 (2000): 139–63.

4. Razzell, *Conquest of Smallpox,* 1.

5. Fulford and Lee, "The Jenneration of Disease," 159.

6. Percy Bysshe Shelley, "The Triumph of Life," in *Shelley's Poetry and Prose,* 276–81. For poetic evocations of vaccination by Southey, Coleridge, and other Blake contemporaries, see Fulford and Lee, "The Jenneration of Disease."

7. Anne Janowitz, *England's Ruins: Poetic Purpose and the National Landscape* (Cambridge, Mass.: Blackwell, 1990); Susan Matthews, "*Jerusalem* and Nationalism," in *William Blake,* ed. John Lucas (New York: Longman, 1998), 89–95; Dominic Rainsford, *Authorship, Ethics, and the Reader: Blake, Dickens, Joyce* (New York: St. Martin's, 1997).

8. Plato, *Phaedrus,* in *The Works of Plato,* ed. Irwin Edman, trans. Benjamin Jowett (New York: Modern Library, 1956), 327.

9. Plato, *Apology,* in *The Works of Plato,* 75.

10. Plato, *The Republic,* 2nd ed., trans. Desmond Lee (Markham, Ontario: Penguin, 1983), 420.

11. Desmond Lee, *Republic,* 420 n.

12. Paul J. Achtemeier, ed., *Harper's Bible Dictionary* (New York: Harper & Row, 1985), 1115; Behrendt, "'The Consequence of High Powers.'" The vital/viral duality appears in Jacques Derrida's description of the rhetoric that supports the valorization of religious discourse: "Writing in the common sense is the dead letter, it is the carrier of death. It exhausts life. On the other hand, on the other face of the same proposition, writing in the metaphoric sense, natural, divine, and living writing . . . is immediately united to the voice and to breath. . . . It is hieratic, very close to the interior holy voice" (*Of Grammatology,* 17).

13. William Cowper, "Expostulation," in *The Poems of William Cowper,* vol. 1, ed. John D. Baird and Charles Ryskamp (Oxford: Clarendon, 1980), 198–202 (my emphasis). Cowper's poem contains other references to the power of discourse to convert the population to a particular ideology; see, for example, 650–59.

14. See Louis Althusser, "Ideology and Ideological State Apparatuses (Notes Toward an Investigation)," in *Lenin and Philosophy and Other Essays,* trans. Ben Brewster (New York: Monthly Review P/NLB, 1977), 127–86.

15. Thus, for example, Derrida writes, "The Socratic *pharmakon* also acts like venom, like the bite of a poisonous snake. . . . And Socrates' bite is worse than a snake's since its traces invade the soul. . . . And when they don't act like the venom of a snake, Socrates' pharmaceutical charms provoke a kind of *narcosis,* benumbing and paralyzing into aporia, like the touch of a sting ray" ("Plato's Pharmacy," in *Dissemination,* trans. Barbara Johnson [Chicago: University of Chicago Press, 1981], 118).

16. Review of *The Trial of Thomas Muir, Analytical Review* 17 (1793): 104.

17. William Godwin, "Of Choice in Reading," in *The Enquirer: Reflections on Education, Manners, and Literature* (1797; reprint, New York: Kelley, 1965), 129–46.

18. *Full Report,* 37–38. Though it is primarily concerned with a call for "universal emancipation and representative legislature," including Catholic Emancipation, the address does ask Irishmen to take up arms to defend their rights; the call to arms, moreover, is specifically framed as a response to the British government's raising of the militia to suppress "all seditious associations" (*Full Report,* 41, 38).

19. Ibid., 39.

20. Regarding the textual production of cultural hybridity, see especially David Lloyd's chapter, "Adulteration and the Nation," in *Anomalous States: Irish Writing and the Post-Colonial Moment* (Durham, N.C.: Duke University Press, 1993). Lloyd's subject, the corruption of national identity under an imperial regime, is in many ways homologous to that of the present chapter, namely the conflict between different constructions of national identity.

21. See John Barrell, *The Infection of Thomas De Quincey: A Psychopathology of Imperialism* (New Haven: Yale University Press, 1991).

22. Lloyd, "Adulteration and the Nation," 96–97.

23. Homi K. Bhabha, "Signs Taken for Wonders: Questions of Ambivalence and Authority Under a Tree Outside Delhi, May 1817," in *The Location of Culture* (New York: Routledge, 1994), 112, 113.

24. Edmund Spenser, similarly, identified the propagation of the alien political structure of the Irish—which, for instance, required that leaders be selected on the basis of merit—with suckling, writing, "first the childe that sucketh the milke of the nurse, must of necessity learn his first speach of her . . . and not only of the speach, but also of the manners and conditions" ("A View to the Present State of Ireland" [1596], in *The Works of Spencer* [*sic*], *Campion, Hanmer, and Marleborough,* 2 vols. [New York: Kennikat Press, 1970], 1:112).

25. David Hume, *An Inquiry Concerning Human Understanding,* in *Hume on Nature and the Understanding,* ed. Anthony Flew (New York: Collier, 1962), 109. Hume refutes the claim that "the WHOLE, considered as one system, is, in every period of its existence, ordered with perfect benevolence. . . . Every physical ill . . . makes an essential part of this benevolent system, and could not possibly be removed . . . without giving entrance to greater ill or excluding greater good," comparing that approach to "preaching" to "a man lying under the racking pains of the gout" about "the rectitude of those general laws which produced the malignant humors in his body" (108–9). Stephen D. Cox suggests that, despite Blake's many differences with "Deists," this is one point on which Blake agreed with them (*"The Stranger Within Thee": Concepts of the Self in Late-Eighteenth-Century Literature* [Pittsburgh: University of Pittsburgh Press, 1980], 142).

26. Hume, *Inquiry Concerning Human Understanding,* 109–10.

27. Cowper, "Expostulation," 95–106.

28. Barrell, *The Infection of Thomas De Quincey,* 15.

29. Cowper, "Expostulation," 372.

30. Steven Blakemore, "Revolutions in Representation: Burke's *Reflections on the Revolution in France,*" *Eighteenth-Century Life* 15 (1991): 9. For example, in Thomas Randolph's "To a painted Mistresse," cosmetics not only implicate the woman in prostitution, but render her "adulterate," suggesting both hybridity and "adultery" (*The Poems and Amyntas of Thomas Randolph,* ed. John Jay Parry [New Haven: Yale University Press, 1917], 12, 3). See also Andrew Marvell's "Mower against Gardens," in which the "Luxurious man, to bring his vice in use, / Did after him the world seduce," transforming the flowers with perfume and cosmetics, so that "[n]o plant now knew the stock from which it came," and producing "[f]orbidden mixtures" and "adulterate fruit" in the "green seraglio" (*The Complete Poems,* ed. Elizabeth Story Donno [Markham, Ontario: Penguin, 1985], 1–2, 11–12, 23, 22, 25, 27).

31. Wollstonecraft, *Vindication,* 99, 99 n.

32. Godwin, "Of Choice in Reading," 135, 140 (my emphasis).

33. Ibid., 141.

34. I prefer the double negative of "not immoral" to "moral" in this instance because of Godwin's central argument in the essay. Godwin suggests that "good" literature excites the mind and is not necessarily moral, particularly since the moral of a piece will depend on the reader's contextualization of the work. He claims, for instance, "Shakespear is a writer by no means anxious about his moral. He seems almost indifferent concerning virtue and vice, and takes up with either as it falls in his way" ("Of Choice in Reading," 138).

35. Edmund Burke, *Reflections on the Revolution,* 213, 185.

36. [Francis Jeffrey,] Review of *Epistles, Odes, and Other Poems,* by Thomas Moore, *Edinburgh Review* 8(July 1806): 456, 458, 459–60.

37. Ibid., 460.

38. Ibid., 457 (my emphasis).

39. There are a number of other instances, including: "the land of snares & traps & wheels & pit-falls & dire mills" (*J,* 13.49); "Here the Twelve Sons of Albion, join'd in dark Assembly . . . Became as Three Immense Wheels, turning upon one-another" (*J,* 18.5, 18.8); "Why should Punishment Weave the Veil with Iron Wheels of War / When Forgiveness might it Weave with Wings of Cherubim" (*J,* 22.34–35); "Albion dark, / Repugnant; rolld his Wheels backward into Non-Entity" (*J,* 39.5–6); "Albions dread Wheels, stretching out spaces immense between / That every particle of light & air" (*J,* 39.9–10); "to winnow kingdoms / The water wheel & mill of many innumerable wheels resistless / Over the Four fold Monarchy from Earth to the Mundane Shell" (*J,* 73.13–15); "Hyle roofd Los in Albions Cliffs by the Affections rent / Asunder & opposed to Thought, to draw Jerusalems Sons / Into the Vortex of his Wheels" (*J,* 74.28–30).

40. Leonard W. Deen, *Conversing in Paradise,* 228.

41. A. G. den Otter has traced the rhetorical strategies deployed in *Jerusalem* in her essay "True, Right, and Good: Blake's Arguments for Vision in *Jerusalem*" (*Philological Quarterly* 72 [1993]: 73–96). While my concerns have some intersection with an informing paradigm of rhetoric—persuading an audience to accede to the orator's viewpoint—I would argue that Blake is doing much more than simply "encourag[ing] his audience to make an informed decision in his favour," as den Otter suggests (74). Blake directs his rhetorical force against culturally specific groups, seeking to alienate them from that which prevents their assimilation into his ideal culture by identifying those elements of their cultures with cancers, infections, and other entities that are readily defined as unmitigatedly bad. The truth and morality of Blake's vision aside, his strategies bear an unpleasant similarity to those of many tyrannies before and since.

42. Matthews, "*Jerusalem* and Nationalism," 83.

43. Blake's valorization of "harmony" appears to be a further departure from his earlier position: as David Punter suggests, "the rejection of 'harmony' common to Blake and Ossian, which we may interpret as a rejection of metaphor and allegory, can be seen as related to Blake's rejection of socially conditioned linguistic and poetic practices" ("Blake: Social Relations," 202). The fundamental difference between the "paltry Harmonies" (*M,* 41.10) that Punter cites and the harmonies of *Jerusalem* is that Blake is ideologically opposed to the former and defines the

latter. The problem is not harmony itself, but the rubric under which it is generated; like discourse, harmony can generate social coherence constructively (vitally) or destructively (virally), and that taxonomy is a politically entangled one.

44. Rainsford, *Authorship,* 50.

45. Damon, *A Blake Dictionary,* 332–33.

46. While Damrosch suggests that "in a horrible image in *Jerusalem* the growing fetus is likened to a spreading malignancy" (*Symbol and Truth,* 204), I would argue that we can read "a ravening eating Cancer growing in the Female" literally, as a reference to uterine cancer, rather than as a ghastly metaphor for a fetus. Cancer takes the place of a fetus in a Gothic parody of procreative propagation that resonates with my discussion of reproduction in chapter 4 of this study.

47. Ferber, *Social Vision of William Blake,* 197.

48. I am, of course, associating the dragon with the serpent, not only because both are reptilian, and they are etymologically linked through the archaism "wyrm," or "worm," but also because of an earlier passage in *Europe* in which the druidic "temple" is described as serpentine (*Eur,* 10.21).

49. In his famous sermon, Latimer writes, "Gods worde is a seede to be sowen in Goddes fielde, that is the faithful congregation, and the preacher is the sower. And it is in the gospel. *Exiuit qui seminat seminare semen suum.* He that soweth, the husbandman, the ploughman went furth to sowe his seede, so that a preacher is resembled to a ploughman. . . . For preachynge of the Gospel is one of Goddes plough workes, and the preacher is one of Goddes plough men" (*Sermon on the Ploughers* [18 January 1549], ed. Edward Arber [London, 1869], 12–13).

50. Stephen Leo Carr, "Illuminated Printing: Toward a Logic of Difference," in *Unnam'd Forms,* 177.

51. Barrell, *Political Theory of Painting,* 254.

52. See Punter, "Blake: Social Relations," 201–2; and note 43, above.

53. With the phrase "narratives in the voice of the disenfranchised," I refer to such works as Maria Edgeworth's *Castle Rackrent* and "Lame Jervas," both of which validate colonialism through what might be termed a subaltern narrator. Edgeworth's narrators sanction and praise the hegemony while decrying those who resist it. Regarding the use of cheap engravings as propaganda, see Colley, *Britons,* esp. 178–82.

54. Matthews, "*Jerusalem* and Nationalism," 99.

CONCLUSION

1. Barrell, *Political Theory of Painting,* 224. Barrell suggests that "it may not be too much of a generalisation to say that in Britain Blake has most often been represented as a humane individual deeply sensitive to the infringement of personal identity by 'mass civilization,' whereas in

America this version of him has been in competition with a more aggressive Blake, the man who goes his own way and walks tall" (224). Steve Clark and David Worrall argue that British Blake studies derives centrally from E. P. Thompson's *Making of an English Working-Class,* while American Blake studies "have flourished within, rather than broken from the idealist tradition established in 1947 by [Frye's] *Fearful Symmetry*" (introduction to *Historicizing Blake,* ed. Steve Clark and David Worrall [New York: Macmillan, 1994], 4). That Frye was a Canadian scholar adds a suggestive complication to such nationalist divisions of Blake studies.

2. Barrell, *Political Theory of Painting,* 225.

3. Ibid., 242.

4. Damrosch, *Symbol and Truth,* 73.

5. See Barrell, *Infection of Thomas De Quincey,* 10–11.

6. Eaves, *Counter-Arts,* 146.

7. Ibid., 143–44.

8. See James L. Resseguie, "Defamiliarization in the Gospels," *Mosaic* 21 (1988): 25–35.

9. Mitchell, "Dangerous Blake," 415, 411, 412.

10. Ibid., 414.

11. Ibid., 410, 414.

12. See Keen, *Crisis of Literature.*

Bibliography

Abrams, M. H. *Natural Supernaturalism: Tradition and Revolution in Romantic Literature*. New York: Norton, 1971.

Achtemeier, Paul J., ed. *Harper's Bible Dictionary*. New York: Harper and Row, 1985.

Adams, Hazard. "The World-View of William Blake in Relation to Cultural Policy." In *Critical Essays on William Blake,* edited by Hazard Adams, 107–17. Boston: Hall, 1991.

——, ed. *William Blake:* Jerusalem, *Selected Poems, and Prose*. New York: Holt, Rinehart and Winston, 1970.

Althusser, Louis. "Ideology and Ideological State Apparatuses (Notes Toward an Investigation)." In *Lenin and Philosophy and Other Essays,* translated by Ben Brewster, 127–86. New York: Monthly Review P/NLB, 1977.

Anderson, Benedict. *Imagined Communities: Reflections on the Origin and Spread of Nationalism*. Rev. ed. New York: Verso, 1991.

Anderson, Mark. "Why Is That Fairy in Europe?" *Colby Library Quarterly* 21 (1985): 122–33.

Ault, Donald. *Narrative Unbound: Re-Visioning Blake's* The Four Zoas. Barrytown, N.Y.: Station Hill, 1987.

——. *Visionary Physics: Blake's Response to Newton*. Chicago: University of Chicago Press, 1974.

Austin, J. L. *How to Do Things with Words*. 1962. Reprint, Oxford: Clarendon, 1975.

Baine, Rodney M. *The Scattered Portions: William Blake's Biological Symbolism*. Athens Ga.: privately printed, 1986.

Barker, Francis. *The Tremulous Private Body: Essays in Subjection*. New York: Methuen, 1984.

Barrell, John. *The Infection of Thomas De Quincey: A Psychopathology of Imperialism*. New Haven: Yale University Press, 1991.

——. *The Political Theory of Painting from Reynolds to Hazlitt: 'The Body of the Public.'* New Haven: Yale University Press, 1986.

——. "Sir Joshua Reynolds and the Englishness of English Art." In *Nation and Narration,* edited by Homi K. Bhabha, 154–76. New York: Routledge, 1990.

Barthes, Roland. "Myth Today." In *Mythologies*. 1957. Translated by Annette Lavers, 117–74. Toronto: Paladin Grafton Books, 1973.

——. *S/Z*. 1970. Translated by Richard Miller. Preface by Richard Howard. New York: Hill and Wang, 1974.

Bataille, Georges. "The Psychological Structure of Fascism." In *Visions of Excess: Selected Writings, 1927–1939,* edited by Allan Stoekl and translated by Allan

Stoekl with Carl R. Lovett and Donald M. Leslie Jr., 137–60. Vol. 14 of *Theory and History of Literature*. Minneapolis: University of Minnesota Press, 1991.

——. *Theory of Religion*. 1973. Translated by Robert Hurley. New York: Zone Books, 1992.

Behrendt, Stephen C. "'This Accursed Family': Blake's *America* and the American Revolution." *The Eighteenth Century: Theory and Interpretation* 27 (1986): 26–51.

——. "'The Consequence of High Powers': Blake, Shelley, and Prophecy's Public Dimension." *Papers on Language and Literature* 22 (1986): 254–75.

——. "History When Time Stops: Blake's *America, Europe,* and *The Song of Los.*" *Papers on Language and Literature* 28 (1992): 379–97.

——. "Paradise Lost, History Painting, and Eighteenth-Century English Nationalism." *Milton Studies* 25 (1989): 141–59.

——. *Reading William Blake*. New York: St. Martin's, 1992.

Bell, John. *Bell's New Pantheon*. 2 vols. 1790. Reprint, New York: Garland, 1979.

Bentley, G. E., Jr. *Blake Records*. Toronto: Clarendon, 1969.

——. "*Rex v. Blake:* Sussex Attitudes toward the Military and Blake's Trial for Sedition in 1804." *Huntington Library Quarterly* 56 (1993): 83–89.

Benveniste, Emile. *Problems in General Linguistics*. Translated by Mary Elizabeth Meek. Coral Gables: University of Miami Press, 1971.

Bernstein, Charles. Preface to *The Politics of Poetic Form: Poetry and Public Policy,* edited by Charles Bernstein, vii–viii. New York: ROOF, 1990.

Bhabha, Homi K. "DissemiNation: Time, Narrative, and the Margins of the Modern Nation." In *Nation and Narration,* edited by Homi K. Bhabha, 291–322. New York: Routledge, 1990.

——. "Introduction: Narrating the Nation." In *Nation and Narration,* edited by Homi K. Bhabha, 1–7. New York: Routledge, 1990.

——. "Signs Taken for Wonders: Questions of Ambivalence and Authority under a Tree Outside Delhi, May 1817." In *The Location of Culture,* 102–22. New York: Routledge, 1994.

Bidlake, Steven. "Blake, the Sacred, and the French Revolution: Eighteenth-Century Ideology and the Problem of Violence." *European Romantic Review* 3 (1992): 1–20.

Bidney, Martin. *Blake and Goethe: Psychology, Ontology, Imagination*. Columbia: University of Missouri Press, 1988.

Bindman, David. Introduction and notes to *The Complete Graphic Works of William Blake,* edited by David Bindman. London: Thames and Hudson, 1986.

Blake, David, and Elliott Gruner. "Redeeming Captivity: The Negative Revolution of Blake's *Visions of the Daughters of Albion.*" *Symbiosis: A Journal of Anglo-American Literary Relations* 1 (1997): 21–34.

Blake, William. *The Complete Poetry and Prose of William Blake*. Rev. ed. Edited by David V. Erdman. New York: Doubleday, 1988.

——. *The Illuminated Books of William Blake*. 6 vols. Edited by David Bindman. Princeton: Princeton University Press, 1998.

——. *Poetical Sketches*. 1783. Reprint, London: Noel Douglas Replicas, 1926.

Blakemore, Steven. "Revolutions in Representation: Burke's *Reflections on the Revolution in France.*" *Eighteenth-Century Life* 15 (1991): 1–18.

Bloom, Harold. *The Anxiety of Influence: A Theory of Poetry*. New York: Oxford University Press, 1973.

———. *Blake's Apocalypse: A Study in Poetic Argument*. Garden City, N.Y.: Doubleday, 1963.

———. "Blake's *Jerusalem:* The Bard of Sensibility and the Form of Prophecy." 1970. In *The Ringers in the Tower,* 64–79. Chicago: University of Chicago Press, 1971.

———. "Commentary." In *The Complete Poetry and Prose of William Blake,* rev. ed., edited by David V. Erdman, 894–970. New York: Doubleday, 1988.

Bolton, Betsy. "'A Garment Dipped in Blood': Ololon and Problems of Gender in Blake's *Milton.*" *Studies in Romanticism* 36 (1997): 61–101.

Bourdieu, Pierre. "Censorship and the Imposition of Form." In *Language and Symbolic Power,* edited by John B. Thompson and translated by Gino Raymond and Matthew Adamson, 137–59. Cambridge: Harvard University Press, 1991.

Bracher, Mark. *Being Form'd: Thinking Through Blake's* Milton. Barrytown, N.Y.: Station Hill, 1985.

———. "The Metaphysical Grounds of Oppression in Blake's *Visions of the Daughters of Albion.*" *Colby Library Quarterly* 20 (1984): 164–76.

Brecht, Bertholt. *Brecht on Theatre: The Development of an Aesthetic*. Edited and translated by John Willett. New York: Hill and Wang, 1964.

Brombert, Victor. "The Happy Prison: A Recurring Romantic Metaphor." In *Romanticism: Vistas, Instances, Continuities,* edited by David Thorburn and Geoffrey Hartman, 62–79. Ithaca: Cornell University Press, 1973.

Brooke, Charlotte, trans. and ed. *Reliques of Irish Poetry*. 1789. Reprint, Gainesville, Florida: Scholars' Facsimiles and Reprints, 1970.

Brossard, Nicole. "Poetic Politics." In *The Politics of Poetic Form: Poetry and Public Policy*, edited by Charles Bernstein, 73–82. New York: ROOF, 1990.

Bruder, Helen P. *William Blake and the Daughters of Albion*. New York: St. Martin's, 1997.

Brunton, Mary. *Discipline*. 1814. London: Pandora, 1986.

Burke, Edmund. *Reflections on the Revolution in France*. 1790. Edited by Conor Cruise O'Brien. Markham, Ont.: Penguin, 1986.

———. "Speech on Opening of Impeachment" (15 February 1788). In *India: The Launching of the Hastings Impeachment, 1786–1788,* edited by P. J. Marshall, 269–312. Vol. 6 of *The Writings and Speeches of Edmund Burke,* edited by Paul Langford. Oxford: Clarendon, 1991.

Butler, Judith. "Imitation and Gender Subordination." In *Inside/Out,* edited by Diana Fuss, 13–31. New York: Routledge, 1991.

Butler, Marilyn. "The Bristol Model: Romanticism as Provincial Nationalism." Paper presented at the biannual conference of the British Association for Romantic Studies, Glasgow, Scotland, 10 July 1993.

Carothers, Yvonne M. "Space and Time in *Milton*: The 'Bard's Song.'" In *Blake in His Time,* edited by Robert N. Essick and Donald Pearce, 116–27. Bloomington: Indiana University Press, 1978.

Carr, Stephen Leo. "Illuminated Printing: Toward a Logic of Difference." In *Unnam'd Forms: Blake and Textuality,* edited by Nelson Hilton and Thomas A. Vogler, 177–96. Berkeley: University of California Press, 1986.

Castle, Terry. "Eros and Liberty at the English Masquerade, 1710–1790." *Eighteenth-Century Studies* 17 (1983–84): 156–76.

———. "Lab'ring Bards: Birth *Topoi* and English Poetics, 1660–1820." *Journal of English and Germanic Philology* 78 (1979): 193–208.

———. *Masquerade and Civilization: The Carnivalesque in Eighteenth-Century English Culture and Fiction*. Stanford: Stanford University Press, 1986.

Caws, Mary Ann. *The Art of Interference: Stressed Readings in Verbal and Visual Texts*. Princeton: Princeton University Press, 1989.

Chase, The. In *Reliques of Irish Poetry,* translated and edited by Charlotte Brooke. 1789. Reprint, Gainesville, Florida: Scholars' Facsimiles and Reprints, 1970.

Clark, David L. "'The Innocence of Becoming Restored': Blake, Nietzsche, and the Disclosure of Difference." *Studies in Romanticism* 29 (1990): 91–113.

Clark, S. H. "Blake's *Milton* as Empiricist Epic: 'Weaving the Woof of Locke.'" *Studies in Romanticism* 36 (1997): 457–82.

Clark, Steve, and David Worrall. Introduction to *Historicizing Blake,* edited by Steve Clark and David Worrall, 1–23. New York: Macmillan, 1994.

Coleridge, Samuel Taylor. *Biographia Literaria or Biographical Sketches of My Literary Life and Opinions*. 2 vols. Edited by James Engell and W. Jackson Bate. Vol. 7 of *The Collected Works of Samuel Taylor Coleridge*. Princeton: Princeton University Press, 1983.

Colley, Linda. *Britons: Forging the Nation, 1707–1837*. New Haven: Yale University Press, 1992.

Cooper, Andrew M. "Blake and Madness: The World Turned Inside Out." *ELH* 57 (1990): 585–642.

———. "Blake's Escape from Mythology: Self-Mastery in *Milton.*" *Studies in Romanticism* 20 (1981): 85–110.

Cowper, William. *The Poems of William Cowper*. Vol. 1: 1748–1782. Edited by John D. Baird and Charles Ryskamp. Oxford: Clarendon, 1980.

Cox, Stephen D. *"The Stranger Within Thee": Concepts of the Self in Late-Eighteenth-Century Literature*. Pittsburgh: University of Pittsburgh Press, 1980.

Crehan, Stewart. *Blake in Context*. New York: Humanities Press, 1984.

Damon, S. Foster. *A Blake Dictionary: The Ideas and Symbols of William Blake*. Rev. ed. London: Brown University Press, 1988.

Damrosch, Leopold, Jr. *Symbol and Truth in Blake's Myth*. Princeton: Princeton University Press, 1980.

De Luca, V. A. "A Wall of Words: The Sublime as Text." In *Unnam'd Forms: Blake and Textuality,* edited by Nelson Hilton and Thomas A. Vogler, 218–41. Berkeley: University of California Press, 1986.

Deane, Seamus. "Civilians and Barbarians." In *Ireland's Field Day,* 33–42. Field Day Theatre Company. Notre Dame: University of Notre Dame Press, 1986.

———. *The French Revolution and the Enlightenment in England, 1789–1832*. Cambridge: Harvard University Press, 1988.

Deen, Leonard W. *Conversing in Paradise: Poetic Genius and the Identity-as-Community in Blake's Los*. Columbia: University of Missouri Press, 1983.

den Otter, A. G. "True, Right, and Good: Blake's Arguments for Vision in *Jerusalem.*" *Philological Quarterly* 72 (1993): 73–96.

Derrida, Jacques. "La Parole Soufflée." In *Writing and Difference,* translated by Alan Bass, 169–95. Chicago: University of Chicago Press, 1978.

——. *Of Grammatology*. Translated by Gayatri Chakravorty Spivak. Baltimore: Johns Hopkins University Press, 1976.

——. "Plato's Pharmacy." In *Dissemination,* translated by Barbara Johnson, 61–171. Chicago: University of Chicago Press, 1981.

——. "Signature Event Context." Translated by Samuel Weber and Jeffrey Mehlman. In *Limited Inc.,* edited by Gerald Graff, 1–23. Evanston, Ill.: Northwestern University Press, 1988.

DiSalvo, Jackie. *War of Titans: Blake's Critique of Milton and the Politics of Religion*. Pittsburgh: University of Pittsburgh Press, 1983.

Dörrbecker, D. W. "Innovative Reproduction: Painters and Engravers at the Royal Academy of Arts." In *Historicizing Blake,* edited by Steve Clark and David Worrall, 125–46. New York: Macmillan, 1994.

Doskow, Minna. "William Blake's *America:* The Story of a Revolution Betrayed." *Blake Studies* 8 (1979): 167–86.

DuPlessis, Rachel Blau. *Writing beyond the Ending: Narrative Strategies of Twentieth-Century Women Writers*. Bloomington: Indiana University Press, 1985.

Eaves, Morris. "Blake and the Artistic Machine: An Essay in Decorum and Technology." *PMLA* 22 (1977): 903–27.

——. *The Counter-Arts Conspiracy: Art and Industry in the Age of Blake*. Ithaca: Cornell University Press, 1992.

——. "Romantic Expressive Theory and Blake's Idea of the Audience." *PMLA* 95 (1980): 784–801.

——. *William Blake's Theory of Art*. Princeton: Princeton University Press, 1982.

Edwards, Gavin. "Repeating the Same Dull Round." In *Unnam'd Forms: Blake and Textuality,* edited by Nelson Hilton and Thomas A. Vogler, 26–48. Berkeley: University of California Press, 1986.

Erdman, David V. *Blake: Prophet against Empire: A Poet's Interpretation of the History of His Own Times*. Rev. ed. Garden City, N.Y.: Doubleday, 1969.

——. "The Symmetries of *The Song of Los*." *Studies in Romanticism* 16 (1977): 179–88.

——. "Textual Notes." In *The Complete Poetry and Prose of William Blake,* rev. ed., edited by David V. Erdman, 786–893. New York: Doubleday, 1988.

——, ed. *Blake and His Bibles*. West Cornwall, Conn.: Locust Hill, 1990.

——. *The Complete Poetry and Prose of William Blake*. Rev. ed. New York: Doubleday, 1988.

Essick, Robert N. *William Blake and the Language of Adam*. Toronto: Oxford University Press, 1989.

——. "William Blake, Thomas Paine, and Biblical Revolution." *Studies in Romanticism* 30 (1991): 189–212.

——. *The Works of William Blake in the Huntington Collections*. San Marino, Calif.: Huntington Library, 1985.

Essick, Robert N., and Joseph Viscomi, eds. *Milton, A Poem and the Final Illuminated Works*. Vol. 5 of *The Illuminated Books of William Blake,* ed. David Bindman. Princeton: Princeton University Press, 1998.

Esterhammer, Angela. "Blake's *Jerusalem* and the Language of Constitutions." Paper presented at the inaugural conference of the North American Society for the Study of Romanticism, London, Canada, 29 August 1993.

———. *Creating States: Studies in the Performative Language of John Milton and William Blake*. Toronto: University of Toronto Press, 1994.

Feather, John P. "From Censorship to Copyright: Aspects of the Government's Role in the English Book Trade, 1695–1775." In *Books and Society in History,* edited by Kenneth E. Carpenter, 173–98. New York: Bowker, 1983.

Ferber, Michael. "Blake's *America* and the Birth of Revolution." In *History and Myth: Essays on English Romantic Literature,* edited by Stephen C. Behrendt, 73–99. Detroit: Wayne State University Press, 1990.

———. "Blake's Idea of Brotherhood." *PMLA* 93 (1978): 438–47.

———. *The Social Vision of William Blake*. Princeton: Princeton University Press, 1985.

Foucault, Michel. *Discipline and Punish: The Birth of the Prison*. 1977. Translated by Alan Sheridan. New York: Random House, 1979.

———. "Nietzsche, Genealogy, History." In *The Foucault Reader,* edited by Paul Rabinow, 76–100. New York: Pantheon, 1984.

———. *The Order of Things: An Archaeology of the Human Sciences*. 1966. Translator not identified. New York: Random House, 1970.

Fox, Susan. "The Female as Metaphor in William Blake's Poetry." *Critical Inquiry* 3 (1977): 507–19.

———. *Poetic Form in Blake's* Milton. Princeton: Princeton University Press, 1976.

Friedman, Susan Stanford. "Creativity and the Childbirth Metaphor: Gender Difference in Literary Discourse." In *Speaking of Gender,* edited by Elaine Showalter, 73–100. New York: Routledge, 1989.

Frosch, Thomas R. *The Awakening of Albion: The Renovation of the Body in the Poetry of William Blake*. Ithaca: Cornell University Press, 1974.

Frye, Northrop. *Fables of Identity: Studies in Poetic Mythology*. New York: Harcourt, Brace, and World, 1963.

———. *Fearful Symmetry: A Study of William Blake*. 1947. Reprint, Princeton: Princeton University Press, 1969.

———. *A Study of English Romanticism*. Chicago: University of Chicago Press, 1968.

Fulford, Tim, and Debbie Lee. "The Jenneration of Disease: Vaccination, Romanticism, and Revolution." *Studies in Romanticism* 39 (2000): 139–63.

A Full Report of the Trial at Bar in the Court of King's Bench, of William Drennan, MD Upon an Indictment Charging Him with Having Written and Published a Seditious Libel with the Speeches of Counsel, and the Opinions of the Court at Large. Dublin: Rea and Johnson, 1794. In *The Trial of William Drennan,* edited by John Francis Larkin, 35–120. Dublin: Irish Academic Press, 1991.

Fuseli, Henry. *The Collected English Letters of Henry Fuseli*. Edited by David H. Weinglass. London: Kraus, 1982.

———. Lectures I–III in *Lectures on Painting*. 1801. In *The Life and Writings of Henry Fuseli,* 3 vols., edited by John Knowles, 2:1–186. 1831. Reprint, London: Kraus, 1982.

Gaskill, Howard. "'Ossian' Macpherson: Towards a Rehabilitation." *Comparative Criticism* 8 (1986): 113–46.

Gellner, Ernest. *Nations and Nationalism*. Oxford: Blackwell, 1983.

Gilbert, Sandra M., and Susan Gubar. *The Madwoman in the Attic: The Woman*

Writer and the Nineteenth-Century Literary Imagination. New Haven: Yale University Press, 1979.

Gillham, D. G. *Blake's Contrary States: The 'Songs of Innocence and of Experience' as Dramatic Poems*. Cambridge: Cambridge University Press, 1966.

Glausser, Wayne. "Atomistic Simulacra in the Enlightenment and Blake's Post-Enlightenment." *The Eighteenth Century: Theory and Interpretation* 32 (1991): 73–88.

Gleckner, Robert F. *Blake's Prelude:* Poetical Sketches. Baltimore: Johns Hopkins University Press, 1982.

Godwin, William. "Of Choice in Reading." In *The Enquirer: Reflections on Education, Manners, and Literature,* 129–46. 1797. Reprint, New York: Kelley, 1965.

Goethe, Johann Wolfgang von. "On the *Laocoon* Group." 1798. In *Essays on Art and Literature,* edited by John Gearey and translated by Ellen von Nardroff and Ernest H. von Nardroff. New York: Suhrkamp, 1986.

Goldberg, Jonathan. *Writing Matter: From the Hands of the English Renaissance*. Stanford: Stanford University Press, 1990.

Goldsmith, Steven. *Unbuilding Jerusalem: Apocalypse and Romantic Representation*. Ithaca: Cornell University Press, 1993.

Goslee, Nancy Moore. "Slavery and Sexual Character: Questioning the Master Trope in Blake's *Visions of the Daughters of Albion*." *ELH* 57 (1990): 101–28.

Gray, Thomas. *The Descent of Odin*. 1768. In *The Works of Thomas Gray in Prose and Verse,* 4 vols., edited by Edmund Gosse, 1:59–65. New York: AMS Press, 1968.

Greenblatt, Stephen. *Shakespearean Negotiations: The Circulation of Social Energy in Renaissance England*. Berkeley: University of California Press, 1988.

Gross, David. "'Mind Forg'd Manacles': Hegemony and Counter-Hegemony in Blake." *The Eighteenth Century: Theory and Interpretation* 23 (1986): 3–25.

Hagstrum, Jean H. *William Blake, Poet and Painter: An Introduction to the Illuminated Verse*. Chicago: University of Chicago Press, 1964.

Hall, Carol Louise. *Blake and Fuseli: A Study in the Transmission of Ideas*. New York: Garland, 1985.

Hazlitt, William. *Lectures on the English Poets*. 1818. Toronto: Oxford University Press, 1952.

Heffernan, James A. W. "Blake's Oothoon: The Dilemmas of Marginality." *Studies in Romanticism* 30 (1991): 3–18.

Hill, Geoffrey. "The Norman Yoke." In *Puritanism and Revolution: Studies in Interpretation of the English Revolution of the Seventeenth Century,* 50–122. London: Secker and Warburg, 1958.

Hilton, Nelson. *Literal Imagination: Blake's Vision of Words*. Berkeley: University of California Press, 1983.

———. "An Original Story." In *Unnam'd Forms: Blake and Textuality,* edited by Nelson Hilton and Thomas A. Vogler, 69–104. Berkeley: University of California Press, 1986.

———, ed. *Essential Articles for the Study of William Blake, 1970–1984*. Hamden, Conn.: Archon, 1986.

Holy Bible. King James Version. Toronto: Collins' Clear-Type Press, 1975.

Horn, William Dennis. "Blake's Revisionism: Gnostic Interpretation and Criticial Methodology." In *Critical Paths: Blake and the Argument of Method,* edited by

Dan Miller, Mark Bracher, and Donald Ault, 72–98. Durham, N.C.: Duke University Press, 1987.

Howard, John. *Infernal Poetics: Poetic Structures in Blake's Lambeth Prophecies*. Toronto: Associated University Press, 1984.

Howard, Seymour. "Blake: Classicism, Gothicism, and Nationalism." *Colby Library Quarterly* 21 (1985): 165–87.

Hughes, Thomas. *Tom Brown's Schooldays*. 1857. Markham, Ontario: Puffin, 1971.

Hume, David. *An Inquiry Concerning Human Understanding*. In *Hume on Nature and the Understanding*, edited by Anthony Flew, 21–163. New York: Collier, 1962.

——. "Of National Characters." In *David Hume: The Philosophical Works*, 4 vols., edited by Thomas Hill Green and Thomas Hodge Grose, 3:244–58. Aalen, Germany: Scientia Verlag, 1964.

Jacobs, Carol. "The Critical Performance of Lessing's *Laokoon*." *Modern Language Notes* 102 (1987): 483–521.

James, David E. "Angels Out of the Sun: Art, Religion, and Politics in Blake's *America*." *Studies in Romanticism* 18 (1979): 235–52.

——. "Blake's *Laocoön:* A Degree Zero of Literary Production." *PMLA* 98 (1983): 226–36.

Janowitz, Anne. *England's Ruins: Poetic Purpose and the National Landscape*. Cambridge, Mass.: Blackwell, 1990.

[Jeffrey, Francis]. "Review of *Epistles, Odes, and Other Poems* by Thomas Moore." *Edinburgh Review* 8 (July 1806): 456–65.

——. "Review of *Specimens of the British Poets; with Biographical and Critical Notices, and an Essay on English Poetry* by Thomas Campbell." *Edinburgh Review* 31 (March 1819): 462–97.

Johnson, Mary Lynn, and John E. Grant, eds. *Blake's Poetry and Designs*. New York: Norton, 1979.

Jones, John H. "Printed Performance and Reading *The Book[s] of Urizen:* Blake's Bookmaking Process and the Transformation of Late Eighteenth-Century Print Culture." *Colby Quarterly* 35 (1999): 73–89.

Joyce, Michael. "Notes Toward an Unwritten Non-linear Electronic Text, 'The Ends of Print Culture.'" *Postmodern Culture* 2.1 (September 1991).

Keach, William. *Shelley's Style*. New York: Methuen, 1984.

Keats, John. *Letters of John Keats*. Edited by Robert Gittings. Oxford: Oxford University Press, 1986.

——. *The Poems of John Keats*. Edited by Jack Stillinger. Cambridge, Mass.: Harvard University Press, 1978.

Keen, Paul. *The Crisis of Literature in the 1790s*. Cambridge: Cambridge University Press, 1999.

——. "Critical Leapfrog: Wordsworth's Canonical Ambivalence." *Critical Mass* 3 (1992): 21–29.

Keynes, Geoffrey, ed. *Blake: Complete Writings*. 1957. Reprint, Oxford: Oxford University Press, 1972.

King, James. "Cowper, Hayley, and Samuel Johnson's 'Republican' Milton." In

Studies in Eighteenth-Century Culture, vol. 17, edited by John Yolton and Leslie Ellen Brown, 229–38. East Lansing, Mich.: Colleagues Press, 1987.

Kowle, Carol P. "Plate III and the Meaning of *Europe.*" *Blake Studies* 8 (1978): 89–99.

Kristeva, Julia. *Revolution in Poetic Language*. Translated by Margaret Waller. New York: Columbia University Press, 1984.

Laqueur, Thomas. *Making Sex: Body and Gender from the Greeks to Freud*. Cambridge: Harvard University Press, 1990.

Larrissy, Edward. "A Description of Blake: Ideology, Form, Influence." In *1789: Reading Writing Revolution,* edited by Francis Barker, et al., 101–9. Colchester, U.K.: University of Essex, 1982.

——. "Spectral Imposition and Visionary Imposition: Printing and Repetition in Blake." In *Blake in the Nineties,* edited by Steve Clark and David Worrall, 61–77. New York: St. Martin's, 1999.

——. *William Blake*. New York: Blackwell, 1985.

Latimer, Hugh. *Sermon on the Ploughers*. 18 January 1549. Edited by Edward Arber. London, 1869.

Leerssen, Joseph Th. "On the Edge of Europe: Ireland in Search of Oriental Roots, 1650–1850." *Comparative Criticism* 8 (1986): 91–112.

Lemprière, John. *Classical Dictionary of Proper Names Mentioned in Ancient Authors Writ Large*. 3rd ed. 1788. Reprint, New York: Routledge, 1984.

Lessing, Gotthold Ephraim. *Laocoön: An Essay on the Limits of Painting and Poetry*. 1766. Translated by Edward Allen McCormick. Baltimore: Johns Hopkins University Press, 1984.

Linkin, Harriet Kramer. "The Function of Dialogue in *The Book of Thel.*" *Colby Library Quarterly* 23 (1987): 66–76.

Lipking, Lawrence. *The Ordering of the Arts in Eighteenth-Century England*. Princeton: Princeton University Press, 1970.

Lloyd, David. *Anomalous States: Irish Writing and the Post-Colonial Moment*. Durham, N.C.: Duke University Press, 1993.

Lonsdale, Roger, ed. *Eighteenth-Century Women Poets: An Oxford Anthology*. Oxford: Oxford University Press, 1989.

Lowery, Margaret Ruth. *Windows of the Morning: A Critical Study of Blake's* Poetical Sketches, *1783*. New Haven: Yale University Press, 1940.

Lucas, John. *England and Englishness: Ideas of Nationhood in English Poetry, 1688–1900*. London: Hogarth, 1990.

Lundeen, Kathleen. "Urizen's Quaking Word." *Colby Library Quarterly* 25 (1989): 12–27.

Maclean, Ian. *The Renaissance Notion of Woman: A Study in the Fortunes of Scholasticism and Medical Science in European Intellectual Life*. New York: Cambridge University Press, 1983.

Macpherson, James, trans. *The Poems of Ossian*. 2 vols. London: Cadell, 1806.

Makdisi, Saree. *Romantic Imperialism: Universal Empire and the Culture of Modernity*. Cambridge: Cambridge University Press, 1998.

Mallet, Paul Henri. *Northern Antiquities*. Translated by Bishop [Thomas] Percy. 2 vols. 1770. Reprint, New York: Garland, 1979.

Mann, Paul. "*The Book of Urizen* and the Horizon of the Book." In *Unnam'd Forms:*

Blake and Textuality, edited by Nelson Hilton and Thomas A. Vogler, 49–68. Berkeley: University of California Press, 1986.

Marvell, Andrew. *The Complete Poems*. Edited by Elizabeth Story Donno. Markham, Ontario: Penguin, 1985.

Mason, Eudo C., ed. *The Mind of Henry Fuseli*. London: Routledge, 1951.

Matheson, C. S. "The Royal Academy and the Annual Exhibition of the Viewing Public." In *Lessons of Romanticism: A Critical Companion*, edited by Thomas Pfau and Robert F. Gleckner, 280–303. Durham, N.C.: Duke University Press, 1998.

Matthews, Susan. "*Jerusalem* and Nationalism." In *William Blake*, edited by John Lucas, 80–100. New York: Longman, 1998.

Maturin, Charles Robert. *Melmoth the Wanderer: A Tale*. 1820. Edited by Alethea Hayter. Markham, Ontario: Penguin, 1984.

McConnell, Will. "Blake, Bataille, and the Accidental Processes of Material History in *Milton*." *CLIO* 26 (1997): 449–72.

McCord, James. "Historical Dissonance and William Blake's *The Song of Los*." *Colby Library Quarterly* 20 (1984): 22–35.

McCreery, Cindy. "Satiric Images of Fox, Pitt, and George III: The East India Bill Crisis, 1783–1784." *Word & Image* 9 (1993): 163–85.

McGann, Jerome J. "The Idea of an Indeterminate Text: Blake's Bible of Hell and Dr. Alexander Geddes." *Studies in Romanticism* 25 (1986): 303–24.

———. *The Romantic Ideology: A Critical Investigation*. Chicago: University of Chicago Press, 1983.

———. *The Textual Condition*. Princeton: Princeton University Press, 1991.

McLuhan, Marshall. *Understanding Media: The Extensions of Man*. Toronto: McGraw-Hill, 1964.

Mee, Jon. *Dangerous Enthusiasm: William Blake and the Culture of Radicalism in the 1790s*. Oxford: Clarendon, 1992.

Mellor, Anne K. "Blake's Portrayal of Women." *Blake: An Illustrated Quarterly* 16 (1982–83): 148–55.

Merriman, Brian. *Cúirt an Mhean-Oíche / The Midnight Court*. 1780. Translated by Patrick C. Power. Dublin: Mercier Press, 1971.

Miller, Dan. "Contrary Revelation: *The Marriage of Heaven and Hell*." *Studies in Romanticism* 24 (1985): 491–509.

Milton, John. *The Complete Poetry of John Milton*. Rev. ed. Edited by John T. Shawcross. Garden City, N.Y.: Doubleday, 1971.

———. *Milton's Prose Writings*. New York: Dutton, 1958.

Mitchell, W. J. T. *Blake's Composite Art: A Study of the Illuminated Poetry*. Princeton: Princeton University Press, 1978.

———. "Dangerous Blake." *Studies in Romanticism* 21 (1982): 410–16.

———. "Visible Language: Blake's Wondrous Art of Writing." In *Romanticism and Contemporary Criticism*, edited by Morris Eaves and Michael Fischer, 46–95. Ithaca: Cornell University Press, 1986.

Moore, Thomas. *The Poetical Works of Thomas Moore*. New York: A. L. Burt, n.d.

Morgan, Sydney. *The O'Briens and the O'Flahertys*. London: Pandora, 1988.

Moskal, Jeanne. *Blake, Ethics, and Forgiveness*. Tuscaloosa: University of Alabama Press, 1994.

Nietzsche, Friedrich. "On Truth and Lying in an Extra-Moral Sense." 1873. In *Friedrich Nietzsche on Rhetoric and Language,* translated by Sander L. Gilman, Carole Blair, and David J. Parent, 246–57. New York: Oxford University Press, 1989.

Nussbaum, Felicity A. "'Savage' Mothers: Narratives of Maternity in the Mid-Eighteenth Century." *Cultural Critique* 20 (1991–92): 123–51.

"Of a National Character in Literature." *Blackwood's Edinburgh Magazine* 3 (September 1818): 707–9.

O'Halloran, Clare. "Irish Re-Creations of the Gaelic Past: The Challenge of Macpherson's Ossian." *Past and Present* 124 (1989): 69–95.

O'Neil, Daniel J. "The Cult of Self-Sacrifice: The Irish Experience." *Éire-Ireland* 24 (1989): 89–105.

Ostriker, Alicia. "Desire Gratified and Ungratified: William Blake and Sexuality." *Blake: An Illustrated Quarterly* 16 (1982–83): 156–65.

Otto, Peter. *Constructive Vision and Visionary Deconstruction: Los, Eternity, and the Productions of Time in the Later Poetry of William Blake*. Oxford: Clarendon, 1981.

Paine, Thomas. *Common Sense*. 1776. Edited by Isaac Kramnick. Markham, Ont.: Penguin, 1982.

——. *Rights of Man*. 1791–1792. Edited by Henry Collins. Markham, Ont.: Penguin, 1983.

Paley, Morton D. *The Continuing City: William Blake's* Jerusalem. Oxford: Clarendon, 1983.

——. *Energy and the Imagination: A Study of the Development of Blake's Thought*. Oxford: Clarendon, 1970.

——. "'Wonderful Originals'—Blake and Ancient Sculpture." In *Blake in His Time,* edited by Robert N. Essick and Donald Pearce, 170–97. Bloomington: Indiana University Press, 1978.

Parker, Patricia. *Literary Fat Ladies: Rhetoric, Gender, Property*. New York: Methuen, 1987.

Percy, Thomas. *Reliques of Ancient English Poetry*. 3 vols. 1765. New York: Dover, 1966.

——. Translator's preface to *Northern Antiquities,* 2 vols., by Paul Henri Mallet, 1:i–xlxvii. 1770. Reprint, New York: Garland, 1979.

Peterfreund, Stuart. "The Problem of Originality and Blake's Poetical Sketches." *ELH* 52 (1985): 673–705.

——. *William Blake in a Newtonian World: Essays on Literature as Art and Science*. Norman: University of Oklahoma Press, 1998.

Plato. *The Republic*. Rev. 2nd ed. Translated by Desmond Lee. Markham, Ontario: Penguin, 1983.

——. *The Works of Plato*. Edited by Irwin Edman. Translated by Benjamin Jowett. New York: Modern Library, 1956.

Plowman, Max, ed. *William Blake: Poems and Prophecies*. 1927. With an introduction by Kathleen Raine. London: Dent, 1984.

Poster, Mark. *The Mode of Information: Poststructuralism and Social Context*. Chicago: University of Chicago Press, 1990.

Pressly, Nancy L. *The Fuseli Circle in Rome: Early Romantic Art of the 1770s*. New Haven: Yale Center for British Art, 1979.

Preston, Thomas R. "From Typology to Literature: Hermeneutics and Historical

Narrative in Eighteenth-Century England." *The Eighteenth Century: Theory and Interpretation* 23 (1982): 181–96.

Punter, David. "Blake: Social Relations of Poetic Form." *Literature and History* 8 (1982): 182–205.

R. R. Review of *An Essay on the Picturesque, as compared with the sublime and the beautiful; and, on the Use of Studying Pictures, for the Purpose of improving real Landscape.* By Uvedale Price. *Analytical Review* 20 (1794): 259–66.

Rainsford, Dominic. *Authorship, Ethics, and the Reader: Blake, Dickens, Joyce*. New York: St. Martin's, 1997.

Rajan, Tilottama. *The Supplement of Reading: Figures of Understanding in Romantic Theory and Practice*. Ithaca: Cornell University Press, 1990.

Randolph, Thomas. *The Poems and Amyntas of Thomas Randolph*. Edited by John Jay Parry. New Haven: Yale University Press, 1917.

Razzell, Peter. *The Conquest of Smallpox: The Impact of Inoculation on Smallpox Mortality in Eighteenth Century Britain*. Newhaven, U.K.: Caliban, 1977.

——. *Edward Jenner's Cowpox Vaccine: The History of a Medical Myth*. Newhaven, U.K.: Caliban, 1977.

Rees, Abraham. *Cyclopaedia; or, Universal Dictionary of Arts, Sciences, and Literature*. 4 vols. London: Longman, 1820.

Renan, Ernest. "What Is a Nation?" Translated by Martin Thom. In *Nation and Narration*, edited by Homi K. Bhabha, 8–22. New York: Routledge, 1990.

Resseguie, James L. "Defamiliarization in the Gospels." *Mosaic* 21 (1988): 25–35.

Review of *The Trial of Thomas Muir. Analytical Review* 17 (1793): 104–5.

Richardson, Alan. *A Mental Theater: Poetic Drama and Consciousness in the Romantic Age*. University Park: Pennsylvania State University Press, 1988.

Richey, William. *Blake's Altering Aesthetic*. Columbia: University of Missouri Press, 1996.

——. "The French Revolution: Blake's Epic Dialogue with Edmund Burke." *ELH* 59 (1992): 817–37.

Richter, Simon. *Laocoon's Body and the Aesthetics of Pain: Winckelmann, Lessing, Herder, Moritz, Goethe*. Detroit: Wayne State University Press, 1992.

Rivero, Albert J. "Typology, History, and Blake's *Milton*." *Journal of English and Germanic Philology* 81 (1982): 30–46.

Roe, Nicholas. *The Politics of Nature: Wordsworth and Some Contemporaries*. New York: St. Martin's, 1992.

Rose, Edward J. "Blake's Metaphorical States." *Blake Studies* 4 (1971): 9–31.

Ross, Marlon B. "Romancing the Nation State: The Poetics of Romantic Nationalism." In *Macropolitics of Nineteenth-Century Literature: Nationalism, Exoticism, Imperialism,* edited by Jonathan Arac and Harriet Ritvo, 56–85. Philadelphia: University of Pennsylvania Press, 1991.

Rothenberg, Molly Anne. "Parasiting America: The Radical Function of Heterogeneity in Thomas Paine's Early Writings." *Eighteenth-Century Studies* 25 (1992): 331–51.

——. *Rethinking Blake's Textuality*. Columbia: University of Missouri Press, 1993.

Rudowski, Victor Anthony. "Lessing *contra* Winckelmann." *Journal of Aesthetics and Art Criticism* 44 (1986): 235–43.

Sandler, Florence. "The Iconoclastic Enterprise: Blake's Critique of 'Milton's Religion.'" *Blake Studies* 5 (1972): 13–57.

Saslow, James M. Notes to *The Poetry of Michelangelo: An Annotated Translation*. New Haven: Yale University Press, 1991.

Schiller, Friedrich. *On the Naive and Sentimental in Literature*. 1795. Edited by Helen Watanabe-O'Kelly. Manchester: Carcanet New Press, 1981.

Schmitt, Cannon. *Alien Nation: Nineteenth-Century Gothic Fictions and English Nationality*. Philadelphia: University of Pennsylvania Press, 1997.

Schorer, Mark. *William Blake: The Politics of Vision*. New York: Holt, 1946.

Scott, Walter. *The Antiquary*. 1816. Vol. 3 of *The Waverley Novels*. Edinburgh: Black, 1873.

——. *Waverley; or, 'Tis Sixty Years Since*. 1814. Edited by Andrew Hook. Markham, Ontario: Penguin, 1985.

Shafer, Boyd C. *Faces of Nationalism: New Realities and Old Myths*. New York: Harcourt Brace Jovanovich, 1972.

Shaviro, Steven. "'Striving With Systems': Blake and the Politics of Difference." *boundary 2* 10 (1982): 229–50.

Shelley, Percy Bysshe. *Shelley's Poetry and Prose*. Edited by Donald H. Reiman and Sharon B. Powers. New York: Norton, 1977.

Shklovsky, Victor. "Art as Technique." 1917. In *Russian Formalist Criticism: Four Essays,* translated by Lee T. Lemon and Marion J. Reis, 5–24. Lincoln: University of Nebraska Press, 1965.

Silverman, Kaja. *The Subject of Semiotics*. New York: Oxford University Press, 1983.

Simpson, David. *Romanticism, Nationalism, and the Revolt against Theory*. Chicago: University of Chicago Press, 1993.

Singer, June. *The Unholy Bible: Blake, Jung, and the Collective Unconscious*. Boston: Sigo, 1986.

Smith, Adam. *Theory of Moral Sentiments*. 1759. Reprint, New York: Kelley, 1966.

Smith, Anthony D. *National Identity*. Reprint, Reno: University of Nevada Press, 1991.

——. "Neo-Classicist and Romantic Elements in the Emergence of Nationalist Conceptions." In *Nationalist Movements,* edited by Anthony D. Smith, 74–87. London: Macmillan, 1976.

——. *Theories of Nationalism*. 1971. 2nd ed. London: Duckworth, 1983.

Smith, Barbara Herrnstein. *Poetic Closure: A Study of How Poems End*. Chicago: University of Chicago Press, 1968.

Snorre Sturlason. *Ynglinga Saga*. In *Heimskringla: The Norse King Sagas*. 1844. Rev. ed., translated by S. Laing, 7–43. New York: Dutton, 1951.

Spenser, Edmund. "A View to the Present State of Ireland." 1596. In *The Works of Spencer* [*sic*], *Campion, Hanmer, and Marleborough,* 2 vols., 1:1–266. New York: Kennikat Press, 1970.

Stacy, R. H. *Defamiliarization in Language and Literature*. Syracuse: Syracuse University Press, 1977.

Stempel, Daniel. "Identifying Ahania: Etymology and Iconology in Blake's Allegorical Nomenclature." *Studies in Romanticism* 28 (1989): 95–119.

Swearingen, James E. "Time and History in Blake's *Europe*." *CLIO* 20 (1991): 109–21.

——. "William Blake's Figural Politics." *ELH* 59 (1992): 125–44.

Tannenbaum, Leslie. *Biblical Tradition in Blake's Early Prophecies: The Great Code of Art*. Princeton: Princeton University Press, 1982.

Tayler, Irene. "Blake's *Laocoön.*" *Blake Newsletter: An Illustrated Quarterly* 10 (1976–77): 72–81.

Thompson, E. P. *Witness against the Beast: William Blake and the Moral Law.* Cambridge: Cambridge University Press, 1993.

Tipler, Paul A. *Physics*. 2nd ed. New York: Worth, 1982.

Tolley, Michael J. "*Europe:* 'To Those Ychain'd in Sleep.'" In *Blake's Visionary Forms Dramatic,* edited by David V. Erdman and John E. Grant. Princeton: Princeton University Press, 1970.

Trumpener, Katie. *Bardic Nationalism: The Romantic Novel and the British Empire.* Princeton: Princeton University Press, 1997.

Vesely, Suzanne Araas. "The Daughters of Eighteenth-Century Science: A Rationalist and Materialist Context for William Blake's Female Figures." *Colby Quarterly* 34 (1998): 5–24.

Villalobos, John C. "A Possible Source for William Blake's 'The Great Code of Art.'" *English Language Notes* 26 (1988): 36–40.

Vogler, Thomas A. "'in vain the Eloquent tongue': An Un-Reading of *VISIONS of the Daughters of Albion.*" In *Critical Paths: Blake and the Argument of Method,* edited by Dan Miller, Mark Bracher, and Donald Ault, 271–309. Durham, N.C.: Duke University Press, 1987.

Wagenknecht, David. Afterword to *Critical Paths: Blake and the Argument of Method,* edited by Dan Miller, Mark Bracher, and Donald Ault, 310–28. Durham, N.C.: Duke University Press, 1987.

——. *Blake's Night: William Blake and the Idea of Pastoral.* Cambridge, Mass.: Belknap, 1973.

Warner, Janet A. *Blake and the Language of Art.* Kingston: McGill-Queen's University Press, 1984.

Warton, Thomas. "Of the Origin of Romantic Fiction in Europe." 1774. In *The History of English Poetry,* 3 vols., with additional notes by Joseph Ritson, George Ashby, et al., 1:i–lvi. London: Tegg, 1840.

Whitted, Brent E. "Locating the Anomalous: Gesualdo, Blake, and Seurat." *Mosaic* 31 (1998): 25–42.

Williams, Nicholas M. *Ideology and Utopia in the Poetry of William Blake.* Cambridge: Cambridge University Press, 1998.

Winckelmann, Johann Joachim. *The History of Ancient Art.* 1764. 4 vols. in 2. Translated by G. Henry Lodge. Boston: James R. Osgood and Company, 1880.

——. *Reflections on the Imitations of Greek Works in Painting and Sculpture.* 1755. Translated by Elfriede Heyer and Roger C. Norton. La Salle, Ill.: Open Court, 1987.

Wittreich, Joseph Anthony, Jr. *Angel of Apocalypse: Blake's Idea of Milton.* Madison: University of Wisconsin Press, 1975.

Wolfson, Susan. "Sketching Verbal Form: Blake's *Poetical Sketches.*" In *Speak Silence: Rhetoric and Culture in Blake's Poetical Sketches,* edited by Mark L. Greenberg, 27–70. Detroit: Wayne State University Press, 1996.

Wollstonecraft, Mary. *A Vindication of the Rights of Woman.* 1792. Edited by Miriam Brody. Markham, Ontario: Penguin, 1985.

Wordsworth, William. *William Wordsworth.* Edited by Stephen Gill. New York: Oxford University Press, 1989.

Wright, Julia M. "'Empire Is No More': Odin and Orc in *America.*" *Blake: An Illustrated Quarterly* 26 (1992): 26–29.

———. "'Greek & Latin Slaves of the Sword': Rejecting the Imperial Nation in Blake's *Milton.*" In *Milton and the Imperial Vision,* edited by Elizabeth Sauer and Balachandra Rajan with an afterword by Homi K. Bhabha, 255–72. Pittsburgh: Duquesne University Press, 1999.

———. "'The Nation Begins to Form': Competing Nationalisms in Morgan's *The O'Briens and the O'Flahertys.*" *ELH* 66 (1999): 939–63.

Youngquist, Paul. "Reading the Apocalypse: The Narrativity of Blake's *Jerusalem.*" *Studies in Romanticism* 32 (1993): 601–25.

Index